Access and Identity Management for Libraries

Controlling access to
online information

Access and Identity Management for Libraries

Controlling access to online information

Masha Garibyan, Simon McLeish and John Paschoud

facet publishing

Published by Facet Publishing
7 Ridgmount Street, London WC1E 7AE
www.facetpublishing.co.uk

Facet Publishing is wholly owned by CILIP: the Chartered Institute of Library
and Information Professionals.

British Library Cataloguing in Publication Data
A catalogue record for this book is available from the British Library.

ISBN 978-1-85604-588-9

First published 2014

Text printed on FSC accredited material.

Typeset from author's files in 10/14 pt Palatino Linotype and Frutiger by Facet
Publishing Production.
Printed and made in Great Britain by CPI Group (UK) Ltd, Croydon, CR0 4YY

Contents

Foreword

It's a pleasure to be able to write a short foreword to this book, which I think will be very useful to librarians, publishers and information technologists trying to gain insight into the complexities surrounding access to licensed networked information resources in settings such as universities or public libraries. This book documents a bit of history that's not well known, a little folklore that I don't think has been written down before, and some tacit knowledge that hasn't been well codified; both are needed to understand where we are today, how we got here, and why.

I'm honoured to have some of the work hosted and co-ordinated by the Coalition for Networked Information (CNI) recognized as a pivotal stage in the development of authentication and access management strategies; I do agree with the authors that the period from around 1997 to 2000 was key in establishing the central ideas and the roadmap, although implementing this roadmap took a long time – surely longer than many of us would have believed in, say, 1999. As you can see, the CNI white paper of which I served as editor (and which is reproduced as Appendix 2 to this book) never made it past a draft stage; things were happening too fast, and there seemed to be little value in perfecting the document. Instead, it paved the way ahead along two distinct roads.

One was technical, and involved the development and deployment of Shibboleth and the organizational frameworks such as InCommon that make the technical mechanisms work. Here I want to recognize the contributions of a number of leaders in the formulation of the white paper, and in the subsequent protocol and software design and implementation work, which quickly moved to other venues, such as Internet2 and later InCommon. They include (but are certainly not limited to) Scott Cantor, Steve Carmody, Michael Gettes, Ken Klingenstein, the late R. L. 'Bob' Morgan, and Oren Sreebny. And I'll apologize now for the many other names that I've omitted here.

The second road was a policy-based one, adding new depth to the very complex issues of individual user privacy in the context of licence negotiations and subsequent operational relationships. The issues here continue to be challenging, particularly as new user demands emerge for bulk downloading of material to facilitate text mining, or simply to populate portable personal libraries on ever-cheaper storage, and these activities increase content provider concerns about accountability. (It is also interesting to note that, while the discussions around the white paper tried to stress a wide range of interorganizational access and resource sharing scenarios, I think almost all of the early implementation work was focused on university community access to library-licensed information resources.) Today we are seeing a great deal of new emphasis on individuals sharing scholarly data across institutional boundaries as a very real and immediate problem, and additional scenarios such as large scale annotation of information collections by various communities emerging rapidly.

I'll conclude with a few brief comments on where we are now, what we've learned, and some of the places to which we may be headed in the near future.

Federated authentication to control access to at least some (generally low-risk) resources seems to be gaining substantial acceptance in higher education – Eduroam is a great case study here, though only after years of hand-wringing by institutional general counsels, auditors, and other risk managers. There is now serious implementation of federated identity with level of assurance guarantees; what remains to be seen is how willing institutions are to rely upon this for providing access to high-risk resources.

It's clear that authentication has reached a crisis point. Passwords as a single-factor authentication technology are rapidly dying (see, for example, Dan Goodin's piece at http://arstechnica.com/security/2012/08/passwords-under-assault) and we are rapidly seeing the deployment of various two-factor authentication methods for large-scale, relatively high-value systems or high-visibility targets; but there are huge numbers of systems that are still not dealing with the problem. Universities have provided select faculty and staff with multi-factor access to high-value systems (for example financial systems, or operationally critical infrastructure management) for years, but are now facing the challenge of rolling this out much more broadly; it will be interesting to see how this works. Campuses that have outsourced services such as e-mail to commercial providers such as Google or Microsoft have been able to benefit quickly from the relatively aggressive work that these commercial providers have done in large-scale deployment of two-factor authentication. One game changer for implementation of multi-factor authentication is the widespread adoption of smartphones, with system-specific apps, text messaging, or automated calling, offering economical alternatives to distributing very large numbers of system-specific special-purpose hardware authentication devices.

While single sign-on has come a long way in the university environment, across the broader array of consumer and professional networked applications individuals now maintain absurd numbers of identities in separate systems. Federated identity and authentication is deploying in the consumer world, using backbone identities such as Facebook (as opposed to those managed by members of InCommon), but with sometimes porous and poorly understood information flows among the various systems involved (though this may not matter that much given the incredible escalation of tracking of behaviour in consumer use of the network overall).

While libraries of all kinds have continued valiantly to create environments where reader privacy can be preserved, their users have demonstrated that they are almost always happy to sacrifice this privacy for the convenience of personalization or a bit of access to content not otherwise available; it is common to see users interacting with an information system where the user is authorized anonymously or pseudonymously via Shibboleth, but then later invited by the content provider to log into a personal 'profile' that he or she has set up. At least libraries can be proud that they are maintaining perhaps the last environment where users can even have an opportunity to choose.

Access (both real-time and retrospective) to aggregated query or interaction streams – the less anonymized the better – has been shown to be of incredible and diverse value again and again, reinforcing that the stakes surrounding use of these streams are very high. Google identifies and predicts infectious disease outbreaks based on geo-tagged query streams; it identifies criminals (see http://blogs.reuters.com/felix-salmon/2013/02/20/the-long-arm-of-the-google for just one set of anecdotes); the Twitter stream is being used to drive high-speed stock trading algorithms and to predict the box-office gross for newly opened Hollywood movies. A very recent scandal involved reporters at *Bloomberg News*, which is a division of Bloomberg Financial, using data from log-on records; the financial industry (and government sectors) that rely heavily on Bloomberg terminals were in uproar, but underneath that, one could see the palpable fear that reporters, or someone, might get access to their actual individual and identifiable *query streams*. I sense that there are some very important and high-stakes policy issues getting ready to surface in this area, which is a whirlpool of conflicting interests, many of them happiest to be operating secretly and through a series of *quid pro quo* understandings.

Finally, I want to mention the emergence of a series of new developments that the Coalition for Networked Information is heavily engaged with; we refer to these variously as 'scholarly identity management' or 'archival name and identity infrastructure.' Briefly, the first of these developments deals with the assembly, preservation, validation and interchange of what one might characterize as *factual biographies* of individuals (living and dead), with emphasis on activities relevant to their scholarly work: publications, patents, grants received, doctorates supervised, awards, etc. The second deals with an even broader and somewhat more historically focused set of factual biographies of individuals that appears in the cultural record as authors, political, artistic or intellectual figures, and their connections to the published literature (as authors or as subjects), to archival holdings, and to the apparatus supporting scholarly investigation (for example, editor's or author's notes). All of this work, but particularly that dealing with current scholarly identity, will have connections to more traditional authentication and identity management, though the nature of those connections is still very much under discussion (for example, the question of levels of assurance in various contexts). I believe that this is going to be one of the new frontiers of identity management, and one that our memory organizations are going to play a key role in developing and supporting.

Clifford Lynch

Acknowledgements

The authors would like to thank Clifford Lynch for writing a foreword to this book and for giving us permission to reproduce his famous white paper on access management principles (first published in 1998); Nicole Harris for her help with Chapter 8 (Federated access: history, current poition and future developments) and general advice; Rhys Smith for his help with Chapter 11 (Library statistics, particularly the information on RAPTOR); Graham Mason and Rebecca Williams (Kidderminster College, UK case study); Andy Ingham (University of North Carolina-Chapel Hill, US case study); David Kennedy (USMAI Consortium, US case study); Tod Olson (University of Chicago, US case study); Peter Austin, Lynne Vautier and Daniel Piczak (Western Australian University Libraries case study); Margaret Stone (UCL, UK case study); Teun Nijssen and Thomas Place (Tilburg University, the Netherlands case study); Paul Williams (The Hive, UK case study). We would also like to thank Helen Carley, our editor, for her support and patience.

Some of the content of this book is based on original content produced as part of the JISC-funded Identity Management Toolkit project and other work that the authors have undertaken for the UK Joint Information Systems Committee.

Masha Garibyan, Simon McLeish and John Paschoud

Note to readers

The main purpose of this book is to give a comprehensive overview of the complexities of providing effective access and identity management (AIM) for libraries, particularly in relation to protected library e-resources. Therefore, other types of access issues, such as providing access for people with disabilities, are not the topic of this book. There are some excellent resources that cover this, including a book by Hernon and Calvert (2005).

The main chapters can be treated as standalone resources that cover a particular aspect of AIM to enable the reader to dip in and out of the book as required; or they can be approached sequentially (they start with quite basic concepts and then progress into greater depth and complexity) for anyone needing a reasonably comprehensive primer because, for example, they may be taking on a role with operational responsibility for AIM within a library. The Glossary that follows this Note will help to make sense of the most important terminology associated with AIM. There are a number of practical case studies at the end of the book that the reader might find useful to get a feel of how other libraries, serving different types of communities of users and in different parts of the world, are implementing their own AIM solutions. We have tried to include enough contextual background to each so that readers may identify which of them were tackling similar problems to their own.

The final section of the book contains a reprint of Clifford Lynch's paper, *A White Paper on Authentication and Access Management Issues in Cross-*

organizational Use of Networked Information Resources, as his work, and this paper in particular, introduced many of the concepts which lie behind modern access management work. Chapter 1 of this book explains why we think it was so significant; but apart from those reasons it also helped to inspire all of us to think up, seek and win government funding for, and then successfully deliver, some of the projects carried out by the London School of Economics and many partner organizations from 1998 onwards, in which we tackled the challenges which AIM presents to libraries – and even overcame some of them.

We hope that it, and what we have added to it in this book, will do the same for others.

Resource

Hernon, P. and Calvert P. (2005) *Improving the Quality of Library Services for Students with Disabilities*, Libraries Unlimited Inc.

Glossary

Access management federation: Managers of the trust framework between groups of identity providers and service providers in many FAM model implementations (Chapter 8).

AIM: Acronym used in this book for 'access and identity management'. For almost all purposes in this context interchangeable with 'IAM' (*passim*).

Athens: National research and education authentication service used in the UK from around 1997 to 2008 (Chapter 8).

Authentication: The process in which a user presents credentials of some sort to prove 'they are who they say they are' (Chapter 3).

Authorization: The process of determining whether an individual should have access to (all or part of) this resource (Chapter 3).

Barcode authentication: The use of the pattern of the digits on a card to identify that the user was issued with it by an organization which has purchased a licence to access a resource. Used by many public libraries for access to online resources (Chapter 4).

Cookie: Short piece of textual data, often encrypted, which a web server can store on a browser to retrieve on subsequent visits from the same user. Often used for creation and maintenance of a session at a website (Chapter 8).

Current Research Information System (CRIS): System for managing and integrating information about research projects, staff, publications, data, etc. (Chapter 12).

Domain name: Human-readable internet address (Chapter 6).

Electronic resource management system (ERM): A software product designed to allow users to discover and access electronic resources; the electronic resource part of a library management system (Chapter 2).

Extensible Markup Language (XML): An open standard defining structured data, widely used on the internet (Chapter 8).

EZProxy: Open-source IP proxy server product (Chapter 6).

Federated access management (FAM): A model for authentication and authorization in which the resource management is separated from the identity/user management (Chapter 8).

Federated identity management (FidM): Term sometimes used as an alternative to FAM, especially in the commercial sector (Chapter 8).

IAM: Acronym used in this book for 'identity and access management' (*passim*).

Identity as a Service (IdAAS): Name given to identity management systems which operate in the cloud (Chapter 9).

Identity management: The processes of managing information about library users; frequently abbreviated in this book to IdM (*passim*).

Identity provider (IdP): In the FAM model, the service which provides the identification of a user to trusted service providers; will typically run IdM processes for registration of users in addition to requiring authentication (Chapter 8).

Internet protocol (IP): The standard which defines how internet traffic is routed from source to destination (Chapter 6).

IP authentication: A mechanism which uses the user's location on the internet (often, in academic institutions, equivalent to on- as opposed to off-campus) to determine whether they are entitled to access a resource (Chapter 8).

IP proxy server: Software which enables a user to access a resource from an apparently different IP address from the one which they are actually using. Frequently used to provide off-campus access to IP-authenticated resources (Chapters 4 and 6).

Joint Information Systems Committee (JISC): UK body which has worked to improve the use of IT by universities and colleges since the mid-1990s (*passim*).

National Research and Educational Network (NREN): An internet service provider specifically providing services to researchers and educators. In the UK, the NREN is JANET (*passim*).

Open standard: A standard which can be read and used by anybody without charge (*passim*).

Password: A secret textual string used for authentication, usually not displayed when used (Chapter 5).

Registration (or enrolment): The initial recording by an identity manager (the library) of details about an individual user (Chapter 3).

Resource/journal/content aggregator: A website which includes electronic content from multiple sources, especially when the sources are journals from several publishers (Chapter 2).

Service provider (SP): In the FAM model, the entity which manages resources and allows accesses to individuals vouched for by trusted IdPs (Chapter 8).

Session: A period during which a user is considered to be authenticated to a resource. On the internet, frequently managed using web cookies (Chapter 8).

Shibboleth: Open-source FAM product used extensively in higher education worldwide, especially for access to electronic library resources (Chapter 8).

Single sign-on (SSO): Any mechanism which allows a user to use a single set of credentials to access multiple resources; a distinction is often made between full SSO and single log-in (where the same credentials are used but need to be presented repeatedly) (Chapter 8).

SCONUL (Society of College, National and University Libraries): A consortium of academic libraries which promotes awareness of their role and helps them to collaborate to improve effectiveness. See www.sconul.ac.uk/page/about-sconul (*passim*).

Social engineering: Any of a large number of methods by which one person persuades another to do what he/she wants, often used specifically where the thing wanted is access to resources or the credentials to gain such access (Chapter 12).

Top level domain (TLD): The most general part of an internet domain name (Chapter 6).

UKOLN (UK Online Network): 'A centre of expertise which advises on digital infrastructure, information policy and data management'. See www.ukoln.ac.uk (Chapter 10).

Username (also known as user ID): A non-secret textual identifier for an individual, usually used with a password for authentication and often for authorization. Does not have to be a 'name', and could be a sequence of digits, hence the alternative term 'user ID' (Chapter 5).

Web services: Mechanisms for transferring information between services/applications on the world wide web (e.g., defining how to ask a weather website to send an XML document with the temperature in Chicago tomorrow afternoon) (Chapter 8).

What is access management, and why do libraries do it?

A (very) brief history of the role of libraries in managing access to information resources, how this underpins what libraries do now and will do in the future, how their role has changed in recent history, and some seminal milestones in the invention of modern access and identity management principles.

Historical role of libraries in managing access to information

> I want a poor student to have the same means of indulging his learned curiosity, of following his rational pursuits, of consulting the same authorities, of fathoming the most intricate inquiry as the richest man in the kingdom, as far as books go . . .
>
> (Select Committee on British Museum, 1836)

These were the words of Sir Anthony Panizzi, arguably the greatest administrative librarian who has ever lived, in his vision for the British Museum Library in 1836. Panizzi was not, at the time, envisaging libraries giving people access to the wealth of information resources beyond books, as they do 170 years later. But perhaps we can now see with the benefit of hindsight that the most perceptive part of that statement may have been 'as far as books go'. Because whilst libraries all over the world have long established their role in making access to books (and most other printed material) free and equal to all, they have not been able to achieve the same accessibility for the material delivered electronically, which already constitutes the majority by volume of information available from some libraries.

Since the first libraries existed, they have had two apparently conflicting purposes: to facilitate access to sources and records of scholarly knowledge; and to restrict such access. The oldest-established form of access management practised by libraries is still in use today in most of them. When information is contained in a printed book, it can be kept on a shelf (chained to it, if necessary) inside a secure building, and the entrance can be guarded to allow only known and authorized users into the building. A few examples of chained libraries still exist, such as the Hereford Cathedral Chained Library in the UK (www.herefordcathedral.org/education-research/library-and-archives/history-of-the-chained-library). If the library has a large number of users, the guard on duty may not know all of them well, so a user might be issued with some special credentials by the library – either to establish his (scholars were invariably 'he') identity, which could be checked against a list of authorized users, or merely requesting the guard to 'permit the bearer access'. This book does not even attempt to examine the motives, politics and other social factors that, now or in the past, have divided the 'information rich' (who can get into the library) from the 'information poor' (who are denied access, even if they can read the language of the books).

The role of libraries in the 21st century

During the relatively short period (of 30 years or less) of the late 20th century when libraries had started including electronic resources alongside print, but the internet and the web had not yet achieved ubiquity, electronic resources were most often held locally on optical discs, computer workstations or file servers, usually inside the library building. In this era there was little difference in access management terms between the few electronic resources and the many books and other paper-based items. If a user could get into the library, he or she could use all the resources there. A few notable exceptions (such as Lockheed Dialog – see www.dialog.com/about/history/transcript.shtml for details) were truly online networked services, but it was normally necessary to access them from a specially configured terminal, via a special (dial-up or leased line) connection.

Charges for access to most of these early online resources also meant that they were often actually used by library staff (who controlled the budgets that paid for them), and not by users directly. One of the authors' memories of that period (as an occasional but computer-literate user of such things in the 1970s) is that the librarians of the time guarded them more closely and jealously than their ancient (and slightly more priestly) predecessors had probably kept ordinary citizens at a respectful distance from the Delphic Oracle – and used a similar amount of intended-to-baffle mumbo-jumbo to hide their own nervousness about using such big magic.

The role of libraries in the 21st century has changed fundamentally. For example, in the past, the information resources held by a library were often those which were generated within the university of which it was a part, or collected by the scholars of the university on their travels, and deposited with the library for safe-keeping. Although academic libraries still have a part to play in storing and making accessible the academic output of their local scholars, now reinvented through the use of institutional repositories, the problem they are now helping people to tackle is fundamentally one of too much information, rather than too little. Libraries that serve a specialized community still acquire and manage collections of printed and electronic resources of particular relevance to their users, but they also serve to filter all of the 'free' information on the web, highlighting what is likely to be of relevance to their users and helping to verify the provenance of its sources. The growing establishment of institutional repositories by libraries brings with it another access management issue, where the library finds itself in a similar role to that of the online publisher – even if the repository is intended to offer free-to-web access (see Chapter 2).

A second important type of access which many libraries are now managing is not to information as such, but to their own networked workstations, as a means of access for their patrons to 'all that's out there' on the 'free' web. This has become an important new role for libraries, particularly public libraries, in helping to equalize access for the 'information poor' of today. Patrons can use this new service of the library to access a far wider range of information and services than the traditional range of printed resources would have contained, and this raises issues of whether (or to what extent and for what reasons) a library should restrict the use of the access facilities it provides. See Chapter 10 for a discussion of the issues for libraries that offer open network and web access and publicly available wireless access to the internet, and some of the technical solutions that can be used to manage this.

Part of the acquisitions role of libraries is the purchase of access to information resources that are online, but not 'free'. For many libraries in the academic, public and business sectors this is (or will soon become) the second biggest line of their annual budget (after staff costs), outstripping annual expenditure on new printed books and periodicals. In terms of managing access to content, the responsibilities of a library may be largely defined by the conditions of such licences.

The history of access management of online information resources

The history of access management of online information resources, and identity management of library users to facilitate this, is conveniently very brief and probably contained within the lifetime of many readers of this book (and certainly that of the writers). None of this was a problem until the birth of the internet in 1983 (Zakon, 2006) that created the ubiquitous interconnection of everything and everywhere (almost). The scale of the problem increased dramatically after the birth of the world wide web in 1991 (Berners-Lee, 1998), which widened usability beyond the small minority who were technically competent in earlier internet protocols.

In 1994 Vint Cerf (1994), accredited as one of the inventors of the principles behind the internet, wrote a spoof history-from-the-future of network developments, in which he envisaged this continuing role of publishers (but not of libraries):

Interestingly, this didn't do away either with the need for traditional publishers, who filter or evaluate material prior to publication, nor for a continuing interest in paper and CD-ROM. As display technology got better and more portable, though, paper became much more of a speciality item. Most documents were published on-line or on high-density digital storage media. The basic publishing process retained a heavy emphasis on editorial selection, but the mechanics shifted largely in the direction of the author – with help from experts in layout and accessibility. Of course, it helped to have a universal reference numbering plan which allowed authors to register documents in permanent archives. References could be made to these from any other on-line context and the documents retrieved readily, possibly at some cost for copying rights.

In one sense, the whole idea of restricting access to information on the web (and, therefore, of needing to manage such restricted access) goes against the principles originally envisaged by Tim Berners-Lee in creating the web, of making information more interlinked and accessible to more people. But, of course, the dominance of commercial uses means that access to a great deal of web content is now restricted (but not necessarily very well managed).

The range of types of online information products available is wider than that of print resources, and the sheer volume of online content (not including that of the 'free' web) available in even a modestly funded library is likely to be many times that of the equivalent in print items that can be stocked. It includes fiction and non-fiction e-books (which more or less emulate their printed counterparts), reference works, such as dictionaries and encyclopedias (which can exploit the medium to be much more useful than their printed predecessors by including dynamic searching and cross-referencing, and content that includes sound and moving images), e-journals (currently still closely related to printed scholarly journals, but starting to lose the print-based concepts of volumes and issues, with some moving to online-only publication), 'raw' data sources (such as output from large scientific equipment, or population census data) and more interactive resources for learning or other processes, which have no obvious printed counterparts.

The role of e-commerce in library access management

E-commerce has driven the development of many of the web-based technologies that have been adopted by libraries for access management, or by the commercial publishers who market online resources to libraries. In nearly all cases publishers recognize and serve a 'retail' market for their products, selling individual licences for access to individuals or small businesses. It's not easy to get information about the comparative volumes of such retail business, and corresponding 'wholesale' licensing via libraries, because publishers (like any other commercial businesses) are in a competitive environment and see such information as commercially confidential.

Many library users, too, are highly familiar with such retail e-commerce – possibly not for access to information resources (they have a library for that!) but for buying almost all other goods and services, and much more. Through buying books from Amazon, personal computers from Dell, or something bizarre from eBay, booking aircraft tickets, train tickets, medical appointments, to dealing with their bank or filing their tax returns, they have gained experience of good and bad user interfaces, and secure and less-secure ways of handing over personal information about themselves and, more significantly to most of them, their money. All of these transactions involve identity and access management (you wouldn't want somebody else's bizarre eBay purchase, would you?), and one thing that such people will certainly be experienced in is using (and probably forgetting) a multitude of usernames and passwords.

This means that libraries and librarians are now dealing with, at least in part, a population of users who may be more familiar than they are with what is possible and impossible, what works and what doesn't. Such web-savvy users will not be tolerant of library services that don't perform as well, regardless of the fact that the library is probably not driven to use technology to keep up with commercial competitors. They also deserve some respite from managing their own identity and access to things, and this is something that we, as information professionals, can offer them.

The 'birth' of access management principles – Clifford Lynch's white paper

Partly because of the commercial origin of much of the content that requires access management by libraries, some of the business models and the technical solutions to implement them don't perfectly match the relationship between publisher, library and library patron. They also fail to cater for new ways in which people quite reasonably want to use libraries, such as without having to visit the physical building of the library (perhaps because the particular library they need to use has its physical building on the other side of the world).

If we wanted to pinpoint a seminal event with which we could define the end of 'the dark ages' of access management, and the birth of current thinking and technology, it would be the meeting of the Digital Library Federation (DLF) on 6 April 1998. Shortly before this meeting, Clifford Lynch of the Coalition for Networked Information (CNI) produced a draft of his white paper (Lynch, 1998) defining the abstract requirements which should be met by access management systems, and outlining some options for further investigation. Lynch's white paper is such a notable cornerstone of this subject that it is reproduced as Appendix 2 of this book.

Of course, it didn't just happen like this, in one place at one particular time. The community of specialists in library and network access management is relatively small now, and it was even smaller then; and small communities talk amongst themselves. If they happen to be composed of people who are intimately involved in the development of the internet, then they talk amongst themselves even if they are spread around the world. Lynch had in fact rehearsed many of the ideas, and the challenges posed by typical scenarios (involving users, libraries and publishers as actors) to various of the possible technology options that were then becoming apparent, in an earlier published paper (Lynch, 1997). Parallel thinking and discussions that helped to evolve these ideas were going on in other national fora and in other library-rooted projects. But the credit for defining the principles on which many developments have since been based, and documenting them in the most coherent way, should go to Lynch, the Coalition for Networked Information, and the Digital Library Federation. Chapter 3 will explain and expand on these principles, and define some of the terminology of identity and access management.

References

Berners-Lee, T. (1998) *The World Wide Web: a very short personal history,*
    www.w3.org/People/Berners-Lee/ShortHistory.html.
Cerf, V. (1994) *A View from the 21st Century,* Internet RFC 1607,
    www.faqs.org/rfcs/rfc1607.html.
Lynch, C. (1997) The Changing Role of Authentication and Authorization in a
    Networked Information Environment, *Library Hi Tech,* **15** (1–2), 30–8.
Lynch, C. (ed.) (1998) *A White Paper on Authentication and Access Management Issues
    in Cross-Organizational Use of Networked Information Resources,* Coalition for
    Networked Information,
    www.cni.org/about-cni/staff/clifford-a-lynch/publications.
Select Committee on British Museum (1836) *Report from the Select Committee on
    British Museum; together with the minutes of evidence, appendix and index.*
Zakon, R. H. (2006) *Hobbes' Internet Timeline,*
    www.zakon.org/robert/internet/timeline.

2

Electronic resources: public and not so public

Many libraries around the globe need to manage access to a variety of internal and external online resources and services, such as proprietary journals and databases, the organization's own resources and data. User permissions information contained in licensing agreements is sometimes unclear and complicated, and so it needs to be managed carefully in order to ensure that users are given access to everything they are entitled to. In addition, users now expect to be able to access online resources irrespective of time and the users' physical location. This chapter looks at the different kinds of online information that need to be protected, the reasons why, and the importance of effective library management of licensing information.

> *The primary purpose of information services has always been and will always be to reduce to a minimum the amount of time required by local users to obtain access to that information they need to do their work.*
>
> R. Atkinson (in Woodward and McKnight, 1995, 71)

Managing access to electronic collections

Many libraries around the world need to manage an ever-increasing number of electronic resources. Library collections are no longer confined to the physical boundaries of the library and are seeing rapid growth thanks to the incredible selection of quality electronic resources that are now available.

While it is impossible for any library to own everything that its users want, electronic resources have opened up opportunities for providing access to a resource while not actually owning it (Moyo, 2002, 49).

Managing access to electronic collections in the 'global electronic information market' (Steele, in Moyo, 2002, 48) faces a number of serious challenges. Back in 1998, Steele suggested that this new information market would have the following features:

• ubiquitous desktop access
• tailored and flexible gateways to information
• ease of access to information with no location barrier
• interchangeability, interoperability and compatibility
• 24-hour access to information, i.e., whenever the user wants it
• public library gateways to the internet providing citizens rights to information
• inclusion of local content alongside global material
• slices of information, e.g. chapters, contributions to symposia, articles, will be the norm for electronic access rather than the simple replication of books or journals
• value-added databases and features in the academic arena such as multimedia hot links
• increasing ease of economic network print delivery with authentication, copyright protection, electronic payment facilities
• customized personal information filters both for data screening and quality ratings
• an increasing jungle of complexity of electronic licensing in the short term
• the academic community reclaiming the copyright and their distribution of their research output to combat rise in costs of much 'essential' electronic information, e.g. in law, medicine and engineering.

Inevitably, the list covers a number of specific issues that relate to managing access in the electronic environment, including 'access to information with no location barrier', '24-hour access to information', 'complexity of electronic licensing' and 'academic community reclaiming the copyright', which are covered in this chapter.

How and where users may want to access e-resources

These days users expect to be able to access the majority of electronic resources to which they are entitled not just on the library premises but from the comfort of their home or any other outside location. There is also an expectation that access should be available at any time of day or night, any day of the week. The majority of, although not all, electronic resources also make it possible for multiple users to access the material simultaneously (Moyo, 2002, 52). However, there are still some resources (and libraries) that allow only single-use access to their e-resources.

There was a time when digital library users were primarily associated with the academic sector (e.g. university students and scholars) but this is no longer the case. Lesk (2005, 371) argues that the users of any library may 'range all over the world and include everyone from children to professional researchers to the retired'. Furthermore, there has been an increase of services built for private interests, such as genealogy and tourism, as well as supporting governmental systems to supply practical information to citizens (Lesk, 2005, 363). More details on the growth of digital library services in scope and availability are given in Chapter 10.

Users may follow a variety of access routes in order to navigate to an online resource that they are entitled to. For example, they may use a library catalogue or library gateway as a starting point, or go via an online learning environment (e.g. WebCT). Undergraduate students often use online reading lists as the first port of call. Some users may choose to navigate directly to the online resource or service, such as an online journal or a large resource aggregator (e.g. EBSCOhost, JSTOR). Other users may use general resource discovery tools (e.g. Google Scholar) and from there, follow a link directly to the online resource.

What needs to be protected, and why

There are a myriad of electronic resources and services that a library may provide access to, internal and external, commercial and freely available. Although not all electronic resources require access management, many do. For the purpose of this chapter we will concentrate on the most common electronic resources that fall under the following two categories (Miller, 2002, 97):

- commercially produced electronic databases, journals and e-books that libraries purchase and license for delivery via the library's web interface, to be accessed both on site and remotely
- digital materials that are produced within the library or organization and made available electronically.

It is important to bear in mind that although some resources are free to access, they may still require access management in order to manage and maintain the collection, for example an institutional repository. Equally, online systems that allow the library to provide access to, and manage, protected electronic resources also require access management, such as library gateways and electronic resource management systems (ERMs).

Commercially produced resources that need to be protected

In this section we will look at commercially produced material that is purchased and licensed by the library and so requires access management in order to ensure that only authorized users can access the licensed content. The three most common types of licensed electronic content are:

- e-journals
- e-books
- data, maps and other special resources.

E-journals

Commercially produced e-journals (also known as online journals, e-journals and online serials) are scholarly journals that are available via electronic submission on a pay-as-you-read or cost-per-access basis (Woodward and McKnight, 1995). Some e-journals are electronic copies of printed journals and some are online-only. There are also some e-journals that are copies of printed journals but contain extra material, such as videos and links to further information. Some e-journal articles miss some of the printed content, such as graphs and notes for authors (Woodward and McKnight, 1995, 72). Access to a protected journal can be via a direct link to the publisher's website or via a subscription-based online database or resource aggregator. Some e-journal articles are available full-text, while others are only available in part, e.g. an abstract.

E-books

Access to e-books is now most frequently obtained by buying titles for reading on dedicated hardware, 'readers' such as the Kindle or Koob. Libraries are increasingly making e-books available to users, usually following a model similar to that for physical books where only a few 'copies' can be borrowed at a time.

Data, maps and other special resources

Another important group of commercially available electronic resources consists of different kinds of data, digital copies of maps and other images, and other special resources, such as statistics. Special resources have benefited greatly from going digital. For example, scientists can now access vast amounts of automatically collected scientific data to find an answer to a problem which would have previously involved setting up and testing complex experiments (Lesk, 2005, 368).

Databases and search platforms

As mentioned earlier, many electronic resources can be accessed directly via the original publisher's website but it is often more convenient to navigate to a resource via an electronic database or a search platform. Libraries often buy access to protected electronic resources in bulk by subscribing to electronic databases in order to lower subscription costs.

There are different types of online databases. Rowley (1998, 104; also in Rowley and Hartley, 2008, 27–8) suggests the following database types:

1 **Reference databases**, which refer the user to another source, such as a document or an organization for additional information, or for the full text of a document. The most common types of a reference database are:
   - **Bibliographic databases**, which include citations, bibliographic references and sometimes abstracts of literature.
   - **Catalogue databases**, which show the stock of a particular library or library network. Some catalogue databases can also provide links to full text documents or further details.
   - **Referral databases**, which offer references to information or data, such as the names and addresses of organizations, or other directory-type data.
2 **Source databases**, which contain the original source data. Source databases can be grouped according to their content:
   - **Numeric databases**, which contain numerical data of different kinds, including statistics and survey data.
   - **Full-text databases**, which contain full-text electronic versions of a

document, e.g. a journal article or a book. Sometimes only a 'slice' of information, such as a book chapter or a report, is available full-text, not the whole document.

- **Text-numeric databases**, which contain a mixture of textual and numerical data (e.g. company annual reports) and handbook data.
- **Multimedia databases**, in which information is stored in a mixture of different types of media, e.g. sound, pictures, animation, video, text and animation.

Many libraries also subscribe to search platforms (e.g. EBSCOhost) that give access to a variety of databases, sometimes across several subject areas. Increasingly, libraries also use commercial (e.g. 360 Search from Serials Solutions) or home-grown search interfaces and gateways to make it easier for users to search paid-for content. Resource gateways help integrate the different products and resources to help users browse through the electronic collection (Guenther, 2000, 60). For the same reason some libraries have library portals (Moyo, 2002, 57). These systems also require access management in order to maintain the collection and to make sure that only authorized users can access restricted content.

Publicly available information that may also require access management

Many institutions, particularly academic ones, now manage an institutional repository in a bid to gain more control over the institution's research input and to lower subscription costs (Lesk, 2005, 368). Several open-source e-repository software applications are now available, notably EPrints and DSpace. Although the content in such a repository is often publicly available (although it is possible to restrict access if needed), access management is still needed in order to manage access rights of individuals who can manage and develop the collection held by the repository, e.g. add or a delete an item or change the search interface.

Some libraries have archives and special collections that they have made available online, by, for example, engaging in a digitization project (Miller, 2002, 101) or in a study that was served by the library (Balas, 2002, 40). Again, even if access to these collections is unrestricted, some access management control needs to be in place in order to manage these collections. Digital archives – both those which contain 'born digital' material, that is, items which have always been digital in nature, and those which consist of digitized material – are rapidly increasing in importance.

There are also other materials that a library may provide unrestricted access to, e.g. old exam papers and dissertations. Some libraries have intranets that contain both restricted and open content (Rowley, 1998, 194). Electronic reading list systems are also gaining popularity amongst academic libraries. All these resources and services may be available to all but they also need access management, as discussed above.

Publishers and licensing issues

In January 2011 Primary Research Group published a survey of library database practices (Primary Research Group, 2011). The survey looked at how 70 academic, special and public libraries in the UK, USA, Europe, Canada and Australia managed their commercial database subscriptions. Amongst other findings, the study found that the surveyed libraries collectively spent over US$1.259 million on paid-for electronic content. Of that amount, 43.72% was spent on consortium contracts. Electronic resources account for a major part of many libraries' overall spending budget. Purchasing and licensing electronic content is complex and requires considerable time and effort (Miller, 2002, 100). Buttler (2003, 70) argues that publishers now use licensing as 'the means' for delivering electronic content.

Licensing issues concerning access

According to Guenther (2000, 59), some of the most challenging aspects of licensing electronic resources are issues concerning access. A licensed electronic resource requires the licensor to give permission for the resource to be used by a defined user population and for a limited period of time (Moyo, 2002, 53). 'Appropriate' (or 'fair') use is defined by the agreed licence and is carried out through the processes of identification and authentication (see Chapter 5). Licence terms also specify how the content can be accessed (e.g. on-site and/or remotely), and who is defined as a 'user' (authorized and unauthorized).

Licensing agreements can be difficult to read, require knowledge of some legal and technical terminology in order to understand the licence terms, and can be vague or confusing. According to Buttler (2003, 70), most licensing activity is to do with close scrutiny of licensing terms and usually ends with 'glazed eyes' and the 'occasional headache'. Defining a user population that is permitted to access the resource can be difficult, particularly if the agreement involves several libraries, such as in a consortium agreement (Moyo, 2002, 53). Some resources only give access to a specified group of users (e.g. staff members) or to a limited number of users. While most academic libraries welcome visitors (Courtney, 2003), it is not always clear what visitors' position is in terms of access. The same goes for other special user groups, e.g. alumni. There can also be limitation on how many users can access the resource simultaneously (concurrent use). Some resources require the user to get in touch with the library to request an individual password in order to access the resource. Access methods are not always clear either (e.g. whether or not the use of a proxy, a technology described in Chapter 4, is allowed). Sometimes a resource is available from different suppliers, each imposing different access conditions. The list of examples can be continued.

Licence terms standardization

A lot of work has been done on licence terms standardization but there is still more that needs to be done. Model licences, e.g. the National Site Licensing Initiative in the UK (NESLi), help to make the licensing process easier. Guenther (2000, 58–60) gives some good tips on making smart licensing decisions. Guenther recommends using the Lib License website (www.library.yale.edu/~llicense) from Yale University and the 'Principles for Licensing Electronic Resources', a collective work by six library associations (www.arl.org/sc/marketplace/license/licprinciples.shtml), to help with licensing decisions. Guenther also advises not to be afraid of negotiating any terms that the library is not happy with. However, while licence negotiations are desirable in order to ensure the best possible access for the end-user, sometimes the library has no choice but to agree with licence conditions that it is not happy with for the sake of securing a good deal or benefiting from a consortium or other shared agreement (Buttler, 2003, 71).

Consortium agreements

Consortium agreements and other joint subscriptions are a popular way of subscribing to electronic content (Moyo, 2002, 49–50). However, as Moyo points out, this one-size-fits-all approach has its challenges, as individual decision-making and autonomy tend to be lost. It can be difficult to bring together user populations of several libraries into one. Moyo uses Penn State University, which operates in 24 locations, as an example of how any joint agreement needs to be thought through to take into account individual needs of users served by each library. Another issue is that sometimes participating libraries use different definitions for their user groups and may need to agree on common user definitions before they can proceed with the agreement (Lynch, 1998, 4). The same applies to other joint agreements, for example resource sharing.

Licensing open content

An altogether different aspect of licensing that libraries may have to deal with is licensing open content. As discussed earlier in this chapter, many institutions now have digital repositories, which means that the library has to act as an online publisher. Even if the content is free, the library needs to make sure that it seeks all the necessary permissions in order to avoid any legal disputes with either the authors or any commercial publishers that may have published the material already. Another example is so called 'orphan works', which may still be in copyright but for which the rights holders are not known or cannot be traced. In 2010 the Joint Information Systems Committee in the UK (the main public body responsible for implementing innovative use of digital technologies) commissioned a project to develop 'The Risk Management Calculator' for open content to help with these issues (www.web2rights.com/OERIPRSupport/risk-management-calculator).

Library management of licences

Considering the complexity and peculiarities of electronic resource collection building and management, it seems sensible that libraries should establish online resource collection policies to guide decision making related to digital content (Moyo, 2002, 51; Miller, 2002, 98). Guenther (2000, 58) suggests applying formal evaluation criteria to all electronic products that are considered by a library.

Another issue is the way libraries handle licensing information. Breach of licensing agreements can have serious consequences, including possible legal action. Also, licensing information being complicated and sometimes difficult to make sense of, it can be hard to make sure that users get exactly what they are entitled to. The way licensing information is kept and managed is sometimes governed by the library's organizational structure. It is not unusual for licensing information to be handled by several members of staff, each responsible for a particular type of resource. For example, the serial librarian might be in charge of everything to do with electronic journals, the data librarian might look after data sources and another librarian would be in charge of indexes/abstracts, free resources, etc. In that scenario, licensing information might be dispersed, which would make it difficult to find the necessary information quickly and easily. In 2005 the authors took part in an electronic resource survey for a project they were engaged in. Amongst other things, the respondents were asked how they managed their licensing information. Of the eight academic libraries that answered the question:

- none had a commercial e-resources management system
- all agreed that they did not have an adequate system for managing licences
- four libraries used Excel or Access databases to manage their licensing information
- six out of eight libraries were thinking of implementing an e-resource management system.

Electronic resource management systems (ERMs)

Grover and Fons (2004, 110) suggest that a library has two basic choices of how to proceed in managing electronic resources. They can either invest human and financial resources in developing an in-house electronic resource management system (ERM) or buy a commercial one.

Some libraries have invested time and effort in developing an in-house ERM and have shared their experience with others. The advantage of having an in-house system is that it can be completely customized to local needs but can be expensive in terms of money and staff time. Schulz (2001, 443–53) gives a useful summary of the pros and cons of developing an in-house e-journal management database for Griffith University in Australia. Schulz points out that although an in-house solution offers the benefit of customization, this option may not be financially viable for many libraries. Also, changes in supported software (e.g. Microsoft Office versions) can lead to additional programming work. Some in-house ERM systems are now available as open-source software, so it is worth shopping around before making the final decision.

In the last few years the commercial ERM market has grown considerably. One of the benefits of purchasing a commercial ERM is that it offers lower long-term costs and provides a solution that can be made available to a wide variety of libraries (Grover and Fons, 2004, 110). However, a commercial ERM may not be entirely customizable to fit the local needs and be easily integrated with the existing library systems. Some commercial ERMs are tied to additional services provided by that company. Maria Collins has produced two excellent articles (2005, 2008) that give a detailed overview of some of the commercial ERMs available today and selection criteria for choosing an ERM. The commercial systems design is largely based on the ERM requirements established by the Digital Library Federation's Electronic Management Initiative (Digital Library Federation, 2004). While the DLF guidelines have given invaluable assistance to commercial ERM developers, it is still important to evaluate each potential ERM very carefully to make sure it fits closely with the local requirements. It is also useful to choose a system which allows the library to display licence terms and conditions in such a way that they closely match access terms used by the library (e.g. authorized user definitions). Another issue is whether access terms and use restrictions are available as free-text entries or are machine-readable to make it easier to run reports and feed into other library and access management systems.

Summary

To summarize, even if an online resource can be accessed without any restrictions, it may still require access management. Licence management of electronic resources is complex and challenging, so it is worth developing an electronic management policy to help with the decision-making process. Investment in an electronic management system, either home-grown or commercial, can make management of electronic licensing information easier.

References

Balas, J. (2002) And What of Special Collections in the Digital Library?, *Computers in Libraries*, April 2002, 40–2.

Buttler, D. (2003) Little of Now Choice: copyright, licensing, and electronic resources (editorial), *Serials Review*, **29** (2), 69–70.

Collins, M. (2005) Electronic Resource Management Systems: understanding the players and how to make the right choice for your library, *Serials Review*, **31** (2), 125–40.

Collins, M. (2008) Electronic Resource Management Systems (ERMS) Review, *Serials Review*, **34** (4), 267–99.

Courtney, N. (2003) Unaffiliated Users' Access to Academic Libraries: a survey, *Journal of Academic Librarianship*, **29** (1), 3–7.

Digital Library Federation (2004) Electronic Resources Management Initiative, www.diglib.org/standards/dlf-erm02.htm.

Grover, D. and Fons, T. (2004) The Innovative Electronic Resource Management System: a development partnership, *Serials Review*, **30** (2), 110–16.

Guenther, K. (2000) Making Smart Licensing Decisions, *Computers in Libraries*, June, 58–60.

Lesk, M. (2005) *Understanding Digital Libraries*, Elsevier.

Lynch, C. (ed.) (1998) *A White Paper on Authentication and Access Management Issues in Cross-Organizational Use of Networked Information Resources*, Coalition for Networked Information, www.cni.org/about-cni/staff/clifford-a-lynch/publications.

Miller, R. (2002) Shaping Digital Library Content, *Journal of Academic Librarianship*, **28** (3), 97–103.

Moyo, L. (2002) Collections on the Web: some access and navigation issues, *Library Collections, Acquisitions & Technical Services*, **26**, 47–59.

Primary Research Group (2011) The Survey of Library Database Licensing Practices, www.primaryresearch.com.

Rowley, J. (1998) *The Electronic Library*, Library Association Publishing.

Rowley, J. and Hartley, R. (2008) *Organizing Knowledge: an introduction to managing access to information*, Ashgate Publishing.

Schulz, N. (2001) E-journal Databases: a long-term solution?, *Library Collections, Acquisitions & Technical Services*, **25**, 449–59.

Woodward, H. and McKnight, C. (1995) Electronic Journals: issues of access and bibliographical control, *Serials Review*, Summer, 71–8.

3

Principles and definitions of identity and access management

In order to understand the principles behind access management, it is useful to examine what constitutes an effective access management system. Clifford Lynch of the Coalition for Networked Information (Lynch, 1998) in his white paper on authentication and access management defined the key conceptual requirements and business relationships between publishers, libraries and users. This chapter also provides an overview of the key processes involved in access management: registration, authentication, authorization and accounting.

Introduction

Management of user access to online resources is something that most libraries need to do, in ways that strike a balance between three sometimes conflicting external pressures:

1 **User demand** Users want to access an information resource, as quickly and easily as possible. (If they don't, why is the library providing it? Measuring the demand for and use of particular resources is the subject of Chapter 12).
2 **Legal restrictions** Usually imposed in the form of conditions attached to the licence or other contract between each resource owner or host and the library. Usually with the objective (from the suppliers' point of view)

of ensuring that their provision of a resource to users of the library is
financially viable, bearing in mind whatever payment is involved.
(There may also be restrictions on who can access some resources, not
necessarily financial and not necessarily imposed by the supplier.)

3 **Technical feasibility (and cost)** Limiting access, rather than making a
resource completely open, will inevitably generate costs for the library
and probably the supplier too. Both will ultimately have to make
decisions on technical solutions that are commensurate with the value of
the resource.

We assume that in general the primary aim of any library is to satisfy the
collective needs of its community of users, and to do so within the limits of
its own finite budget and other resources; and entirely within the letter and
spirit of any applicable laws. The main practical aim of this book is to
support libraries and library managers in making well informed decisions
about appropriate technical solutions, whilst not attempting to delve deeply
into the reasons for user demand, nor the reasons why resource suppliers or
owners may impose particular licence restrictions. However, proper analysis
of how users behave in typical information-seeking scenarios, and the
economic or other motives for resource owners to impose the conditions
they do, will also help to understand how access can be controlled in ways
that balance the financial and legal demands that a library must meet, whilst
minimizing the barriers apparent to users.

Managing access? . . . or identities? . . . or both?

Few libraries and librarians would feel happy with a situation in which they
had only a vague idea of what specific printed items were included in their
stock. It would be almost inconceivable for a library not to make significant
investment in systems and staff time to keep close track of where (inside the
library) or in whose safekeeping (outside the library) every one of those
items was at any time.

This task disappears (in most senses) as physical printed resources are
replaced by online resources. But any library such as that of a university
with a defined membership, or any kind of organization in which some
individuals have more rights of access than any member of the public, has
the parallel problem of knowing who all of those members are. Even if there
is no qualification of who can use the facilities of a library (i.e. it's truly a
public library), the process of keeping track of items on loan can only work

if the library knows something about the people who borrow them.

The processes of managing information about library users is known as identity management, and the processes of identity management and access management are so interconnected and interdependent that it's virtually impossible to write about just one of those topics and ignore the other. The path of least resistance (and hopefully most usefulness) that the authors of this book have therefore taken is to conflate both, and to use the convenient abbreviation 'IAM' to describe our topic of identity and access management.

Although for a library, identity management could be regarded as merely a means to the end of access management, for any library that is part of a larger organization, such as a university, college or school, it's quite likely that the registration of members of the organization (students and staff, for example) will be the responsibility of departments and staff outside the library, such as personnel or student registry. Although the library is an important consumer of the identity information such outside departments collect and manage, its role as a creator and manager of identity information has a much lower profile (and nowadays is likely to be mainly confined to the registration of external visiting users).

The business relationships

For access to commercially marketed online resources, a library will negotiate a licence with each supplier for an appropriate level of access for its users. The job of licence or contract negotiation and management (and access management) can be made simpler for a library by using an aggregation service as an intermediary, which can offer a bundle of related material (science or law journals, for example) from a number of different original publishers, but the contractual relationship will almost certainly be between the library and its supplier.

At least an implicit contractual relationship will also normally exist between the library and each patron or user. This will normally be embodied in an agreement signed by an individual on enrolment, either with the library or with a larger organization (a school, college, university or business) of which the library is a part.

The relationships between supplier, library and end-user are illustrated simply in Figure 3.1.

Although the undertakings that a user gives to a library may include respecting copyright and any other restrictions imposed on the use of resources from third-party suppliers made available by the library, there

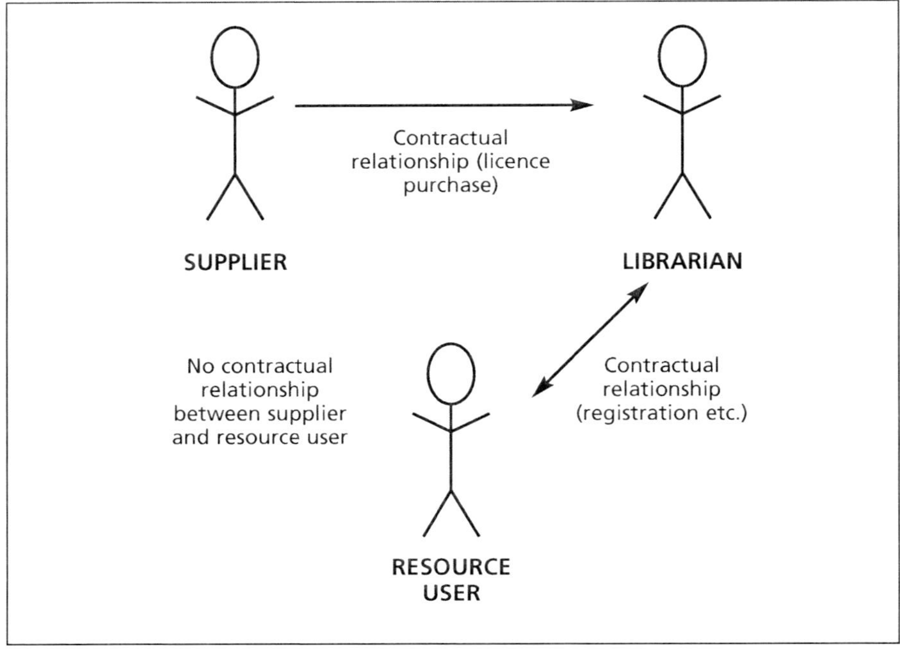

Figure 3.1 *Business relationships*

is unlikely to be any direct relationship between an individual library user and any resource supplier to the library. This may seem a trivial distinction but is vitally important when determining the responsibilities for different IAM processes and to what extent information about individual users should be shared with a resource supplier. It's complicated by the fact that some suppliers of online resources will also have large bases of individual 'retail' users (or customers) – with whom they *do* have direct contractual relationships.

The processes of identity and access management

It's convenient to regard IAM as structured into four important processes:

- registration
- authentication
- authorization
- accounting and monitoring.

Registration and authentication will usually be apparent to the user and involve some interaction with him or her. Authorization and accounting may not be. The distinction between them is necessary because they may happen at different times and also because they may be the responsibility of different parties involved in connecting the user with a resource.

Registration

Registration (or enrolment) is the initial recording by an identity manager (the library) of details about an individual user. The information needed will normally include enough to identify and distinguish that individual from others in the 'real world', such as names, date of birth and a photograph. A registration process may include the requirement to produce some existing form of photographic identification such as a passport, national identity card or driving licence.

Registration will usually be a once-only process for any individual, with any one library. To avoid duplicate records it may be necessary to check details of a 'new' user against all existing user records. For example, it is not uncommon for an individual to have a series of relationships with an organization like a university: appearing first as a potential undergraduate student, then as a student, then (possibly after a gap) enrolling at the same institution for a postgraduate course; and then perhaps turning up again later as an academic staff member. Some of the identifying details of an individual may well change during the average human lifetime: names (on marriage or for other reasons), gender, and certainly appearance. For this purpose an organization may add its own unique identifiers to each registered user record, and *never* re-use any such identifier.

For recognition and unique identification of a registered user most libraries today still issue their own card or other token – adding to the burden of many such cards carried in the average purse or wallet! As well as identifying details visible to staff of the library this may embody one (or more) forms of machine-readable information, carried on a printed barcode, a magnetic stripe or solid-state memory readable via contacts or very-short-range radio (RFID tags). This may identify either the user (most often via the issued unique identifier), or the card or token.

The reason for identifying a card, rather than the user who owns it, is because cards can be (and so often are) lost by users, and will need to be replaced. The identifier of a lost card can be flagged as such when a replacement is issued, whilst the user retains the same unique identifier. Most commonly the need for a machine-readable token is to rapidly identify a user to staff-operated and automated issue-return systems. Secondly, a token may be read by gates or turnstiles to allow access to physical library premises. Where the library is part of a larger organization, such as a university, the same card is likely to identify a student or staff member for other purposes and for access to other services or other physical areas outside the library itself.

Just a few academic and public libraries are considering moving away from the idea of issuing their own machine-readable identifying cards or tokens to users, and instead recognizing other commonly used tokens. In London, the UK capital, almost all users of public transport services carry an Oyster card (Transport for London, 2011) to pay for bus and train journeys. Each card is uniquely identified and the identifier (but not other information specific to travel and fares) can be read by commercially available RFID readers. Several University of London colleges and other academic institutions in London have considered recognizing the Oyster card presented by a user on registration, thus eliminating their own costs of producing (and replacing) machine-readable cards.

In addition, and specifically for access to online resources, the registration process will usually include informing each user of a unique identifier as a username, and an individual password. The username will not necessarily be the same as the unique user identifier mentioned above, but is likely to be more memorable and composed of, for example, the users' own name and initials.

A user password should ideally be known *only* to the individual whose it is, and should be unknown to library or any other staff involved in issuing it. Passwords should not even be 'known' to the computer systems which issue them in the first place or those that can recognize and verify them when used. How this can be done is explained in more detail in Chapter 5. On registration, a default password may be issued which the user must change before any further use.

Authentication

When a (registered) user attempts to access a protected online resource, they will often be faced with an 'authentication challenge'. Authentication is the process in which a user presents credentials of some sort to prove 'they are who they say they are'. There are many different kinds of credentials which can be used; anything which belongs to the user and not shared with anyone who is not permitted to access the protected resource is usable; usernames and passwords in combination are a commonly used example. There may be several possible 'levels of assurance' (EDUCAUSE, 2007) of user authentication, giving greater or lesser certainty of the identity of the user. Different levels typically require different kinds of credential, and the registration process needed to obtain credentials which give a higher level of assurance is typically more onerous.

Authorization

Having established (to an appropriate level of certainty) that an online user is indeed the individual they claim to be, authorization is the process of determining whether this individual should have access to this resource. For some resources (such as an editable wiki) there may be several possible levels of authorization to which different users are entitled ('read', 'write', 'edit', etc.), and different types of user may be entitled to access different parts of a resource (e.g. staff and students are likely to be able to see different resources in a virtual learning environment).

Accounting and monitoring

Accounting or monitoring of IAM is usually a back-office process, invisible to users but necessary to the administrative staff of both a library and a resource supplier. Routinely this will be to collect statistics or billing data. If unauthorized access is suspected, the same facilities and data collected can be used to investigate which user accounts may have been compromised.

Identifying the person using a resource – or not

The processes of IAM, and the different things that people want to do using online resources, generate a number of different requirements that a resource, the owner of a resource, or the library providing access to a resource should be able to identify the person accessing it, for a number of different reasons. Correspondingly there may be good reasons for a user in some circumstances *not* to be identified.

The business relationships between users and a library, and between the library and each of the resources suppliers with which it has licences, may determine whether the identities of individual users should be disclosed to the owner of a resource or whether the library has a responsibility to maintain the anonymity of individual users.

There are many perfectly legitimate and respectable reasons why a user of online resources may wish to (and should be entitled to) remain anonymous. Many fields of scientific research are fiercely competitive and a researcher in, say, the pharmaceutical industry could be concerned about the potential for competing companies to gather information on his current interests from the papers he was accessing. In some countries academics are still fearful of government monitoring of readers of sources considered 'politically incorrect'.

Obligations to protect personal data about users

A library, like most other organizations holding personal information in most countries of the world, will have legal obligations to deal with that information in fair and reasonable ways. In the UK the relevant legislation is the Data Protection Act 1998 (The National Archives, 2011). This is based on the requirements of the European Directive on Data Protection (EUR-Lex, 1995) and parallel legislation imposing broadly similar responsibilities on 'data controllers' is in force in all countries of the European Union. There is no single piece of legislation that deals with data protection in the USA. Instead there are several Federal laws that cover data protection issues, such as the Children's Online Privacy Protection Act of 1998 (COPPA, 1998) and the Health Insurance Portability and Accountability Act of 1996 (HIPAA, 1996). One increasing problem of legal compliance with data protection is the potential for globalization and 'off-shoring' of some IT facilities or processes – where personal data may be exported to a country with different legal expectations.

The processes and business relationships involved in IdM may often require the release of some data about a user to a third party. This raises the challenge of obtaining *informed consent* (European Commission, 2011) from the user for each such transfer – whilst adding as little as possible to (what many users will perceive as) barriers to the user's quick and simple access to the resource they want. Surveys and experiments (Furnell et al., 2000) have shown that many users are prepared to sacrifice personal privacy and their right to give informed consent, in return for greater ease of use – but perhaps without understanding all the consequences.

Summary

As part of their business, libraries need to provide access to resources for their users. As these resources are increasingly electronic, this means that libraries need to be involved in the processes of identity and access management, albeit in many cases principally as a component part of a larger organization which will already carry out IAM.

IAM can be divided into four areas: registration, which deals with the initiation of a relationship between the library and a user; authentication, which concerns the establishment of the identity of a user to a third party; authorization, which involves the provision of access to (all or part of) a resource to an authenticated user if that user is permitted to use it; and accounting and monitoring, which are used to measure the usage of a resource.

Many authentication processes will reveal the actual identity of a user to the resource he or she is attempting to access. This may not be necessary for the logic needed for making authorization decisions by the resource owner, and in this case, legal and moral obligations for dealing with personal data may mean that it makes sense to find a mechanism which allows authentication and authorization without releasing personal information about the user.

The topics introduced here form the subject of much of the remainder of this book.

References

COPPA (1998) The Children's Online Privacy Protection Act of 1998, www.ftc.gov/ogc/coppa1.htm.

EDUCAUSE (2007) *The Importance of Establishing Levels of Assurance*, www.educause.edu/Resources/TheImportanceofEstablishingLev/154978.

EUR-Lex (1995) Directive 95/46/EC of the European Parliament and of the Council of 24 October 1995 on the Protection of Individuals with Regard to the Processing of Personal Data and on the Free Movement of such Data, http://eur-lex.europa.eu/LexUriServ/LexUriServ.do?uri=CELEX:31995L0046:EN:HTML.

European Commission (2011) Article 29: Data Protection Working Party (Opinion 15/2011 on the definition of consent), http://ec.europa.eu/justice/policies/privacy/docs/wpdocs/2011/wp187_en.pdf.

Furnell, S., Dowland, P., Illingworth, H. and Reynolds, P. (2000) Authentication and Supervision: a survey of user attitudes, *Computers and Security*, **19**, 529–39.

HIPAA (1996) The Health Insurance Portability and Accountability Act of 1996, www.gpo.gov/fdsys/pkg/PLAW-104publ191/html/PLAW-104publ191.htm.

Lynch, C. (ed.) (1998) *A White Paper on Authentication and Access Management Issues in Cross-Organizational Use of Networked Information Resources*, Coalition for Networked Information, www.cni.org/about-cni/staff/clifford-a-lynch/publications.

The National Archives (2011) Data Protection Act 2008,
    www.legislation.gov.uk/ukpga/1998/29/contents.

Transport for London (2011) *What is Oyster?*, www.tfl.gov.uk/tickets/14836.aspx.

4

Current access management technologies

This chapter gives an overview of some current access management technologies and the advantages and disadvantages of using a particular technology.

In this chapter, we give a brief introduction to material which will be covered in more detail in Chapters 6–9 of the book, in order to give an overview of the various ways in which access management can be carried out for electronic resources. Relevant references will be given in the more detailed discussions of each of these mechanisms later on.

IP address

The simplest and least sophisticated form of online access management relies on information which is part of every internet access: the IP address. Its basic nature is indicated by the name, as 'IP' is short for 'internet protocol', one of the most important of the fundamental building blocks of the internet. An IP address is a sequence of numbers which is used to identify the source or target of a communication online; domain names such as www.google.com can be 'resolved' into IP addresses so that they can be found and accessed, and an internet service provider (ISP) will assign a computer an IP address when it arranges internet access for it.

The assignment process relies on the ISP being registered as the manager

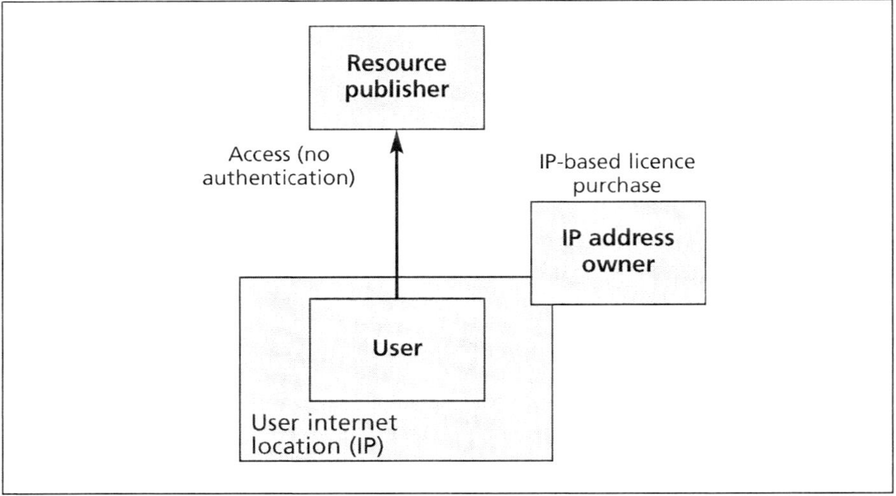

Figure 4.1 *IP address authentication*

of a group of IP addresses, and this fact makes it possible for the IP address
to be used as an access management technology, it being a simple matter for
a server to be configured to allow or block access to it from lists of IP
addresses. A college or university will have such a group of IP addresses
and, by arrangement with the publisher of a resource, can obtain access for
users who access the internet from on-campus computer equipment. Figure
4.1 demonstrates the process of IP address authentication.

While easy to set up, access control by IP address is lacking in the flexibility
needed for the modern environment. While being a nice, easy solution for
access from on campus, requiring little administration and no work from
users once they are logged on to the campus network, it does not allow access
from home users, or any means by which specific users or groups of users can
be identified, thus barring the use of such services as personalization or access
control at a more granular level than just 'in' or 'out'.

An additional problem with IP addresses is caused by the fact that they
have a fixed length. This means that there are only a certain number. For a
long while, a new version of IP addressing has been in existence to solve this
problem, and today it is rapidly reaching the point where it will be needed.
This means that the IP addresses that ISPs can assign will soon be of the new
type, and therefore will bear no relation to the older type, meaning that all
existing IP address-based access management rules will need to be updated.
For more details, see Chapter 6 .

Barcode patterns

Many vendors who sell licences to access online resources to public libraries (which tend to have limited technical resources) use barcode patterns as a simple means of access control for users not physically on the library premises. The idea is simple and easy to implement; the library describes how the codes on the cards given to members are structured (e.g. 'DD990- followed by 12 digits'), and this information is used to determine whether a user comes from a library which has a current licence or not, granting or prohibiting access accordingly. The pattern matching can be given extra sophistication if the barcode has a mechanism for error detection (like an ISBN, where 1 times the first number, plus 2 times the second, and so on, reading 10 for X, always adds up to a multiple of 11), which can be incorporated in the pattern matching. Figure 4.2 demonstrates the process of barcode authentication.

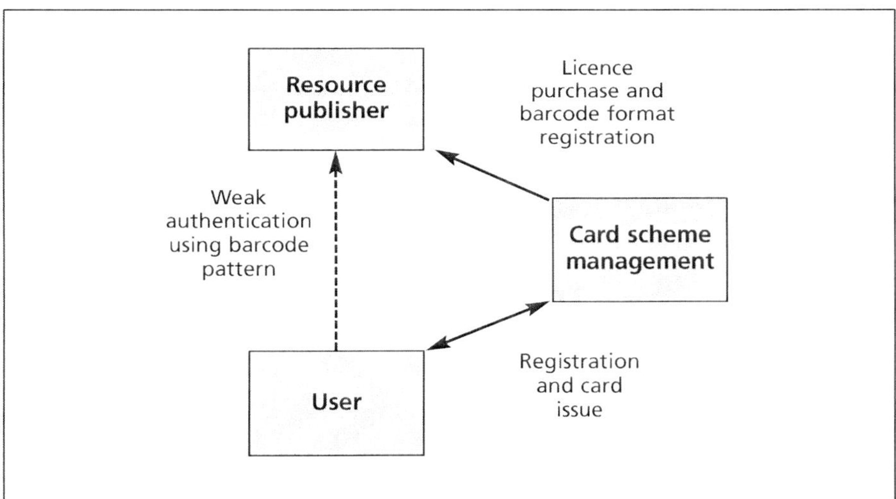

Figure 4.2 *Barcode authentication*

Barcode patterns do not act as a mechanism for authenticating the user, because they not only fail to distinguish between currently valid and invalid codes but cannot determine that the code is entered by the owner of the library card or even if they have guessed a valid pattern for one of the licensed libraries for access to the resource. However, they are easy to set up and use, requiring less technical knowledge than IP address ranges.

Proxy servers

A proxy server (or more fully, IP proxy server) is a service which extends the

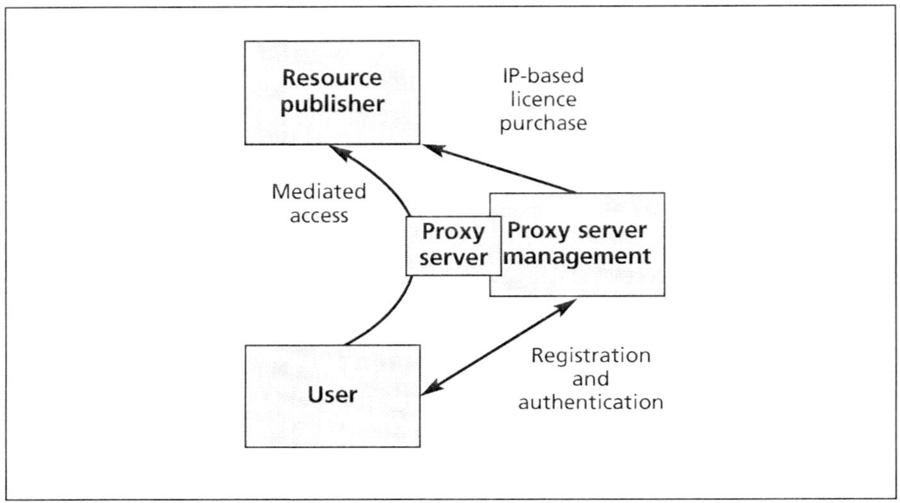

Figure 4.3 *Proxy servers*

usefulness of IP address-based access management, though that is not its only use. Essentially, a proxy server acts as a gateway between the user and the internet, or part of the internet, and as far as any services the user accesses are concerned, the user's IP address originates at the proxy server rather than at their real-world location. This allows remote users to access IP-restricted resources by appearing to be in a location from which access is permitted when in fact they are not. In order to ensure that only permitted users access the resource, a proxy server will require authentication to prove that a user is permitted access. While increasing the range of IP address-based access control, proxy servers do nothing to address the issues of distinguishing between different types of user. Figure 4.3 gives an overview of how proxy servers work.

Shared passwords

Shared passwords used to be a fairly common mechanism for controlling access to electronic resources. This method simply means that a username and password are required for access to the resource, but the same username/password combination is used by more than one person. Without further elaboration, this method of access control is simple to use, and simple for a resource publisher to set up. However, it has problems with security, especially with the need to remove access from users who are no longer privileged to access the resource. Another problem is that users do

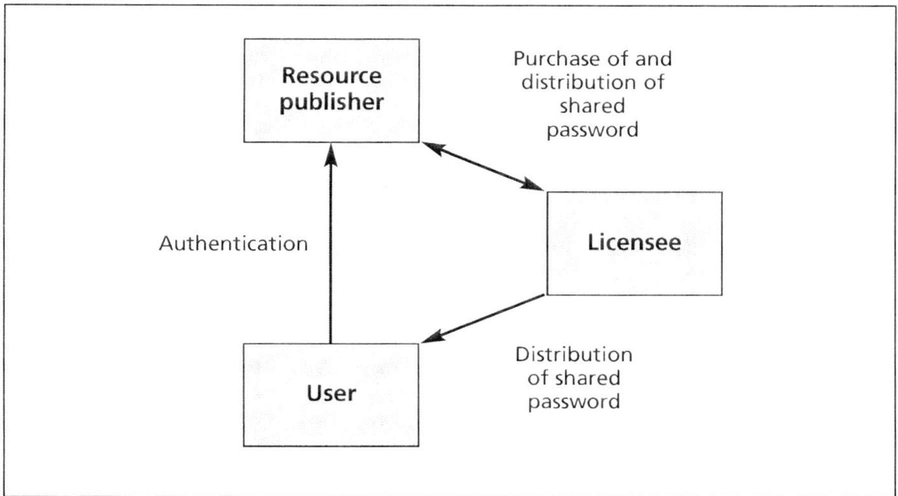

Figure 4.4 *Shared passwords*

not like the proliferation of passwords, and generally aim to make their lives easier at the expense of security (e.g. by writing down the password). With federated access as an alternative, this access control mechanism has largely faded from the access control map. Elaborations of this method can include passwords which have short expiry periods (such as ones based on the current month). Such passwords can still be used for the support of events (e.g. to provide access to the internet for conference delegates), when the password expires after the event concludes. Figure 4.4 demonstrates how shared passwords work. For more details, see Chapters 7 and 8.

User registration with publishers

Another method which was commonly used in the past was direct user registration with publishers, a process familiar still from many consumer-oriented sites. A user would complete an online form, and specify a password which would then grant access to the resource. Some confirmation would almost certainly be required, especially when a user wanted to register to a site to which they would have access paid for by another party (as would be the case when the user was a member of an organization which had purchased a licence to access the resource). With this method of access management, granular access is possible, because each user has a different username, though there are potentially problems in trying to use other information provided by the user (such as student/staff status or academic department

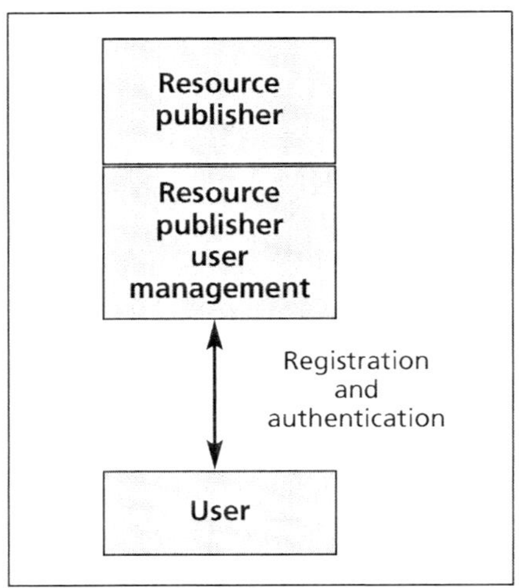

Figure 4.5
User registration with publishers

membership) for access control, as this would typically not be checked with the user's home organization.

This requires a certain amount of effort on the part of the user, and the likelihood that the user will act in an insecure manner (e.g. by using a password which was also used for other resources or selecting an easy-to-guess password) is quite high. Additionally, the publisher has to manage the expiry of users with whom they have only a fairly remote direct relationship (through the registration form, as opposed to through the purchase of a licence).

Figure 4.5. demonstrates how user registration with publishers might work.

Federated access

Federated access is a model for access control in which the authentication and authorization are separated and handled by different parties. If a user wishes to access a resource controlled by a service provider (SP), then they log into an identity provider (IdP), which passes information to the SP indicating successful authentication. If the SP trusts the IdP, then it will grant the user access to the resource. More complex forms of federated access involve the use of attributes (information about the user passed from IdP to SP, which can be used to make access decisions) and can include extra services such as trust federations and discovery services (where the user selects which IdP to use to connect to the SP).

The major advantage of this approach is that the roles of the SP and IdP are restricted to realms in which they should have special knowledge and expertise: resource management and identity management, respectively. Where the IdP is an organization which already carries out large-scale identity management processes for other reasons, this is a large potential time saving for the SP. Federated access can also provide greater privacy, including the possibility of anonymity for users (by only passing on attributes required for access to the resource they wish to use). Figure 4.6 looks at the process of federated access.

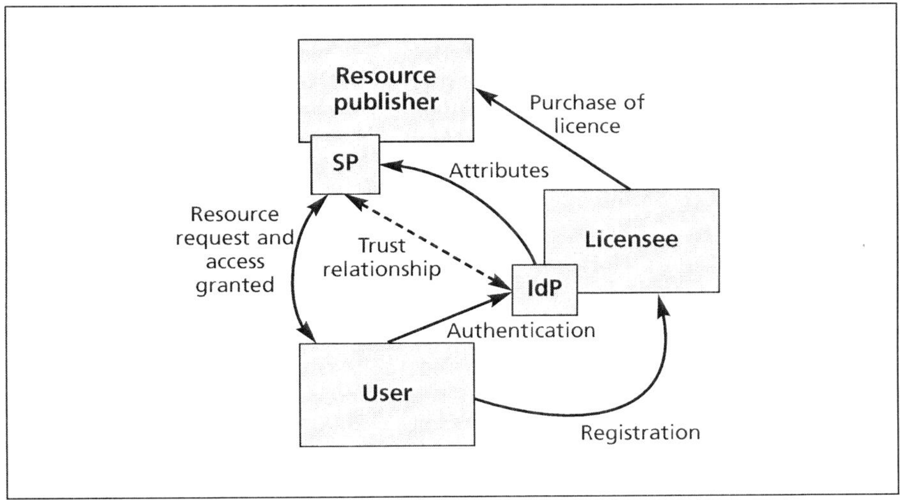

Figure 4.6 *Federated access*

A wide variety of federated access technologies exist, varying in details of the model. Familiar examples include Kerberos, Facebook and Google authentication, and Shibboleth, which is widely used in academic institutions.

Federated access software can, however, be difficult to set up for both IdP and SP, and integration with existing processes may also be hard to manage. It also requires the IdP to ensure that its processes for identity management are in fact robust and accurate, something which may not have always been the case when these processes evolved, particularly for users other than the standard staff and students (such as contractors, associates and alumni). Users can also find it confusing, especially when having to make choices of IdP, and an element of user education needs to be undertaken. For more details, see Chapters 7 and 8.

Summary

Table 4.1 provides a quick overview of the pros and cons of the technologies introduced in this chapter.

Each technology has positive and negative aspects; in practice, these can help a decision to be made about which of them might be appropriate in a given real-world situation, where there may be requirements for good security to protect a resource, but less need for security if the resource is less

Table 4.1 *Summary of the pros and cons of the most popular access management technologies*

Technology	Pro	Con
IP address	Easy to use; easy to manage; reasonably secure.	Inflexible; no granularity; no scope for personalized services; soon to require major overhaul.
Barcode patterns	Easy to use; very easy to manage; allows external users to access resources.	Insecure; no granularity; no scope for personalized services.
Proxy servers	Fairly easy to use; fairly easy to manage (established technology); allows external users to access resources; secure.	No granularity; no scope for personalized services.
Shared passwords	Fairly easy to use; fairly easy to manage.	No scope for personalized services; granularity limited; difficult to manage; likely to be used insecurely.
User registration with publishers	Fairly easy to use; easy for institutions to manage; allows personalized services; allows granular levels of access down to individual user.	Very hard for publishers to manage properly; likely to be used insecurely; difficult to allow access to some subgroups of users but not to others.
Federated access	Integrates with existing user/resource management processes; allows personalized services; can allow anonymity and enhance privacy; allows granular levels of access down to individual user and including groups of users; secure.	Can be hard to set up; users can find federated access confusing.

valuable, or where there may be little technical resource for management of the technology, or where requirements for ease of use are paramount.

References for the various access management technologies can be found in the chapters which describe them in more detail.

5

Authentication technologies

This chapter examines the different approaches to authentication, as well as what is considered good practice. It also gives an overview of some of the available technologies for authenticating a user.

'Something you know, something you have, or something you are'

As explained in more detail in Chapter 3, the four main components of access control used in most information systems are:

1 **Identification** (also called registration): 'Who are you?' – the user provides information to identify him/herself, e.g. e-mail address, user ID, name or username.
2 **Authentication** 'Are you who you say you are?' – the user verifies his/her identity or which organization he/she comes from.
3 **Authorization** 'What are you allowed to do?' – the process of determining what the identified and authenticated user is allowed to access and what operations he/she is allowed to carry out. In case of licensed information resources, this is based on user profiles and licensing permissions.
4 **Accounting** The process of collecting statistics and/or billing data. The

same tools can also be used to investigate which user accounts may have been compromised due to unauthorized access.

In this chapter we focus on the authentication aspect of access control.

Authentication is a process of establishing the user's right to an identity, in other words, the right to have a name (Lynch, 1998). While identification is usually non-private information provided by the users to identify themselves and can be known by system administrators and other system users, authentication requires private information (Zviran and Elrich, 2006). Names used to authenticate a user do not need to correspond to real names used by the user in real life (Lynch, 1998). Authentication is the first step towards protection of electronic library resources and information systems, so it is important to get it right in order to avoid security issues later.

There are many ways of authenticating a user, most commonly by means of a username and password, but can include any other method of demonstrating identity, such as a smart card, retina scan, voice recognition or fingerprints.

Menkus suggested dividing authentication methods into three types (in Zviran and Elrich, 2006, 5):

1 **Knowledge-based authentication** 'Something you know', e.g. password or PIN (personal identification number). It is based on private information supplied by the user.
2 **Possession-based** 'Something you have', e.g. smart card tokens. It is based on private objects that the user possesses.
3 **Biometric-based** 'Something you are', e.g. fingerprint, iris scan or digital signature. It is based on physiological or behavioural characteristics of the user as a living person.

Figure 5.1 gives an overview of the three main types of authentication method.

Authentication technologies overview

There are many authentication technologies available, so in this chapter we will examine and compare the most commonly used ones.

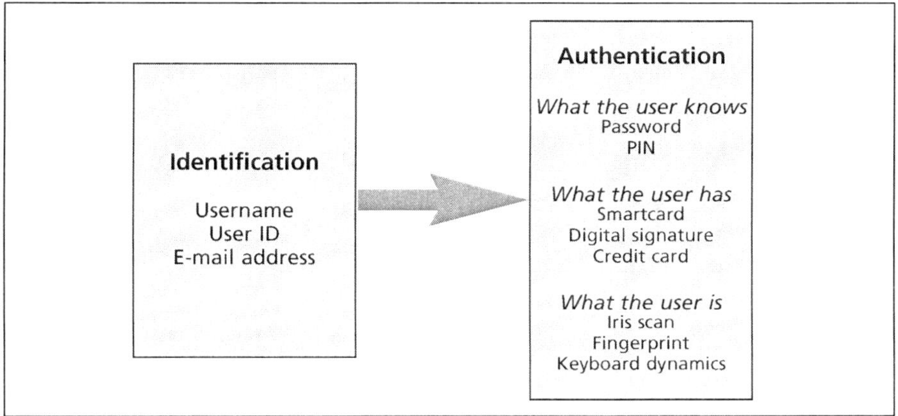

Figure 5.1 *Authentication methods*

Knowledge-based authentication

Knowledge-based authentication is based on private information supplied by the user, such as a password or PIN.

Password authentication

Password is the traditional and most widely used type of authentication. Password authentication has been used by libraries for a long time and has its distinct advantages and disadvantages.

A password is a secret word or a series of characters that have to follow some predefined rules (e.g. be a certain length and contain a mixture of letters and digits). Passwords have been used since ancient times as a way of ensuring authorized access. A secret password used in biblical times was what gave the name to one of the most rapidly developing access management technologies, now used by most academic libraries in the UK and many other countries – Shibboleth (see Chapter 8).

Passwords can take many forms. For example, a password can be a string of random characters, a phrase (known as a pass-phrase), a graphical character or even a sentence (known as a pass-sentence). Passwords can be generated by the user ('user-generated passwords') or assigned by the operating system ('system-generated passwords').

Advantages and disadvantages of using password authentication

The main reason why password authentication is so popular is that it is reasonably easy for system administrators to implement and for end-users to use. Password authentication is also one of the cheapest ways to provide security and doesn't require special hardware, so many organizations use password authentication for these reasons rather than because it provides the best protection (Stoller, 2009; Spector and Ginzberg 1994). However, password authentication is also known to suffer from several pitfalls. Stoller (2009, 44) rightly applies the famous phrase 'can't live with them, can't live without them' to people's difficult relationship with passwords.

Many deficiencies of password authentication are due to limitations of human information processing (Zviran and Elrich, 2006; Yan et al., 2004). These days most people have to remember and maintain at least several passwords (for a bank account, cash machine, Facebook, university ID, etc.), which can be a real burden. Ideally, passwords should be difficult to guess and easy to remember. That poses a real dilemma. The most secure password is a random string of characters that includes a combination of letters, numbers and other characters (Zviran and Elrich, 2006). Passwords like this are often computer-generated and not chosen by users. They are difficult to guess by others but are also difficult to remember (Spector and Ginzberg, 1994). That is why users tend to either write these passwords down, which reduces their security, or change them to something they find easier to remember – but is also easier to crack.

An approach which is now quite common is to use a secured password store, in which encrypted copies of passwords are permanently saved, accessible to a web browser (or other software) to use for authentication without user intervention when the user opens the store. This means that users can have complex passwords, and only need to remember the one which decrypts the store.

Several studies in password security have been carried out over the last 20 years. The studies show that many passwords can be cracked by a determined hacker. Some passwords can even be bypassed by relatively inexperienced intruders using free internet tools (Furnell et al., 2000; Stoller, 2009). Password data stolen by computer hackers and made public has been used to analyse the choices (see, e.g. Impervia, 2010) which people make when setting passwords, and shows that they continue to be very predictable and susceptible to a 'dictionary attack', where a digital dictionary is used to systematically suggest words to use as the password.

Password authentication on a large scale can be difficult to administer. In many cases, internet password management has been handled by the resource publishers, who have no direct relationship with the users. The problems which arise from this include difficulties in ensuring that the user is who he or she claims to be (a serious issue where the resource in question is not paid for by the user directly but is made available under the terms of a licence purchased by others), and the lack of an easy way of de-activating users who have left the authorized community (Shillum, 2004). These issues and others were important drivers for the development of the federated access model (see Chapter 7).

Passwords are sometimes shared by users. For example, since users often have to use different passwords for different systems they don't always see anything wrong with sharing a password with another user, provided it doesn't give access to their personal information (and sometimes even when it does!). In case of library resources this may result not only in compromised security but also in a serious breach of a licensing agreement. For example, this was the case with the Athens service (see Chapter 8), which 'only' provided access to library resources, and so some users felt there was no harm in sharing their Athens password with another user. This can also be true of more obviously important passwords.

Ways of improving password security

There are a number of ways of improving password protection.

1 **Following rules** A number of rules for choosing and maintaining passwords are suggested by Smith (in Zviran and Elrich, 2006, 7; Furnell et al., 2000, 530):
    *   **Non-dictionary words** Asking users to select non-dictionary words helps prevent dictionary attacks. According to Furnell et al., a dictionary-based attack can identify a password in less than 20 minutes even on dictionaries with up to one million words.
    *   **Long enough passwords with mixed types of characters** Including both upper/lower case and symbols (# ! %, etc.) in passwords increases the number of character combinations that have to be tried in order to break the password. Having passwords that are at least eight characters long also helps make the password stronger.
    *   **Password aging and not re-using** Changing passwords regularly and not re-using old passwords make it more difficult for an intruder to guess the password. It is good practice to establish a password aging policy that compels users to change their passwords periodically.

- **Complex yet easy-to-remember passwords** Passwords based on more complex data structures that are familiar to users, such as creating acronyms from a personal sentence known by a user or a mnemonic phrase, are more secure and yet are relatively easy to remember (Yan et al., 2004). Using pass-sentences – a collection of words with semantic meaning, can also strengthen passwords. The user can choose a sentence with his or her own associations to make it easier to recall it later (Spector and Ginzberg, 1994).
- **Passwords should not be shared and should not be written down** This seems obvious but is surprisingly often done by users, as already mentioned above.

2 **User education** Anne Adams and Martina Angela Sasse note (in Yan et al., 2004, 25) that users are not enemies of security, but collaborators who need appropriate information and help in order to maintain system security. The organization responsible for the user's identity management can give advice on secure password construction and maintenance which will improve password security. Users can be guided through the password creation process and made aware if they are choosing a weak password. However, it should be noted that even with the most effective user education, there will always be a significant proportion of users who will refuse or fail to follow the suggested guidelines (Yan et al., 2004; Furnell et al., 2000).

3 **Human authentication** Increasingly, authentication mechanisms involve human authentication as part of the authentication process. This is done in order to protect users against automated programs used by hackers. The user is presented with a picture that shows some characters, which the user has to type in correctly in order to finish the log-in process (the 'captcha' system). The assumption is that an automated program would not be able to recognize the characters in the picture.

4 **One-time passwords** One-time passwords are sometimes used for authentication over the internet, implemented by using smart cards (see 'Possession-based authentication' on page 46).

5 **Reducing the number of passwords the user has to remember** Having multiple passwords makes it difficult for users to remember them and use the right techniques for increasing password protection (Yan et al., 2004). Single sign-on technologies minimize the need for multiple passwords and when used to protect a range of different services may reduce the risk of password sharing (as users are less likely to share a password that also gives access to their personal information, not just

library resources). There is, of course, a corresponding danger that one password chosen by a person for many different services or resources will, if stolen, give the same range of access to the thief. The same password registered and used with different services may be more easily remembered but multiplies the probability that it could be lost by or stolen from one of those organizations and then used with others. However, mature single sign-on technologies such as Shibboleth-based federated access (see Chapter 8) do not depend on actually disclosing a user's password (nor any other authentication credentials used) to all (or indeed any) of the services for which it may be used as authentication.

Password types

There are different types of passwords and different ways of classifying them (Zviran and Elrich, 2006):

1 **Primary and secondary passwords** Zviran and Elrich suggest categorization based on the level of authentication, distinguishing primary and secondary passwords. Passwords that are used as the first level of authentication (e.g. to gain access to top-level resources, such as databases) are often referred to as primary passwords. Passwords that are used for further access control (e.g. to gain access to sensitive information) are referred to as secondary passwords.

2 **Question-and-answer passwords** Question-and-answer passwords are also referred to as security questions or secret questions. Typically the user is presented with several randomly selected questions taken from a pre-defined set of questions stored by the operating system. Access is only granted if the answer matches the user's answer stored in his profile.

There are two types of question-and-answer passwords: *cognitive passwords* and *associative passwords* (also known as word association passwords). With *cognitive passwords* users are presented with a rotating set of questions about highly personal facts and information, e.g. the name of their first school (Zviran and Haga, 1990). The aim is to create passwords that are simultaneously easy to remember and hard to guess. With *word association passwords*, users are asked to provide the system with a set of word associations, consisting of both cues and their associative responses (Pond et al., 2000). To gain access, users must provide the correct associated responses to rotating cues taken from a set of cues stored by the system (Zviran and Elrich, 2006).

Question-and-answer passwords are also the model which serves as the basis for the 'captcha' system used on the internet (and explained above) to attempt to prove that a submitter of data (such as a comment on a blog post) is human, where the user works out the letters in a distorted pattern or responds to a simple question.

Possession-based authentication

Possession-based authentication is based on private objects that the user possesses. The most popular possession-based authentication technologies are smart cards and identity tokens, and digital signatures.

Smart cards and other identity tokens

Tokens are usually divided into memory tokens and smart tokens. Memory tokens, as the name suggests, store information but do not process it (Zviran and Elrich, 2006). Special devices are used to write and to read the data to and from tokens. The most common early type of memory token was a magnetic card, although magnetic stripes are being gradually replaced on cards with contact or contactless chips. Memory tokens are often used together with a knowledge-based mechanism, such as the user's PIN or password. Combining two methods of authentication provides better security than using just one method alone. Memory tokens are not very expensive to produce.

Smart cards, on the other hand, can process information, as they incorporate one or more integrated circuits (Zviran and Elrich, 2006). Smart cards are also mostly used together with a knowledge-based mechanism, such as the user's PIN. The card (or other physical container) needs to be physically presented to the computer in order for the authentication mechanism to work. Authentication of the card involves execution of cryptological algorithms. Due to their flexibility and cryptographic capacity smart cards are used in many e-commerce applications. Due to their complexity smart cards are more expensive than memory tokens but offer a higher level of security.

Smart tokens can also take the form of a small device (often in the form of a key fob or standard-sized credit card) with a small alphanumeric display and an accurate clock included in its electronics. Each time it is activated the device will display a one-time password or number which the user must type and which the remote system (such as an online bank account service) can verify, usually for a limited period of between a few seconds and a few minutes before the one-time code expires. This avoids the need for any specialized reader connected to the terminal device used by the user, which in turn reduces the risk that such a device could be used by criminals to capture and 'replay' the code, within the expiry period.

There are different types of one-time passwords. Some one-time passwords are based on complex mathematical algorithms to generate a series of one-time passwords from a secret shared key. This makes those passwords near impossible to guess, which benefits system security. There are also time-synchronized one-time passwords that change constantly at a set time interval (e.g. once every five minutes). Some sort of synchronization between the client's token and the authentication server is required in order for time-synchronized passwords to work. Some one-time passwords are based on events, which means that once used, a new password is generated.

Token technology requires a lot of resources and effort to deploy and maintain (Yu, 2007). According to Gamby (2010), security tokens are costly for large populations of users and hard to manage for users outside the organization, for example customers and contract workers. In order to use token technology, organizations have to first purchase the tokens, put in place processes for provisioning them, and educate users on their physical protection and usage.

Biometric authentication

Authentication based on 'what the user is' is referred to as biometric authentication. Biometric authentication uses certain physiological and/or behavioural characteristics of the user, e.g. the user's face or mouse dynamics (Bhargav-Spantzel et al., 2007). Because biometrics uses unique or at least very diverse characteristics of living people, as opposed to keys or passwords they possess or know, biometrics cannot easily be shared, forgotten, lost, stolen, duplicated or overheard, which significantly improves security (Monrose and Rubin, 2000).

In general, biometric authentication systems depend on the digitization and storage of one or more samples of the user's personal attribute to be recognized, and then (at each authentication attempt) a repeat of the digitization process on the personal attribute 'presented', and a process of matching that against the stored sample(s) (Bolle, Connel and Ratha, 2002; Monrose and Rubin, 2000; Zviran and Elrich, 2006).

Biometric technologies are currently technically more complex and usually more costly than other methods, because they often require special hardware. Because of their technical complexity, allowing communication from outside locations can be a problem (Spector and Ginzberg, 1994). Biometrics is also not readily accepted by users, as it requires unique personal information, which can be seen as intrusive. Biometric devices, therefore, offer a compromise between high security/low user acceptance and low security/high user acceptance (Furnell et al., 2000). Another issue with biometric technologies is that unlike other methods, such as passwords and tokens, it is not possible to re-issue a biometric characteristic should it be stolen or compromised (Bolle, Connel and Ratha, 2002). Also biometric technologies suffer from some degree of false match or false non-match (i.e. accepting a match when there is no match and vice versa). This can happen for several reasons, e.g. dirty scanning equipment, poor lighting, the user's physiological changes due to surgery or accident (Zviran and Elrich, 2006).

There are two types of biometric devices: physiological and behavioural biometrics.

Physiological biometrics

Physiological biometrics is based on the user's physical attributes, such as:

- **Fingerprint** A computerized version of the traditional fingertip identification is the most commonly used type of physiological biometric device.
- **Hand geometry** Physical dimensions of a hand are measured using a small camera and compared with a previously stored image (Furnell et al., 2000).
- **Iris scan** A snapshot of the iris is taken by a camera and matched to a previously saved profile.
- **Facial scan** This is based on attributes of the face, bone structure, nose shape, and eye width (Zviran and Elrich, 2006).

Behavioural biometrics

Behavioural biometrics is based on user behavioural characteristics that are learned or habitual movements. The best known are:

- **Keystroke or keyboard dynamics** The process of analysing the way a user types at a computer terminal by monitoring the keyboard inputs in order to identify a recognizable pattern (Monrose and Rubin, 2000). Keystroke dynamics analysis is one of the cheaper biometric options, as the main tool required is the user's keyboard.
- **Mouse dynamics** Users can be identified by the way they use the mouse (Furnell et al., 2000).
- **Voice/ speech recognition** Based on the user's voice pattern, it recognizes slight differences in speech sounds and patterns.

There has been significant growth in the use of biometrics for personal authentication, such as the data captured and stored on the passports of many countries and routinely checked at borders. The US Department of Homeland Security 'US-VISIT' programme has probably been one of the most significant ways in which large numbers of people have encountered the customer-facing end of biometric identity authentication (US Homeland Security, 2011). More recently (from September 2010) 'Aadhaar', the Indian government programme to implement a national identity card for all Indian citizens, has been capturing biometric data from several thousand individuals per day (UIDAI, 2011).

Fictional authors and filmmakers (examples include the movies *Face Off* (1997) and *Minority Report* (2002)) have devised ingenious (and sometimes grisly) ways in which ubiquitous biometric authentication systems (usually protecting something more exciting than library resources) might be circumvented; but in reality there have as yet been only a few (albeit equally grisly) documented cases of attempted or successful theft and misuse of biometrics, such as the theft of a car owner's finger to bypass a fingerprint-activated security system (BBC, 2005).

Authentication by third parties

Authentication systems can be based at the home institution or provided by a third party. A third party solution can be either proprietary (e.g. the Athens authentication system) or open-source (e.g. the A-Select authentication system). Athens has already been discussed in this chapter. The A-Select authentication system (A-Select in short, see Chapter 8) is an open source system for authenticating users in a web environment. There is a growing number of applications that have been A-Select enabled, e.g. Blackboard and WebCT learning environments, Microsoft Sharepoint,

Oracle portal. Outsourcing an authentication solution to a third party has both advantages and disadvantages. For example, while outsourcing to a third party may make system implementation and maintenance easier, it will reduce the level of control the home organization has over the system. With proprietary solutions, subscription costs might be an issue, while with open-source solutions long-term support and system development need to be taken into account.

Choosing an authentication system

Choosing and implementing an authentication system that suits the organization's specific needs can be a challenge. There are several factors that need to considered (Furnell et al., 2000, 529):

- effectiveness
- ease of implementation
- ease of use
- user attitude and acceptance.

Another issue that needs to be taken into account is, of course, cost.

We have, hopefully, demonstrated that there is no one method that can be considered perfect. While knowledge-based authentication (e.g. password protection) is relatively inexpensive and easy to implement, it is not very secure. Token and biometric authentication methods are more secure but are more expensive to implement. They are also not readily acceptable by users, particularly biometric authentication. Zviran and Elrich (2006) offer a helpful chart that shows the ranking of the three authentication types according to the four factors suggested above.

Research shows that users have a strong preference for passwords (Furnell et al., 2000), so it is likely that passwords are here to stay. Some authors suggest combining all the three types of authentication for optimum protection but this is not something many organizations can afford, due to high cost (Stoller, 2009). Two-factor authentication systems that combine two methods of authentication (e.g. password and token authentication) is more realistic (Bolle, Connel and Ratha, 2002). The 'chip and pin' authentication used with debit and credit cards relies on the possession of the card (with its built-in chip containing a secret code) and the user's knowledge of the PIN number (an exceptionally simple password) is an important example. Tokenless two-factor authentication technologies are now being developed.

Instead of using a dedicated hardware device to deliver one-time passwords, an alternative out-of-band device (a means of communicating with the user that is independent of the technologies and networks in use for the authentication session) that the user owns and is already familiar with, such as the user's mobile phone, is used instead (Gamby, 2010). However, Stoller (2009) rightly points out that no matter how sophisticated the selected authentication technologies become, they do not remove the need to manage the data collected during the authentication process, or the task of carefully monitoring user activities once they gain access.

And, finally, the level of user authentication for access to library (or any) resources needs to be proportionate to what is being protected. As Clifford Lynch points out, that while any authentication solution needs to be 'reasonably secure', authentication strength is a somewhat 'subjective question' (Lynch, 1998, 5). Authentication is only a part of the overall access management system design and implementation. Lynch argues that it is important to keep things in perspective, as although 'most of the resources being access controlled, while certainly valuable assets, do not represent imminent dangers to public safety or national security if access control is breached' (Lynch, 1998, 6).

Summary

Authentication is a process of establishing the user's right to an identity, which may or may not correspond to their real world identity. Authentication methods have been classified into three types: knowledge-based (something the user knows), possession-based (something the user has) and biometric-based (something the user is). Within each type a variety of technologies are used to carry out authentication, of which the most widely used in the electronic world is currently the use of a password, an example of knowledge-based authentication. Smart cards are commonly used as a possession-based mechanism, while biometric-based authentication mechanisms include the scanning of fingerprints or other bodily features and the use of behavioural measurements, such as keyboard dynamics. Third parties can also be involved in authentication processes. Which authentication method is chosen depends on effectiveness, ease of implementation, ease of use, user attitude and acceptance and cost. Different mechanisms will score differently in each of these areas, and the application involved will determine how much high scores in one are to be counted against low scores in another.

References

BBC (2005) Malaysia Car Thieves Steal Finger,
http://news.bbc.co.uk/1/hi/world/asia-pacific/4396831.stm.

Bhargav-Spantzel, A., Squicciarini, A., Modi, S., Young, M., Bertino, E. and Elliott, S. (2007) Privacy Preserving Multi-factor Authentication with Biometrics, *Journal of Computer Security*, **15** (5), 529–60.

Bolle, R. M., Connel, J. H. and Ratha, N. K. (2002) Biometric Perils and Patches, *Pattern Recognition*, **35**, 2727–38.

Furnell, S. M., Dowland, P. S., Illingworth, H. M. and Reynolds, P. L. (2000) Authentication and Supervision: a survey of user attitudes, *Computers & Security*, **19** (6), 529–39.

Gamby, R. (2010) *SMS Two-factor Authentication for Electronic Identity Verification*, SearchSecurity, Tech Target, http://searchsecurity.techtarget.com/tip/SMS-two-factor-authentication-for-electronic-identity-verification.

Impervia (2010) *Consumer Password Worst Practices*, The Impervia Application Defence Center white paper,
www.imperva.com/docs/WP_Consumer_Password_Worst_Practices.pdf.

Lynch, C. (ed.) (1998) *A White Paper on Authentication and Access Management Issues in Cross-Organizational Use of Networked Information Resources*, Coalition for Networked Information, www.cni.org/about-cni/staff/clifford-a-lynch/publications.

Monrose, F. and Rubin. A. (2000) Keystroke Dynamics as a Biometric for Authentication, *Future Generation Computer Systems*, **16**, 351–59.

Pond, R., Podd, J., Bunnell, J. and Henderson, R. (2000) Word Association Computer Passwords: the effect of formulation techniques on recall and guessing rates, *Computers & Security*, **19** (7), 645–56.

Shillum, C. (2004) The Growing Authentication Problem: does Shibboleth technology provide the answer?, *Elsevier Library Connect Newsletter*, **2** (1), 1–2, http://libraryconnectarchive.elsevier.com/lcn/0201/lcn020105.html.

Spector Y. and Ginzberg, J. (1994) Pass-sentence – a New Approach to Computer Code, *Computers & Security*, **13**, 145–60.

Stoller, J. (2009) Authentication – Passwords and Beyond, *CMA Management*, **82** (9), 44–6.

UIDAI (2011) Aadhaar: the UID brand name and logo, http://uidai.gov.in/index.php?option=com_content&view=article&id=145&Itemid=2.

US Homeland Security (2011) US-VISIT programme,
www.dhs.gov/files/programs/usv.shtm.

Yan, J., Blackwell, A. F., Anderson, R. and Grant, A. (2004) Passwords Memorability and Security: empirical results, *IEEE Security and Privacy*, September/October, 25–31.

Yu, S.-C. (2007) RFID Implementation and Benefits in Libraries, *The Electronic Library*, **25** (1), 54 – 64, www.emeraldinsight.com/journals.htm?articleid=1593795&show=abstract&.

Zviran, M. and Elrich, Z. (2006) Identification and Authentication: technology and implementation issues, *Communications of AIS*, **17**, 2–30.

Zviran, M. and Haga, W. (1990) Cognitive Passwords: the key to easy access control, *Computers & Security*, **9**, 723–36.

6

Authorization based on physical location: how does the internet know where I am?

A large proportion of access decisions (or authorization decisions) are based on the physical location of the user. The design of the internet means that it is quite difficult for a resource host to know, for sure, where a user is in the physical world. This chapter explains how the topology of the internet relates to the geography of the real world, and how services can make access decisions by making a 'reasonable guess' about the location of a user based on an IP address.

Introduction

The internet is based on technical protocols which allow the traffic which uses the network to find its destination. While humans rely on the domain name system, the computers which actually handle the routing of data use the more fundamental and more systematically structured IP address system. As well as providing the (non-physical) location of devices attached to the internet, this underlying structure can be used to determine physical location too, and this is the basis for some of the simplest forms of access control, even if the structure itself is quite technical and has a complex history.

Domains and domain names

Domain names are effectively the basis for human-understandable interaction with the internet. People are familiar with typing URLs (uniform resource locators), such as http://en.wikipedia.org/wiki/Rivera_Plate (obtained from Wikipedia's random article function), into web browsers in order to access the resource.

A URL can be broken up into several pieces. The first piece is the choice of how to access the resource (here http, which is the basic protocol used on the web), then the domain name (here en.wikipedia.org) which indicates the location of the resource, classically a single server attached to the internet, and then the 'path', the specific location of the item required on the server (here /wiki/Rivera_Plate), a single web page or a call to software to generate a viewable page (as in this case). A complete domain name such as en.wikipedia.org is known as a 'fully qualified' domain name. Not only does the URL move from the general to the specific, but so does the domain name itself – though it does so from right to left instead of left to right, for historical reasons. In the example, the most general part, known as a top level domain (TLD), is 'org', more or less indicating a non-commercial organization which is either American or international in scope. (The caveat will be explained below.) Next comes 'wikipedia', which is one such organization, and then 'en', which is more specific (in this case, the English language site for wikipedia). Figure 6.1 gives an overview of domains and domain names.

(How) is all this governed?

In the 1980s (Mockapetris, 1983), there were originally two types of TLD, one group of two-letter abbreviations for the countries of the world, and the other consisting of seven generic three-letter codes: 'com' (commercial), 'edu' (educational), 'gov' (government), 'int' (international), 'mil' (military), and 'net' (networking, or technical), and 'org' (organizations). The two-letter country domains are taken from the ISO-3166 standard (ISO-3166 Maintenance Agency, 1974 onwards), with a small number of exceptions, of which the most commonly seen is the United Kingdom: 'uk' rather than 'gb'.

The overall system of TLDs is overseen by the Internet Corporation for Assigned Names and Numbers (ICANN) (www.icann.org/), an American not-for-profit organization set up by the US government in 1998, when it wished to distance itself from the management of the internet. The number of generic TLDs has gradually increased to the current level of around 20, and is likely to increase explosively over the next few years, following proposals put forward at the 32nd International Public ICANN Meeting in

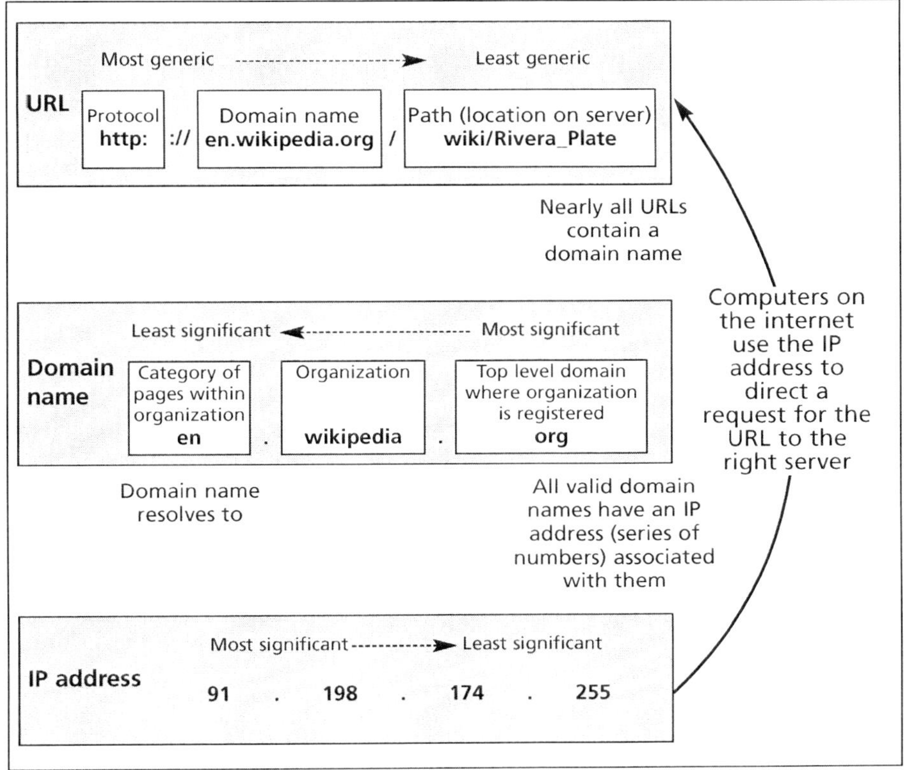

Figure 6.1 *Domains and domain names*

2008 (http://par.icann.org), as described in the *gTLD Applicant Guidebook* (ICANN, 2012), which basically permit any organization to apply to register a new TLD.

Each TLD has an associated registrar, which accepts registrations for second level names within their top level domain, usually charging a small fee to do so. They can delegate their authority so that some other body becomes the registrar for a second level domain. For example, in the UK the registration authority for the '.uk' TLD is Nominet UK (www.nominet. org.uk/). Originally, strict rules were often enforced by naming authorities, to try to ensure that domains such as '.co.uk' contained only registrations for actual companies, but over time this type of restriction has been lifted, so that almost any name can now be used as long as it does not infringe the rights of others (e.g. it is not permitted to register a trademark which belongs to someone else) (Nominet, 2012, Section 7). Moreover, some country TLDs have been used to make money for the naming authority, or because they make the domain part of a phrase in English; this is the case with 'go.to', registered within the Tonga TLD, for example.

IP addresses

Having described domain names as the basic human interface to the internet, the obvious question which arises is 'what are they an interface to, precisely?' What is the underlying structure of the internet? The answer to this question is given by one of the most fundamental building blocks for the internet: the aptly named internet protocol (IP). Discussion of this is obviously going to be rather technical, but it is necessary to understand something about IP in order to understand how some types of access management on the internet work.

The internet protocol and the definition of an IP address

Part of a collection of standards known collectively as the Internet Protocol Suite, IP is responsible for the way in which data travels around the internet. The data is divided up into 'packets' or 'datagrams', each of which has a header containing metadata including the source and destination of the packet. At each point in the journey, the computer managing the navigation process (known as 'routing') will send it on to another computer which is basically the routing computer's best guess as a location closer to the destination.

The crucial aspect of routing in IP is the method used to determine the location on the internet of other computers around the world, and this is decided through the use of the 'IP address'. An IP address is a collection of numbers defining an 'addressable' (that is, accessible) location on the internet, and they currently are of two basic types, as defined in versions 4 and 6 of the Internet Protocol Standard (abbreviated as IPv4 and IPv6 respectively).

IPv4 and IPv6

IPv4 (Information Sciences Institute, 1984) was published in 1981 (it was in fact the first version of a protocol with the name, but the number was chosen to reflect earlier related protocols). It defines addresses for internet locations in the form of a quartet of binary numbers, usually printed for human consumption as decimal numbers between 0 and 255, with stops ('.') to indicate the divisions: 192.39.215.2, for example.

There are various ways of describing ranges of IP addresses of this form; one of the most common is to refer to all 16,777,216 addresses sharing the same first number as a 'class A', all 65,536 sharing two initial numbers as a 'class B', and the 255 sharing three initial numbers as a 'class C'. As with domain names, IP addresses are assigned to organizations and computers, and organizations the size of universities would typically own one or more class B addresses.

The problem with IPv4, recognized in the 1990s, is that the number of available addresses cannot cope with the expansion of the internet. There are only 4,294,967,296 addresses available, not even enough to assign each individual on the planet a personal address, let alone to cope with the explosion in internet-connected devices in the days when phones, fridges and televisions can access the internet. Additionally, historical choices meant that some organizations pivotal in the development of the internet before 1981 had been assigned a whole class A block, one in 256 of all IP addresses, even though by the 1990s they had a much less important role in the internet than this would suggest, aggravating the shortage (see IANA, 2012). In 2000, Stanford University (USA), for example, returned their class A address to the IANA, which manages IP addresses, to help alleviate the shortfall in available addresses (Marsan, 2000).

This led to the publication of a new version of IP, IPv6 (Deering and Hinden, 1998) in 1998. (IP version 5 was the unofficial name for an experimental protocol which was never widely used.) In IPv6, the addresses have been expanded to an octet of binary numbers (each still in the range 0 to 255), which increases the number of available addresses to the point where every atom on the planet earth could be given a specific address. An IPv6 address is usually quoted in hexadecimal rather than decimal notation. That is, instead of using the digits 0 to 9 as in decimal, the letters a to f are also available, giving sixteen digits rather than 10. So an IPv6 address will look like 1a:f3:24:9b:38:f1:04:c7.

The problem which has arisen, which has delayed the adoption of IPv6 across the internet, is that not all the software which has been developed to handle routing for IP across IPv4 addresses can be used for routing for IPv6 addresses. New software needs to be written, and installed on every device connected to the internet. The high cost of doing so has led to the adoption of temporary measures which have allowed the use of IPv4 in more creative ways without having to replace the most fundamental software governing the internet, as well as freeing up many unused addresses such as the class A blocks mentioned above. These measures include: dynamic addresses, in which computers which could be attached to the network are only assigned temporary IP addresses using the Dynamic Host Configuration Protocol (DHCP) (Droms, 1993), when they actually are connected rather than having permanent addresses configured; and Network Address Translation (NAT), which allows the use of large numbers of local IP addresses by computers without the internet having to assign addresses for each of them, using localized routing solutions (Srisuresh and Holdrege, 1999). This has left IPv6 in use mainly on test networks or in pilot implementations.

But we are now reaching the point where IPv6 is starting to be adopted on a larger scale for production systems. It has, for example, been usable for routing on JANET (the UK academic internet provider, or NREN) as a production service since 2006 (Chown, 2006). This means that it now needs to be taken into account in any discussion of IP.

Domain Name System (DNS) resolution

The connection between the human-friendly domain system and the computer-friendly IP address is the role of Domain Name System resolution.

In the early days of the internet, it was possible for each computer to store a list of all the other computers connected to the internet (or the precursors of the internet) that it needed to know about. This was done with a file named 'HOSTS.TXT', which consisted of a list of names (not necessarily full domain names, but possibly nicknames for quick and convenient access) with their associated IP address. Each line of the file consists of a host name and an IP address. This file, now sometimes just named 'hosts' is still in existence in computer operating systems today, but little used. Standard HOSTS.TXT files would have to be distributed to every computer online each time the network changed in order for the networking to continue in operation.

The introduction of the domain names described in the first section of this chapter was a consequence of the hosts files becoming too complex for easy distribution around the internet. DNS resolution is handled by special computers, named 'name servers' or 'resolvers', which know how to access a large number of domains. Each domain name has a registration record, which is stored in several resolvers, though not all. However, each resolver also knows where more information can be found about domains it does not have a local listing for. For example, a resolver based at the University of Bath (UK) would have a list of all the local domains which are part of 'bath.ac.uk', and probably many other common domain names, but would pass queries about domains it does not know about, such as www.japantimes.co.jp, to other servers.

Many DNS servers will create a cache of the IP addresses to which requested domain names resolve, which makes the resolution process quicker but can cause problems when the IP address associated with a domain name changes. The use of caches has unfortunately proven to be vulnerable to an attack method known as 'DNS cache poisoning', in which data is introduced into a DNS server cache in order to re-route requests for common domain names to hosts controlled by the hacker, often for the purpose of loading malicious software onto the computer making the request (see, for example, Dougherty, 2008).

As well as having a HOSTS.TXT file, each computer also has a 'RESOLV.CONF' file (or equivalent). This basically lists the IP addresses of a small number of DNS resolvers, generally those set up by the internet service provider the computer is connected to or by the organization which owns the computer. So when accessing a website, say, the first stage is to find a resolver in the resolv.conf file, then send a request to the resolver to find the IP address of the web server at the required domain.

What may seem slightly strange about DNS resolution is that, because every item of information passed across the internet is turned into a series of zeros and ones, DNS resolution consists of turning one series of zeros and ones into another. But it is the controlled nature of the second series which makes the whole process of connecting to another computer across the internet possible.

Access control using IP addresses

When an IP request packet reaches a server, the information included in the packet includes the source IP address from which it originated. (Some exceptions are discussed later.) The server can make this information available to applications it hosts, and these applications can then make access control decisions based on the IP address from which the original request was made.

While it is possible to use single IP addresses for the purpose of access management, it is usually groups of them that are used, especially when use of the DHCP protocol can make it impossible to use an IP address to accurately identify an individual computer from one session to the next. So it is common for access to be allowed to several class B or class C blocks of addresses. Sometimes more complex collections of IP addresses are needed, for example to allow the fourteen computers in one particular room access to a resource, but no others. This can be done but is beyond the scope of this book.

In the context of a university library managing access to electronic resources, IP addresses make a convenient and simple way to pick out the computers which are actually on campus from ones anywhere else on the internet. This means that many resource providers will allow the registration of groups of IP addresses from which browsers are allowed access to the resource without any request for authentication whatsoever, on the assumption that computers allowed access through the campus network will belong to members of the university as defined in the resource's licence agreement.

The differences between IPv6 and IPv4 mean that with the use of the newer standard, any existing IP-based authorization to any resource, external or internal, will need to be redefined; otherwise, users who expect to be able to access a resource will no longer be able to do so. IPv4 has been in use for so long that there are likely to be many places in which it has been configured to be used for access control. All will need to be updated as part of the move towards the newer standard.

IP proxies

Earlier, we mentioned that there were some exceptions to the rule that the destination of an IP packet has access to its source IP address. The use of IP proxying is one important case where this happens. There are various types of IP proxy, but the purpose of all of them is to make the destination for IP packets believe that the packet came from a different source from the one it actually started at. The technology for doing this can be used for a wide variety of purposes, including the promotion of anonymity and avoidance of censorship (e.g. www.torproject.org), but in access management it is generally used to widen the locations which can be used to access a resource which is restricted by IP address, by allowing legitimate users of the resource to authenticate themselves to a service which then re-routes the IP packets from the user to the resource so that the resource believes that they came from a source with an IP address which should be allowed access: in other words, a user with an IP address from off-site appears to a resource to have an IP address which is on-site.

Virtual private networks

A virtual private network (VPN) is a service offered by many organizations to off-site members. A VPN is a network service which needs to be configured on a computer which uses it, but will then route some IP packets (exactly which depends on configuration) so that they travel via an on-site VPN server and so that the resource being accessed believes that the on-site server itself is the source of the packet using the VPN server as an IP proxy. The accuracy of this belief is dependent on a requirement for the user to authenticate in order to gain access to the VPN.

Many VPN implementations for IP use Secure Shell (SSH) (Barrett, Silverman and Byrnes, 2005) tunnelling or similar protocols such as the Microsoft Point-to-Point Encryption protocol (MPPE) (Pall and Zorn, 2001) to provide security. Tunnelling is a mechanism where one protocol is used to carry information expressed in another protocol, using a trick named 'encapsulation'. As far as the network is concerned, all the data which is passing across uses the encapsulating protocol, in this case SSH/MPPE, and the hidden data is decoded and processed at the destination, in this case the VPN server. The point of the encapsulation in this case is to use an encrypted protocol, and the tunnelling process means that the actual requests made by the VPN user are hidden from the open internet and can only be understood by the VPN server which is the destination of the SSH/MPPE session.

As well as security, the advantages of a VPN are that users of one are able to use any protocol which runs on IP, so that they are often used to allow administrators of services access to them from off-site who require access using something other than the web protocol HTTP; and that, once configured, they can be used without further intervention from the user. The disadvantages of a VPN are that configuration of the client computer is a fairly technical operation, and can be difficult for users to accomplish; and that the VPN server acts as a single point of failure, that is, if the VPN server is out of action, then there is no VPN.

Remote desktop services

A remote desktop service is just that. Special client software needs to be installed on a computer, and is used to access a remote desktop service inside an organization. A window on the user's desktop then appears and mimics what would be seen on a computer on-site, providing the applications which would be seen on a typical computer in the organization, including web browsers, e-mail clients, word processors and so on. This is not precisely IP proxying, as any access attempt made through the web browser on a remote desktop really does originate inside the institution, but like the other services discussed here, it does provide a mechanism by which an off-site user can appear to be on-site.

Remote desktop services are fairly easy to set up and configure by the user, but the client software is often a very slow application even over fast broadband, as a lot of data needs to be passed between client and server. Their use can be frustrating due to the lack of connection between the main desktop and the remote desktop (e.g. for web browser bookmarks), and because the applications available from a remote desktop service are typically fairly limited and may differ from the ones to which a user is accustomed.

EZProxy

The two services discussed so far will allow IP proxying for any application. EZProxy, on the other hand, is specific to the web (and is not precisely an IP proxy). It is free software originally developed by Chris Zagar from Estrella Mountain Community College (USA), and is now owned by OCLC (www.oclc.org/us/en/ezproxy/default.htm). It will work with any modern web browser without modification. (There are also web browser-specific IP proxying products which use plug-ins and extensions.) Essentially, EZProxy is a server to which users authenticate, and which then will make web requests on behalf of the user, relaying the returned data to the web browser run by the user. So as far as the resource provider is concerned, all the accesses come from the EZProxy server, using the EZProxy server IP address. The user no longer accesses the resource provider directly; all the URLs that are used will direct the user to the EZProxy server instead. So to access www.sciencedirect.com over EZProxy, the user might be directed to http://sciencedirect.ezproxy.ox.ac.uk and authenticate there, not to Science Direct but to the EZProxy server at the University of Oxford (UK), using their credentials supplied by the university. Any links which appear on the page that the user has accessed are rewritten by the software, so that clicking on one will carry the proxying process out again, for a new URL.

EZProxy is probably the easiest IP proxying technology to use, but still has similar limitations to other methods of making a user's IP address appear to come from a different location. It can also be confusing when a user wishes to access a subscription site when they have discovered the link in a search engine, so the URL used to access the resource doesn't have the special form needed to pass through the proxy server.

IP spoofing

IP spoofing is another technological way to make it appear to the destination of an IP packet that the source of the packet is somewhere other than the real source. It is generally more associated with illicit computer use than with legitimate access to resources.

How it works

As already described, each IP packet contains the IP address which was the source of the request. This is used by the server which receives the request to work out where any response should be sent. Since the source IP address is set by the IP software used by the computer sending the request, it is possible to set up the software to send a different IP address from the real one; this is IP spoofing.

Since the server relies on the return address to send a response, this will therefore be sent to the wrong address, and (in almost every case) it will not be received by the real requester. This restricts use of IP spoofing. It is commonly used for attacks on computers where the attacker does not have any need to receive a response, including Denial of Service attacks, where large numbers of requests are sent to servers, with the aim of forcing their owners to take them off the internet or making them inaccessible to legitimate users. The major legitimate use of IP spoofing is similar, where large numbers of requests are sent to servers to test how they would behave in real-life situations with many users, before making the server live to real access.

A second, more relevant, illicit use of IP spoofing is to break through IP address-based authentication. In modern systems, little can be done this way when a response is expected, as it would be, for example, in a request from off-campus to obtain an electronic web-based resource which is restricted to on-campus IP addresses. Some older Unix servers included mechanisms which would, for example, permit remote execution of commands with IP-based authentication. This would be virtually unheard of today even for the more trusted local machines, as it is clearly a major security hole – the remote commands could include destroying or overwriting the information stored on the server, or making sensitive information accessible on the open internet for the attacker to harvest.

Most IP spoofing attacks can be prevented using modern software, avoiding IP-based authentication, which gives high levels of access, and by good practice configuration of routers (so that packets which arrive at the local network from the external internet but which claim to come from local

IP addresses are blocked). IPv6 also includes built-in measures which act as protection against IP spoofing attacks.

Benefits and problems of using IP address-based licensing

IP address-based licensing is easy to set up and configure, both in the institution and at the resource provider, and involves no work for on-campus users at all. However, allowing access to legitimate users who happen not to be on-campus can be complex for the user to setup, or make their access to the resource unacceptably slow. It has drawbacks, including the possibility of access by individuals who are not members of the institution but have temporary network accounts, such as consultants and contractors, and inflexibility for use with complex access requirements, as it will not allow different levels of access to different categories of institutional member (unless they can be given different IP addresses), and it will not allow for such extra services, such as personalization, without additional authentication.

Summary

Use of the internet depends on the interaction between the human-friendly domain name system and the underlying computer-friendly IP address system, both of which have a long and complex history. Both allow the determination of the location of an internet user or server, with some limitations, and this can be used to allow or deny access to the server. Various solutions exist to make this more friendly for a modern user base; which requires the ability to access resources from anywhere, essentially by making the resource determine the user location as the one which is permitted access even when they are somewhere else. Some of these solutions are easier to use than others, but they all have drawbacks, including use by users who are not supposed to access the resource but who happen to be in the right place, and inflexibility for complex access management decisions.

Many of the topics covered above are described in a great deal more technical detail in the TCP/IP Guide (Kozierok, 2005).

References

Barrett, D. J., Silverman, R. E. and Byrnes, R. G. (2005) *SSH, the Secure Shell: the definitive guide*, 2nd edn, O'Reilly.

Chown, T. (2006) *IPv6 Technical Guide*, UKERNA, https://community.ja.net/system/files/487/ipv6-tech-guide-for-web.pdf.

Deering, S. and Hinden, R. (1998) *RFC 2460: Internet Protocol, Version 6 (IPv6) Specification*, Internet Engineering Task Force, http://tools.ietf.org/html/rfc2460.

Dougherty, C. R. (2008) *Vulnerability Note VU#800113: multiple DNS implementations vulnerable to cache poisoning*, US Computer Emergency Readiness Team, 8 July 2008, www.kb.cert.org/vuls/id/800113.

Droms, R. (1993) *RFC 1531: Dynamic Host Configuration Protocol*, Internet Engineering Task Force, http://tools.ietf.org/html/rfc1531.

IANA (2012) *IANA IPv4 Address Space Registry Version 2012-04-23*, www.iana.org/assignments/ipv4-address-space/ipv4-address-space.xml.

ICANN (2012) *gTLD Applicant Guidebook Version 2012-01-11*, http://newgtlds.icann.org/en/applicants/agb/guidebook-full-11jan12-en.pdf.

Information Sciences Institute (1984) *Internet Protocol: DARPA internet program protocol specification*, http://tools.ietf.org/html/rfc791.

ISO-3166 Maintenance Agency (1974 onwards) *ISO's Focal Point for Country Codes*, www.iso.org/iso/country_codes.htm.

Kozierok, C. M. (2005) *The TCP/IP Guide Version 3.0*, www.tcpipguide.com.

Marsan, C. D. (2000) Stanford Move Rekindles Net Address Debate, *Network World*, 24 January 2000, www.networkworld.com/news/2000/0124ipv4.html.

Mockapetris, P. (1983) *RFC 882: domain names – concepts and facilities*, Internet Engineering Task Force, http://tools.ietf.org/html/rfc882.

Nominet (2012) *Terms and Conditions of Domain Name Registration – Effective from 1 May 2012*, Nominet UK, www.nominet.org.uk/disputes/terms/newtermsandconditions.

Pall, G. and Zorn, G. (2001) *RFC 3078: Microsoft Point-To-Point Encryption (MPPE) Protocol*, Internet Engineering Task Force, http://tools.ietf.org/html/rfc3078.

Srisuresh, P. and Holdrege, M. (1999) *RFC 2663: IP Network Address Translator (NAT) terminology and considerations*, The Internet Society, http://tools.ietf.org/html/rfc2663.

7

Authorization based on user identity or affiliation with a library: who you are? Or what you do?

Traditionally, most authorization decisions have been based on the user's identity but in recent years a new generation access management infrastructure based on the user's role(s) within the organization has emerged. This approach offers a number of advantages, such as increased internet security and opportunities for fine-grained authorization. This chapter examines how role-based authorization works and the benefits of using this approach.

Basing access on identity, or on affiliation with a library

The traditional method of obtaining access to electronic systems and resources is based on an extremely simple authentication model: a user establishes their identity to the system (e.g. by providing a username and password pair) and that identity is processed by the system to decide what type of access to grant.

In recent years, the requirements of electronic resource access have exposed weaknesses in this model in its simplest form, and so new models have been developed to meet the needs of the internet. A brief description of some of the problems encountered in this model follows.

Identity-based authentication requires effort from the user

With a multiplicity of electronic resources all separately managing authentication and access, there is no support for single-sign-on between the resources, and the user needs to maintain many separate credentials for access. This often takes the form of needing to remember many usernames and passwords, something which leads to insecure practices (password re-use, keeping old and possibly compromised passwords in use, writing down or storing plain text copies of passwords, etc.) as a means to aid memory.

Identity alone does not give enough information to make informed access decisions

The traditional authentication model has been established for access to electronic resources since the earliest days of shared access computer systems: The Compatible Time Sharing System (CTSS), developed at the Massachusetts Institute of Technology (USA), had a LOGIN command which requested a password from the user as long ago as 1961 (Walden, 2011). Its simplicity, so far as users are concerned, is its great strength but it has a price, which is that the resource/service provider (whether Facebook or the smallest publisher website) needs to have a way of calculating the access rights for the user based on this single piece of information. Effectively, this means that some kind of table of the user rights associated with each identity needs to be maintained by the resource provider, and this is a complex business when the number of identities permitted to use the system could be in the millions.

The problem is clear: the resource/service provider potentially needs to maintain a large quantity of extra information for each user beyond the simple fact of successful authentication. Sometimes, this is precisely what is needed (e.g. when a collection of editable resources allows access only to individuals invited by other authors, as is the case for services like GoogleDocs). But usually the possible access rights within the system will be based on memberships of specific groups of individuals (such as students or staff in a university, as membership categories in the university library).

Not only is there no need for the service provider to be able to narrow down the identity of someone requesting access to a specific individual, but the system which does so requires the duplication of work carried out elsewhere. In the case just mentioned, the university has many reasons to accurately manage details of who its students and staff are, in a timely fashion; while the resource provider is doing the same work just for access to the resources, and for all those organizations which have purchased licences.

Identity gives more information than is needed to make informed access decisions

At the same time, the personal information about a user is precious to them, and he/she has a right to privacy. A username is a unique identifier, and as such provides a key to the discovery of this personal information. In simple federated models, such as the common use of authentication relating to a large commercial provider of internet-based services offered by many websites ('Login with Facebook or Google ID'), the identity used to authenticate can be available to the resource provider and at the same time links back to profiles and self-published personal information. Sometimes the username itself can be personal data, as it is when an e-mail address is used for this purpose, something which is very common.

Thus, the use of simple authentication directly to the resource gives away data which the resource provider has no reason to know, as it is not actually important to the question that they are actually asking: 'Can the user access this resource or not?'

Role-based authorization

Federated models of authentication and authorization

The initial step away from the models in which the resource provider needs to manage the identities of its users is federation. This essentially means that authentication and authorization are separated from each other, and it is a basic step which allows agent-based single-sign-on protocols to work. Essentially, the user authenticates to an identity provider, which then (in some way) passes a token indicating that authentication has been successful to the service provider. This enables the service provider to provide authentication protected services without having to verify credentials itself; the credentials involved do not necessarily have to be username/password pairs.

Federated access models are now used frequently online, in which the authentication is not to the system which contains the resource, but to an 'identity provider', and this provider then communicates with the service (or 'resource provider') on behalf of the user.

One of the best known early versions of such a model is Kerberos, an authentication protocol designed at MIT in the 1980s and still widely used today: it is built into popular operating systems, including Windows from Windows 2000 onwards. The first public version of Kerberos, version 4, is specified in Miller et al. (1988); a detailed but less technically demanding description can be found at Learn Networking (2008). Taking Kerberos as a fairly typical example of a single sign-on protocol using federation, the mechanism for obtaining access to a resource is to authenticate to a trusted server, which then brokers access to a ticket-granting server, which then produces electronic tickets for the user which are used to obtain access to resources. An important feature of Kerberos is that it is able to support machine–machine authentication, which is why it is pervasive in modern operating systems. On the other hand, a major difficulty with Kerberos and other agent models is that the resource provider needs to install software which will accept Kerberos tickets, but another is more germane to our theme: the service provider still needs to manage information for each identity in order to handle authorization decisions in services where there is anything other than the simplest authorization decision to make (that is, where the situation is more complex than authenticated users permitted to access the whole resource). Kerberos is also not a protocol which affords anonymity to its users, though there is an extension to Kerberos which does (Zhu, Leach and Hartman, 2011).

More modern federated access protocols include OpenID (OpenID community, 2007). This will be familiar to most internet users, as it is the protocol used to provide authentication to services through Google and MySpace accounts, along with several others, including LiveJournal, where the protocol originated in 2005.

To use OpenID, a person creates an account at an OpenID provider, and then visits a site (known, in OpenID terminology, as a relying party) that accepts OpenID. When challenged to authenticate, the user reveals the name of the provider with which they have registered, usually by clicking on an icon representing their home provider from a collection that the relying party displays to indicate which providers it will accept. The user's browser is then directed back to the chosen provider to authenticate. There are two modes of operation for OpenID at this point; both are quite complicated, but if successful, the relying party receives credentials identifying the user which it can trust came from the provider. The credentials identify the user in terms of their registration with the provider, so they do not necessarily give away the user's real-world identity.

OAuth is another protocol ostensibly similar to OpenID, and is used by services which appear alongside OpenID ones in icon collections online, including Facebook and Twitter. However, OAuth allows greater anonymity. Instead of passing details identifying the user from the provider to the relying party, OAuth sends a token which is valid for a limited time and which contains no identifying information about the user. At the time of writing, version 2 of OAuth (Hammer, 2012) is being developed, focusing on extending its authentication standard beyond web browsers to phones and desktops; it will not be backwards compatible with version 1, which was written in 2006.

A further step in the devolution of authentication and authorization

More devolved still is role-based access, which is a type of federated access in which the identity provider does not communicate the identity established with the user to the service provider, but sends a collection of roles (represented as short textual labels known as 'attributes') to the service provider, which then gives access according to the roles it receives. The type of roles involved here can include the affiliation the user has with a library, so that (for example) the resource provider can assign access rights differently for library members of different types.

Shibboleth (www.shibboleth.net), well known in the academic library community, is an important and fairly typical implementation of a role-based authorization mechanism. Shibboleth is one of several to use a standard named Security Assertion Markup Language (SAML) (www.oasis-open.org/committees/tc_home.php?wg_abbrev=security) to securely transfer information about the process of authentication and authorization between components; an 'assertion' is basically a statement like 'This user authenticated at this identity provider with username and password at 07:24:32 on 10 May 2012', or 'This service provider would like to be sent the following list of information about the user involved in the session identified by unique session ID 874a9e09d098b.' It is also closely related to a range of single-sign-on services for the web, which are grouped under the WebISO name (http://middleware.internet2.edu/webiso).

As with most federated access software, Shibboleth is designed for web browsers and requires several redirections to establish a trusted link between the identity and service providers. This is used to transmit attributes, short pieces of textual information about the user, which effectively publish a list of roles to the service provider and which makes it possible to obtain access where permitted without revealing the user's identity to the service provider (for example, for a resource where a university library has purchased a licence, and all the resource provider needs to know is that the user is a member of the university). The assumption behind Shibboleth is basically that the user is affiliated to some organization which then creates collections of attributes to describe them. It originated in the academic community, where most individuals will be affiliated to a university or similar institution, which would be such an organization.

Additional extra work is needed to distribute metadata describing a collection of identity providers and service providers, enabling them to establish bilateral trust relationships; this distribution is the work of a '(trust) federation'. This is at the cost of making the authentication process very complex to follow, so it is worth describing it in some detail.

Shibboleth has an extra component which will usually come into play, at least for attempts to authenticate to a service provider for the first time (it can be bypassed in certain circumstances). This is the Discovery Service, which may be embedded into the service provider's software or could stand alone. When a user accesses the service provider's website, their browser is re-directed to the discovery service. This has copies of the metadata collections for each federation of which the service provider is a member, and displays to the user a list of the identity providers which are also listed in the metadata, or makes it possible to choose one in some other way, such as filtering a list using keywords provided by the user. When the user makes a selection, their web browser is redirected to the identity provider they have chosen, in such a way as to indicate the service provider that they are attempting to access.

Once at the identity provider, the user authenticates themselves in some way. Then the web browser is redirected to the service provider once more, this time with a short-lived token like that used in OAuth authentication, but also with a collection of (encrypted) attributes. The attributes can be gathered from a variety of sources, including directories of users in an organization and group management software tools. The identity provider can be configured to release different collections of attributes to different service providers, or even to different resources hosted by the same service provider, according to configured 'attribute release policies'.

Finally, the service provider receives the collection of attributes and the token, which enables it to be sure that an identity provider it trusts has released these attributes to it, and that it can therefore be sure that the identity provider is asserting that these attributes are accurate. (Maintaining accurate and up-to-date attribute information is a requirement made by many federations before they will grant membership to new identity providers.) The service provider can then confidently use the attribute values to make access decisions about the resources it makes available.

Matching roles against licence conditions

The affiliation of a user to an organization is not only useful in providing a significant measure of verification for attribute values. It also enables the information in the attributes, identifying the roles held by a user, to be matched by the service provider against the terms of licence agreements that have been made between its owner and the user's organization.

Many licences for electronic resources simply require that a user is a 'member' of the organization that has purchased the licence. This can usually be very easily asserted by the identity provider set up by that organization, and is often linked to such requirements as having an account which provides access to the organization's local area network. There can be issues with the precise definition, but possessing an attribute which asserts the user's membership of the organization is basically enough to give the user access to the whole of such a resource.

Other licences can place more complicated conditions on users, and then essentially the requirement is for the identity provider's organization to assign an attribute value to those users who it believes fulfil the licence conditions, whether this is for members of staff (as opposed to both staff and students), or those from a particular department within an institution.

More complex identity management is needed to create and maintain the data which can be used to make possible such fine-grained access management as these licence conditions require. One tool which is starting to be used for this purpose is a group management system. This, as the name implies, allows the creation and management of large numbers of groups, crucially not just those which can be derived from existing data about users (such as departmental affiliation or course registrations, in the academic context), but also custom groups which can capture relatively informal collections of users or groups which are not maintained electronically elsewhere (such as individuals who have a particular certification or who are fire marshals). Additionally, operations can usually be defined to derive new group memberships from existing groups, such as union (the collection of users who are members of one or more groups from a list) and intersection (the collection of users who are members of all the groups from a list) – and a concept of inheritance (where a group can contain other groups as members as well as individual users): the point of such operations is that these derived groups do not need to be managed separately from those which are used to define them; a new member of the groups used to define a derived group will automatically be a member of the derived group. Clearly, setting up such a system can be complex and difficult, so the expense involved needs to be matched against gains which could be made (such as fine-grained licence agreements which are cheaper than ones which grant access to large numbers of users with no interest in the resource). For more on group management systems, see Chapter 12.

Benefits of role-based authorization

Role-based authorization is usually dependent on the user being a member of an organization which manages their identity and can confidently make assertions about their roles within that organization. (This is not universal, as there can be identity providers which cater for individuals who are not part of an organization of this kind, such as independent consultants who need access to systems protected by a service provider which uses role-based authorization.) The assumption that this is the case leads to important benefits for both identity provider and service provider.

Who manages what aspects of authentication and authorization

Where individuals are a member of an organization, that organization needs to manage their identity within the institution; in an educational setting, this includes such details as the courses they are taking and changes in status (for example, applicant to undergraduate, undergraduate to postgraduate, postgraduate to staff, in a university setting). The organization needs to do this work already, whether or not the information stored about the individual is used for authorization. Additionally, they need to manage the credentials which the individual uses to authenticate to the local services the organization provides, whether it is a username and password for a local network or a smart card to obtain access to electronically locked doors.

At the same time, the publisher of a resource has to understand the resource in detail, and will have an idea of the value of access to different parts of it. The organization and the publisher will come together to agree the terms of a licence agreement allowing the members of the organization access to the resource.

This is the situation which occurs in any authentication and authorization scenario where organizational membership and licensing is involved. The important benefit of role-based authorization is that it uses all this information to allow the publisher to electronically enforce the details of the licence agreement with the organization, without the organization needing to take on the extra burden of understanding the details of the resource or the publisher needing to take on the extra burden of needing to manage the identity of individuals with whom it has no direct formal relationship.

Roles change while identity does not

The management of users should not be under the control of the service provider, because they just do not have the information to keep their management up to date. When an individual changes status, or is made a member of a new group within the organization of which they are a member, it is unlikely that this fact is passed on to every publisher of every resource to which the organization has purchased a licence for access. So the publisher's service provider will continue to provide access to the individual as though they were still in their older group or had their older status. If the individual involved has left the organization, this means that the publisher is effectively giving away their resource to them for free, and that is not good business practice. With role-based authorization, this problem goes away, so long as the organization has reasonable identity management procedures.

Roles can provide privacy and security

When roles are used for authentication, the identity provider is able to send precisely those attributes which are needed by the service provider to establish what the user is permitted to access. This in turn means that it is possible to protect the privacy of the user, and, in particular, role-based authorization lends itself to anonymous legitimate access to protected resources, where no information uniquely identifying the user is sent to the service provider, and to pseudonymous access, where the only identifying information is just a token which allows the user to be identified from session to session as the same individual, without giving away who that user is.

The use of roles in a federated access profile increases the security and control of the service provider, by ensuring that access can only be obtained by those legitimately entitled to it. This is of course dependent on trust in the identity provider's user management processes, but these are almost certain to be better than the service provider's chances of accurate management of users it has no direct relationship with, which is what it would have to rely on if identity-based authentication and authorization were used instead.

Roles can encapsulate complex scenarios

In the early years of the 21st century, most electronic resource access management still lies at one extreme or other of the continuum which runs from access to everything or nothing at one end to individually tailored access to specific items within the resource at the other. (Examples would be an archive which requires authentication but then gives access to all contents equally, or a resource in which users create resources and then share them with other users by inviting them individually to access them.) It is perhaps in the middle, though, that the full power of role-based authorization can be most clearly seen.

For complex resources where access can depend on several factors (e.g. some items need users to be certified as having completed a training course, or are available to third-year students from departments designated as pilots for a specific research project carried out in several universities as a consortium), role-based access gives the flexibility to get the right users to be able to access the right items without having to devise user groups specifically for the purpose.

To give an example, while it may seem sensible to have roles like 'people who are permitted to open the electronic lock on the door of room 7.24A with a smart card', this can prove more difficult to maintain in the long run than groups like 'members of linear programming research group', for which there can be more flexible uses and where the membership list is more intuitively obvious – it is not immediately possible to tell, for example, whether the people identified by the two roles just listed are in fact the same as each other, while knowing that members of the research group should have access to the room is much more useful for long-term maintenance of the access control.

As libraries seek to reduce the costs of their electronic resource provision, complex rights which restrict access to smaller groups of users are likely to become more common. For this to work, of course, there needs to be agreement between identity provider and service provider on the meaning of relevant roles and the identifiers used to indicate that an individual has the role.

Summary

The traditional method for access control for electronic resources, where each individual has credentials which are presented to the resource owner, can work well for resources where different parts of the resource involved are accessible only to small numbers of users, but for most resources this involves unwelcome work for the service provider to manage the identities of the users who currently should have access to the resource, and unwelcome work for the user, who has to maintain a multiplicity of credentials. Federated access protocols, in which authentication and authorization are separated and handled by identity and service providers respectively, means that the service provider can specialize in resource management and leave the identity management to the identity provider. However, many forms of federated access still pass information to the service provider which breaches user privacy, while the service provider still needs to maintain information about which users have access to which parts of the resource. In an organizational context, where the organization will already carry out substantial identity management activities that are likely to include the information needed to match a user's roles in the organization to license agreements, role-based authorization models provide a mechanism for service providers to use the information about a user's roles to manage authorization without necessarily even knowing the identity of a user.

References

Hammer, E. (ed.) (2012) *The OAuth 2.0 Authorization Framework draft-ietf-oauth-v2-26*, Internet Engineering Task Force, http://tools.ietf.org/html/draft-ietf-oauth-v2-26.

Learn Networking (2008) *How Kerberos Authentication Works*, blog article, http://learn-networking.com/network-security/how-kerberos-authentication-works.

Miller, S. P., Neuman, B. C., Schiller, J. I. and Saltzer, J. H. (1988) Section E.2.1: Kerberos Authentication and Authorization System. In *Project Athena Technical Plan, MIT Project Athena (Version 4)*, ftp://athena-dist.mit.edu/pub/kerberos/doc/techplan.txt.

OpenID community (2007) *OpenID Authentication 2.0 – Final*, http://openid.net/specs/openid-authentication-2_0.html.

Walden, D. (2011) Interview with Dick Mills. In Walden, D. and Van Vleck, T. (eds), *The Compatible Time Sharing System (1961–1973) Fiftieth Anniversary Commemorative Overview*, IEEE Computer Society, 26–31, www.multicians.org/thvv/compatible-time-sharing-system.pdf.

Zhu, L., Leach, P. and Hartman, S. (2011) *RFC 6112: anonymity support for Kerberos*, Internet Engineering Task Force, http://tools.ietf.org/html/rfc6112.

8

Federated access: history, current position and future developments

Federated access has become a widespread access control paradigm, of particular importance to the academic library community. How did it reach this position, and what is its future?

Single sign-on and the origins of federated access management

Early work in federated access management grew out of work in the 1990s to create single-sign-on (SSO) services, both for the web and for other protocols, and in commercial and academic settings. In this chapter, the term is used interchangeably with federated identity management (FIdM), which is generally used in the commercial sector for similar technology.

Commercial single sign-on

Two companies founded in 1999 were among the first to produce software which allowed FIdM (Pang, 2005). NewCo, soon renamed Covisint, was set up by as a co-operative venture by several US car manufacturers, and developed FIdM in the context of commercial electronic data interchange (EDI) – which at the time principally used non-internet networking – for the management of the supply chain, allowing suppliers access to their customers' systems and vice versa. A second company, Yodlee, introduced a form of single sign-on through its consumer financial software, allowing users to manage multiple financial accounts through a single interface.

A third important single-sign-on product was Microsoft Passport, launched in 1999. The aim of this product was ambitious even then: to provide a single-sign-on service which would cover the whole of web commerce (Microsoft, 1999). This has an architecture based on central Microsoft-run identity providers, and provides an authentication service similar to those available from Facebook and other major websites more recently (described in Chapter 7). The main difference is that Passport went beyond authentication and was able to pass sensitive data such as physical addresses and credit card details, which was then intended to be used for purchases, to requesting servers. Passport was heavily criticized over privacy and security, and suffered embarrassing problems when the domain name for the authentication service was not renewed on time, resulting in the failure of authentication worldwide, until a user paid the modest fee on their behalf (Chaney, 2000). Between 1999 and 2012, Passport underwent five name changes, and the 2012 equivalent is known as Microsoft Account (more details are available on the Wikipedia page, https://en.wikipedia.org/wiki/Microsoft_Passport).

Single sign-on in the academic sector

In the academic sector, several universities in the USA also carried out development of single-sign-on solutions, focusing on the world wide web. The best known are Pubcookie (www.pubcookie.org) and Central Authentication Service (CAS) (www.jasig.org/cas). Pubcookie was developed at the University of Washington from 1998, and CAS by Yale at around the same time; both were open-source applications from early on.

The architecture of (the 2012 versions of) both web SSO systems is similar; for a more detailed description than there is space for here, see Pubcookie (2002) and CAS (2009). In Pubcookie, there is a central log-in server, which interacts with users, and shares a unique symmetric key (a type of cryptographic key which is used both to encrypt and decrypt data) with each application server, which host the applications that the users wish to use. The user attempts to access an application, and the application server creates a web browser cookie that is encrypted with the symmetric key, which is presented to the log-in server and decrypted when the user's web browser is forwarded there. The user then logs in, and the log-in server then creates another encrypted cookie which is presented to the application server, which allows access if this cookie can be decrypted and is valid.

CAS uses what is conceptually the same architecture, but can operate without cookies, though without single sign-on (cookies being used to avoid having to log in multiple times in the same session, whenever a new application is accessed). The URLs used to redirect the browser between the authentication server (serving the same function as Pubcookie's log-in server) and the application's web server contains the encrypted information directly, instead of this being stored in a cookie.

Issues with early single sign-on

Each of these types of single sign-on was developed to support a particular need, which meant that extending it beyond that need would prove difficult. CAS and Pubcookie were designed to work inside an educational institution, where dynamic cross-domain trust between the components (identity and service providers, in FAM terms, or authenticators and consumers of authentication tokens, in other words) was not needed. Thus, there was no way to extend this single sign-on to important academic use cases such as access to electronic journals hosted by publishers outside the institution (the use of cookies in SSO architectures effectively enforces this limitation, because they should not be accessible to web servers outside the domain which set them).

The solutions from Covisint and Yodlee were proprietary in nature, and were not designed to be compatible with solutions from other vendors, once these appeared. To make them compatible, it was necessary to have a mechanism for standardizing the structure and meaning of the information exchanged between the various parties involved in FIdM in each competing system. Thus there was a requirement for a non-proprietary standard for the interchange of FIdM data between domains and across business sectors.

The development of standards
SAML and SAML profiles

This issue led to the next important development, the creation of standards for FIdM, of which the best known is Security Assertion Markup Language (SAML) (OASIS, 2008). This is a low-level, XML-based, language in which assertions (which have meanings such as 'this is a machine', 'the identity of this individual was established with a username and password at 2:30 AM GMT on 28 October 2012', 'this person is certified to be a student at the

University of Columbia') can be securely passed between the participants in FIdM. In SAML terminology, the originator of an assertion is the 'asserting party', and the recipient the 'relying party'; the entity which is the subject of the assertion is the 'principal'.

Key to the use of SAML for FIdM is the establishment of trust between the parties involved. SAML itself does not specify how trust should be established, so implementations of SAML can differ in this respect. Workflows and paradigm use cases are the other major differences between implementations, with (for example) Shibboleth taking advantage of the existence of institutional membership as the major form of relationship between an individual and an identity provider in the academic sector, while more general models which have been designed for commercial use (such as the Liberty Alliance) cannot make this type of assumption about users. The difference between SAML and the work of the Liberty Alliance was described by Ray Wagner of Gartner in terms of entry into a cinema: 'SAML is the movie ticket. The way you walk up to someone and hand them your ticket to get into the theater is Liberty' (quoted in Scalet, 2012).

The relationship between SAML and this type of extra specification is governed by what is known as a SAML 'profile'. Each SAML profile is intended to support a specific use case, such as web browser single sign-on. It describes the assertions that are to be used, which may not be all those available in SAML, the 'protocols' that are to be used to request assertions and receive responses, and the underlying 'bindings', the communication mechanisms that are to be used to carry the requests and responses (an example of which would be SOAP, a common mechanism for carrying technical information about web services, over HTTP, the protocol which is the basis of the world wide web). (This paragraph draws heavily on the description in OASIS, 2008).

A prominent SAML profile was the Web Service Identity Model (ID-WSF) defined by the Liberty Alliance, now part of the Kantara Initiative (which no longer maintains the profile). Early work on this, following the founding of the Liberty Alliance in 2001, was not only carried out before the creation of SAML (version 1.0 released in July 2002), but was one of the formative influences on the standard. This profile uses its own terminology, defining means for information supporting a proposed transaction to pass between the 'sender', the 'recipient', the 'invoker' and the 'target identity', all of which can be different (e.g. when a travel agency wishes to view and update a customer's online calendar as part of their trip booking service – the example use case described in the introduction to the profile), or which can include the same real-life party in more than one role. The full profile and associated work is defined in a number of documents at http://projectliberty.org/liberty/resource_center/specifications, with an overview in Liberty Alliance (2008).

The Kantara Initiative continues to maintain a list of certified SAML interoperable solutions (Kantara Initiative, 2012).

WS-Security, WS-Federation and WS-Trust

WS-Federation (Nadalin and Kaler, 2006), and WS-Trust (Nadalin et al., 2012) are all part of the WS-Security framework, which adds security functionality to web services. Version 1.0 of WS-Security appeared in 2004, defining the basic mechanisms for securing web services messages.

WS-Federation allows the establishment of trust between entities, which then permits the exchange of security tokens between them, and which finally allows access to information. 'WS-Federation includes mechanisms for brokering of identity, attribute discovery and retrieval, authentication and authorization claims between federation partners, and protecting the privacy of these claims across organizational boundaries' (Goodner et al., 2007). WS-Trust defines methods for issuing and validating security tokens, and how to broker trust relationships. All these functions are needed for FIdM, while WS-Federation itself is basically equivalent to SAML in the functionality it defines.

Like SAML, WS-Security and WS-Trust are managed by OASIS (https://www.oasis-open.org/committees/tc_home.php?wg_abbrev=wss), and some interoperability between the standards is possible – WS-Security implementations can interpret and use SAML assertions (see Goodner et al., 2007, Appendix A).

The best known software tool which uses WS-Federation is Microsoft's Active Directory Federation Services (ADFS). The earliest version of ADFS to be released was part of Windows Server 2003 R2, in 2005. ADFS effectively allows web single sign-on with attribute-based authorization to Microsoft servers across organizational boundaries (Microsoft, 2005).

Federated access in academia

PAPI

PAPI (standing for Point of Access to Providers of Information) is open-source FAM software developed by RedIRIS (the Spanish NREN). It was the 'first federated digital identity infrastructure in production worldwide' when initially deployed in 2001 (https://www.rediris.es/actividades/papi/). It has an apparently similar architecture to ADFS and Shibboleth, with authentication servers (identity providers in the more common FAM model) and Points of Access (service providers). Multiple points of access can be configured to control access to a single web server – and this is where the difference comes, in that the organization running the authentication server also controls the access levels that authenticated users have to remote resources at points of access. This is effectively the same situation as that with other FAM architectures when attributes managed and certified by the identity provider are used to determine levels of access at the service provider (see PAPI Development Team, n.d.).

Internet2, Shibboleth and InCommon

PAPI remains a relatively minor part of the academic FAM community. The major player is Shibboleth, FAM software developed by Internet2 (www.internet2.edu). Internet2 is a collaborative venture between US universities originally set up in 1996 'to solve common technology challenges, and develop innovative solutions in support of their educational, research, and community service missions' (Internet2, n.d.), one strand of which, the Middleware Initiative, 'focuses on developing interoperable identity and access management infrastructures for research and higher education' (www.internet2.edu/middleware/index.cfm).

The most prominent output of the Middleware Initiative is Shibboleth, Internet2's open-source FAM software, now run as a separate consortium (https://shibboleth.net). Early versions of Shibboleth appeared in 2001.

Shibboleth uses SAML, and, as already mentioned, its architecture makes the assumption that a user has a more or less permanent home identity provider (IdP), which can make reliable assertions about him or her because of their relationship – in other words, a user is affiliated to an organization like a university. Indeed, this ability to make assertions in the form of attributes (that is, snippets of information describing the user) makes it possible to use Shibboleth to access protected resources anonymously, with the SP having the assurance that the user is entitled to use the resource without ever knowing who they are as an individual.

However, Shibboleth is quite flexible in many ways. It does not specify an authentication mechanism to use in its identity provider, though most installations use LDAP either directly or indirectly through a Web ISO solution such as CAS or Pubcookie. It also does not make any restrictions on the type of attribute information which can be passed, though again most installations use one main choice: eduPerson (eduPerson, 2012), also an Internet2 Middleware Initiative project. This is a schema (collection of attributes) that is specifically designed for the description of individuals in higher education institutions. Key attributes include eduPersonAffiliation, which distils the relationship between a person and an institution into a small number of specific values, and eduPersonTargetedId, which is a unique identifier that picks out an individual without providing private information about them, so that services which rely on recognizing a previous user on return visits (such as personalization settings on a publisher's website, including saved searches and so on) can do so without the need for personal information.

Shibboleth also does not specify how trust between IdPs and SPs is to be arranged. The Shibboleth profile assumes only that there is trust between the pair of entities, one IdP and one SP, involved in the establishment of an authenticated session, and that they know certain information about each other – public cryptographic keys, and how to communicate with each other (i.e. the locations of the communication endpoints on the internet). This information is known as trust metadata. Where a group of IdPs and SPs get together and share metadata between them, they become a 'trust federation'. Trust federations may have additional rules which are not necessarily technical (requirements about how the institutions behind IdPs manage their users, for example), and may allow the use of software other than Shibboleth, so long as Shibboleth and it are interoperable.

The best known federation worldwide is InCommon (www.incommon. org), which is the North American federation and which initially consisted of key Internet2 members involved in Shibboleth development.

With the advantage of adoption by key players in the large American market, Shibboleth has gone on to become the dominant FAM product in higher education, especially for access to electronic journals, being supported by all the large academic publishers, and many of the small ones, acting as service providers. Figure 8.1 explains how Shibboleth works.

This diagram shows a common architecture for Shibboleth use, with labels appropriate to version 2.0 onwards, for one of the most frequently encountered use cases; other configurations and options are possible. For more details, see https://wiki.shibboleth.net/confluence/display/SHIB2/FlowsAndConfig. Dotted arrows indicate prior not-entirely-technical arrangements which need to be made for Shibboleth to work; organizational boundaries are indicated by dashed lines. Most of the stages are carried out

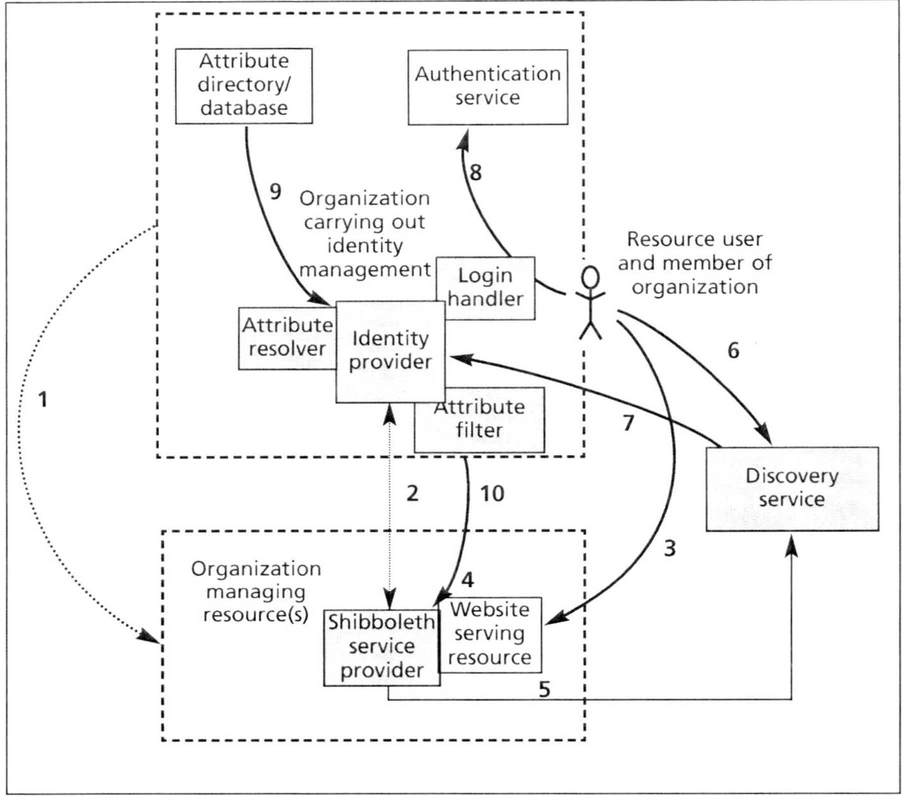

Figure 8.1 *Shibboleth diagram*

using browser redirects, but for clarity the user is only shown to be involved in activities which require interaction.

The numbers indicate the order of events for the granting of access to a previously unauthenticated user: (1) purchase of licence; (2) establishment of trust relationship (e.g. through common membership of a federation); (3) unauthenticated user attempts to access resource; (4) request processed by SP (which is integrated into web server software); (5) request forwarded to Discovery Service for user to choose relevant IdP; (6) user chooses IdP of organization; (7) user forwarded with request for authentication to IdP; (8) user authenticates against organizational authentication service through the Login Handler component of the IdP; (9) IdP obtains attributes describing the user from Attribute Service via Attribute Resolver; (10) user forwarded back to resource website (and SP) with session data and a filtered set of attributes (as configured in the Attribute Filter component of the IdP) which give necessary information for the granting of access.

FAM in the UK

In 2001, the authentication and authorization situation in UK higher education was very different to that in the US or Spain. In the late 1990s, the University of Bath developed an authentication system called Athens, which was adopted as part of the UK's National Information Services and Systems (NISS) (Joint Information Systems Committee, 1997), which was operated by a company named Eduserv (everything2, n.d.). Athens was then the main authentication scheme used by the whole of the UK academic sector for over ten years.

Athens was essentially a central database of usernames and passwords, with individual institutions sending updated lists of users and passwords (or shared usernames and passwords) when needed. Most institutions used existing credentials (often library card numbers and PIN numbers associated with them) as the basis for Athens usernames; a per-institution prefix was used to avoid clashes in usernames. If shared passwords were used, these would generally be changed annually. Once the credentials were set up, Athens essentially offered single sign-on access to their libraries' e-resources, and users no longer needed to remember different usernames and passwords for each resource accessed.

Athens administration was simple and required little technical input from institutions: the administrator for Athens was usually a librarian rather than a member of computing services, and information about new usernames was fed to Athens in the form of spreadsheets. Athens also provided useful information about the usage of electronic journals, something which was not easy to do in a FAM environment (more detail on this issue is given below and in a case study). However, Athens was criticized over security, and expense: although individual institutions did not pay directly, Athens was paid for by JISC (see Glossary) on an annual basis, and publishers had to pay to license the software used to allow Athens users access to their data.

Thus, by 2001, JISC were seeking to move to a new system for authentication, and, as part of the Angel project (www.angel.ac.uk) arranged for the London School of Economics (UK) and Edina, a JISC-funded content provider based in the University of Edinburgh (UK), to evaluate PAPI and Shibboleth as candidates. This led to pilot projects to install Shibboleth IdPs and to set up a prototype trust federation (SDSS, 2004–7, http://edina.

ac.uk/projects/sdss) for the UK academic sector. The next step was a full-scale federation developed from SDSS, the UK Access Management Federation (UK AMF – www.ukfederation.org.uk), which was launched in 2006. In 2012, there were 917 members (www.ukfederation.org.uk/content/Documents/MemberList#), including every institution providing higher or further education in the UK. JISC funding for Athens ceased in 2008, and was replaced by funding for the UK AMF as a free service to the UK academic community. While most UK AMF members use Shibboleth software, Eduserv continued to provide important services in authentication to the UK academic sector, including outsourced IdP software in their OpenAthens product, which was used by around 30% of IdPs in the UK AMF in 2012 (Williams, 2012). To avoid confusion with OpenAthens, the original Athens model is frequently referred to as 'classic Athens'.

Federations worldwide

The USA and the UK are not the only parts of the world to have trust federations for the academic sector. There is now an international group to promote co-operation between federations, REFEDS (https://refeds.org), and 34 federations worldwide are listed on their wiki in November 2012 (https://refeds.terena.org/index.php/Federations). These federations use a wide variety of governance models, and have different rules for members, mainly because of differences in local culture. (The funding models for InCommon and the UK AMF, already mentioned, are examples of how disparate these can be.)

Almost as soon as more than one federation was in existence, the question of how they could work together was raised, and representatives from several federations attended a meeting organized by the UK JISC in Upper Slaughter, Gloucestershire, UK in October 2004 (Joint Information Systems Committee, 2004). There are clear reasons why it is useful to have at least some interoperation: multinational organizations, particularly large publishers like Elsevier, have to register with (academic sector) federations in each country in which they operate if they wish to work with FAM entities in that country, a time-consuming process, much of which needs to be repeated if changes are made to their FAM installations that require the details to be updated. The difficulties in maintaining membership in multiple federations are due to differences in policies between the federations, and their compliance with different local legal frameworks.

EduGAIN (Educational Global Authentication Infrastructure, www.

edugain.org) is one project aiming to tackle these problems. This aims to allow an organization to register once, and then be able automatically to join federations which are EduGAIN partners. Ensuring that the policies written for EduGAIN prove acceptable to the various partners is more of a challenge than the technical requirements of membership (Schofield, 2012). Related work has been carried out by REFEDS, resulting in the production of the PEER software (for metadata management) and the REEP repository (storing metadata in a central location for use by multiple federations) (REFEDS, 2012).

FAM developments to 2012

Work on FAM in the academic sector has tackled several problems, particularly in reference to use of the Shibboleth software. These can be grouped into three areas: usability, manageability, and integration.

Usability

Early end-users of the FAM model for access to electronic journals found it difficult to understand, and experienced problems with the usability of some features of the model, especially in the use of Discovery Services. This issue has been tackled by user education, including the production of updated library guides for users to reflect the use of FAM (such as the work described at www.angel.ac.uk/ShibbolethAtLSE/shibendusers/index.html), for example. Technical development has improved the presentation of the WAYF in Shibboleth (WAYF stands for 'Where Are You From' – now redesigned it has been renamed the Discovery Service). Many libraries also use what are known as 'WAYFless URLs' in their catalogues, which incorporate the user's IdP details in the URL used to access a resource, removing the need for them to be sent to the Discovery Service at all (providing that the user who found the link in the catalogue is a member of the institution which runs the catalogue). WAYFless URLs have themselves a number of issues, in particular fragility with respect to changes at the SP; these have been addressed by the development of WUGEN by the UK AMF, due to be launched soon (Smith, 2012, slide 17). Another change which has been encouraged, both in the UK alone through JISC (Smith, 2010) and more widely by REFEDS (Harris, 2012), is uniformity in the presentation of log-in challenges by publishers, to make it easier for users to know which log-in method they should be using.

Manageability

The issues to do with manageability have affected library management of FAM in general and the system administrators who oversee the installation and configuration of Shibboleth in particular. The latter issue has been tackled in the continuing development of Shibboleth and its documentation, especially with the release of version 2.0 in 2008 (Carmody, 2008).

In non-federated architectures, log information would indicate precisely what a user has done, and could easily be analysed to provide statistics describing the use of resources, including differentiating between services (such as individual journals) hosted on a single website. FAM essentially makes this impossible, as the required log information is distributed between the IdP and SP, so that full analysis would require detailed access to both sets of logs. The use of anonymous and pseudonymous access makes it even more difficult to analyse the accesses attributable to particular users or groups of users. This has meant that library management has been unable to easily discover the levels of usage of the electronic services which they pay for. This need has been addressed by the development of RAPTOR software (https://iam.cf.ac.uk/trac/RAPTOR), which produces analysis of the log files of a variety of products including the Shibboleth IdP, and which can give detailed information about access to each SP (e.g. the difference in usage level between different departments within the institution). RAPTOR is currently in use in pilots by several UK universities (see Chapter 11 for more on RAPTOR).

Integration

There are two basic directions in which work on FAM integration has taken place, excluding the cross-federation initiatives already mentioned. The first is in support for FAM in a wider range of products, including both publisher websites and software such as EZProxy, wikis and repositories. This has made it possible for FAM to be used for such purposes as sharing resources between teams that cross the borders of institutions, as many research projects do. A list of software which is compatible with Shibboleth can be found at www.9starinc.com/solutions/saml-apps?ref=pnappc.

The other type of integration is to make it possible for different FAM products and architectures to interoperate. The possibilities of such integration are often limited by the differences between the assumptions made in the development of the architectures. One example where work has been carried out since 2006 is integration between Shibboleth and Microsoft FAM products such as ADFS. Some of the difficulties to be encountered in this integration work can be seen from (Oxford Computer Group, 2007).

The future of federated access

There are two fairly clearly signposted developments which are likely to happen in the near future, and lead to major changes in the federated access landscape as it affects libraries.

New federated access initiatives

While Shibboleth and products which interoperate with Shibboleth currently have a dominant position in federated access for the academic world, the adoption of the FAM paradigm in other sectors could well mean that other products would become preferred due to high visibility, or even regulatory pressures. Currently, there are two main initiatives which could affect the UK FAM community in this way.

The first of these is the UK government's Identity Assurance Programme, run by the Cabinet Office. This uses a FAM architecture, and is behind the online identity registration service operated for the Department of Work and Pensions for Universal Credit; seven identity providers with which claimants can register are being used for this purpose (Department of Work and Pensions, 2012). Beyond the UK, similar work using FAM principles is under way, including the USA's National Strategy for Trusted Identities in Cyberspace (www.nist.gov/nstic) and the EU Project STORK pilots (www.eid-stork.eu).

Secondly, there are initiatives supported by large computing firms, many of which are unwilling to fully adopt SAML because of its complexity; of these, the currently most visible is OpenID Connect (https://openid.net/connect), being developed as a replacement for OpenID. Companies supporting this work include Facebook, Yahoo, and Google. The ideas behind OpenID Connect are simplicity and adherence to (or creation of new) standards, which means that some difficult issues (such as the trust models used) are not yet fully resolved.

Beyond federated access for the web

Shibboleth is designed to work for access to web-based resources, but there is a perceived requirement for FAM access to non-web applications, such as those which are found on the desktop: then one log-in will act as single sign-on to everything which is used in a session, whether or not it is accessed using a browser. This may well affect not just the organization-wide use of FAM technology, but form part of the library's toolkit for providing services in a world where the user's own devices (phones, tablets, etc.) and social networking continue to become ever more important.

Project Moonshot (www.project-moonshot.org) is one initiative currently working to make this possible. The requirement which motivates Project Moonshot is the provision of access to academic researchers (local and remote) to data produced in collaborative projects, stored in protected directories, with analysis and manipulation tools other than a web browser, and using operating systems including both Linux and Microsoft Windows. A pilot service for users to test Moonshot will be run from April 2013 (Chapman, 2012).

Summary

Single sign on technology began in the commercial sector, but was quickly adopted and adapted for the academic world. The convergent needs of universities led to the development of a wider approach to single sign on, which was not dependent on membership of a single institution, and this model is known as Federated Access. Federated Access is dependent on the adoption of common standards across a "trust federation", and important standards include WS-Federation / WS-Trust and Security Assertion Markup Language, the former being largely used in Microsoft environments and the latter common elsewhere. SAML is the basis for the most widely known implementation of Federated Access to the library community, Shibboleth. This was developed in the United States by the Internet2 consortium of universities, and was then adopted by the UK academic community as the replacement for the Athens authentication software, before rapidly spreading around the world. Work has continued to enhance Federated Access models and implementations with adoption outside the academic sector and beyond the web browser being two major current areas of development.

References

Carmody, S. (2008) *Shibboleth v2.0 is Now Available*, post to shibboleth-users e-mail list, 19 March, https://lists.internet2.edu/sympa/arc/shibboleth-users/2008-03/msg00289.html.

CAS (2009) *CAS 1 Architecture*, www.jasig.org/cas/cas1-architecture.

Chaney, M. (2000) *The Passport Payment*, Michael Chaney's personal web page, www.doublewide.net.

Chapman, J. (2012) Janet's Moonshot Service Pilot – register your interest now, post on Moonshot Project blog, 14 November 2012, https://community.ja.net/groups/moonshot/article/janets-moonshot-service-pilot-register-your-interest-now.

Department of Work and Pensions (2012) *Providers Announced for Online Identity Scheme*, DWP Newsroom, 13 November 2012, www.dwp.gov.uk/newsroom/press-releases/2012/nov-2012/dwp118-12.shtml.

eduPerson (2012) *eduPerson Object Class Specification* (201203), 2012 version, http://middleware.internet2.edu/eduperson/docs/internet2-mace-dir-eduperson-201203.html.

everything2 (n.d.) *Athens (thing)*, article on everything2 wiki, http://everything2.com/index.pl?node_id=1888399.

Goodner, M., Hondo, M., Nadalin, A., McIntosh, M. and Schmidt, D. (2007) *Understanding WS-Federation*, IBM and Microsoft white paper, http://download.boulder.ibm.com/ibmdl/pub/software/dw/specs/ws-fed/WS-FederationSpec05282007.pdf?S_TACT=105AGX04&S_CMP=LP.

Harris, N. (2012) *Making Federations Work Together More Effectively*, presentation at FAM 2012 conference, Birmingham, 6 November, www.eduserv.org.uk/newsandevents/events/2012/fam12/stream-four.

Internet2 (n.d.) *Internet2 Overview*, www.internet2.edu/resources/AboutInternet2.pdf.

Joint Information Systems Committee (1997) *Review of Network Services*, 1 September, www.jisc.ac.uk/media/documents/aboutus/committees/acn/report97.pdf.

Joint Information Systems Committee (2004) International Middleware Meeting (including archive of position papers from organizations represented), www.jisc.ac.uk/whatwedo/programmes/middleware/international.aspx.

Kantara Initiative (2012) *SAML Interoperable Implementations, Tools, Libraries, Services*, Kantara Initiative, https://kantarainitiative.org/programs/iop-saml.

Liberty Alliance (2008) *Liberty Alliance Web Services Framework: a technical overview*, version 1.0, http://projectliberty.org/liberty/content/download/4120/27687/file/idwsf-intro-v1.0.pdf.

Microsoft (1999) *Microsoft Passport: streamlining commerce and communication on the web* (interview with Microsoft Senior Vice President Brad Chase), Microsoft News Center, 11 October, https://www.microsoft.com/en-us/news/features/1999/10-11passport.aspx.

Microsoft (2005) *Overview of ADFS*, Windows Server Library, http://technet.microsoft.com/en-us/library/cc755828%28v=WS.10%29.aspx.

Nadalin, A., Goodner, M., Gudgin, M., Turner, D., Barbir, A. and Granqvist, H. (2012) *WS-Trust 1.4*, http://docs.oasis-open.org/ws-sx/ws-trust/v1.4/ws-trust.html.

Nadalin, A. and Kaler, C., (eds) (2006) *Web Services Federation Language (WS-Federation)*, version 1.1, http://download.boulder.ibm.com/ibmdl/pub/software/dw/specs/ws-fed/WS-Federation-V1-1B.pdf?S_TACT=105AGX04&S_CMP=LP.

OASIS (2008) *Security Assertion Markup Language (SAML) V2.0 Technical Overview*, OASIS Security Services (SAML) Technical Committee, www.oasis-open.org/committees/download.php/27819/sstc-saml-tech-overview-2.0-cd-02.pdf.

Oxford Computer Group (2007) *Achieving Interoperability between Active Directory Federation Services and Shibboleth*, white paper, www.jisc.ac.uk/media/documents/programmes/amtransition/microsoft.pdf.

Pang, L. (2005) *A Manager's Guide to Identity Management and Federated Identity*, ISACA Journal, **4**, www.isaca.org/Journal/Past-Issues/2005/Volume-4/Pages/A-Managers-Guide-to-Identity-Management-and-Federated-Identity1.aspx.

PAPI Development Team (n.d.) *A Detailed Description of the PAPI Protocol*, redIris, https://papi.rediris.es/rep/PAPI_Protocol_Detailed.pdf.

Pubcookie (2002) *How Pubcookie Works*, Pubcookie wiki, www.pubcookie.org/docs/how-pubcookie-works.html.

REFEDS (2012) *PEER FAQ*, REFEDS wiki, https://refeds.terena.org/index.php/PEER_FAQ.

Scalet, S. D. (2012) *The Truth About Federated Identity Management*, CSO Identity and Access blog, 26 July, www.csoonline.com/article/221034/the-truth-about-federated-identity-management.

Schofield, C. (2012) *eduGAIN: State of the U*, presentation at FAM 2012 conference, Birmingham, 6 November, www.eduserv.org.uk/newsandevents/events/2012/fam12/stream-four.

Smith, R. (2010) *Service Provider Interface Study*, JISC Collections, https://www.jisc-collections.ac.uk/Reports/Service-provider-interface-study.

Smith, R. (2012) *Update on RAPTOR – understanding usage information for e-resources*, presentation at FAM 2012 conference, Birmingham, 6 November, www.eduserv.org.uk/newsandevents/events/2012/fam12/RAPTOR.

Williams, M. (2012) *UK Federation Operator: Update,* presentation at FAM 2012 conference, Birmingham, 6 November, www.eduserv.org.uk/newsandevents/ events/2012/fam12/uk-federation#resources.

9

How to choose access management and identity management products and services

This chapter gives an overview of the proprietary access management and identity management system procurement process. It also looks at some of the proprietary technologies available.

Introduction

Once an organization has developed a programme of identity and access management work, and has constructed a realistic roadmap for the work, it may wish to procure some identity and access management systems and/or services. Any identity and access management implementation is likely to involve a range of different products, technologies and services in order to fulfil the organization's specific requirements. Therefore, the products chosen may vary widely from organization to organization, based on the organization's individual needs.

It is possible that a complete solution will be required or it may be that only some of the components need to be procured from commercial sources, while others can be obtained from open-source providers or developed in-house. Some organizations may choose to outsource their identity and/or access management to a third party. From a library's point of view, it is important that any identity and/or access management systems procured by the library fit in with the wider organization's procurement plan and the general IT infrastructure.

This chapter is designed to help libraries understand the procurement process for identity and access management systems, and provide an introduction to some of the more popular commercial solutions currently on the market. It draws heavily on Chapter 10 of the *Identity Management Toolkit* produced by the UK Joint Information Systems Committee (JISC, 2012), 'Selecting supplier solutions for Identity Management'. The original Toolkit was written, tested and produced by four UK partners: Kidderminster College, the London School of Economics and Political Science, the University of Cardiff and the University of Bristol, and gives an excellent introduction to the identity and access management system procurement process. The Toolkit was updated by the same project staff, some still working at the above institutions and some (including the authors of this book) engaged as independent consultants.

The identity management roadmap should inform several aspects of the process of choosing an appropriate solution for the organization. It should:

- indicate whether the preferred identity management architecture involves a central identity management system or working to integrate existing systems which handle parts of the identity management requirements of the institution (such as the software used by HR and the finance department, and the mechanisms used to create accounts on various systems)
- indicate how the identity management work that the organization is planning should be prioritized
- indicate general requirements for software solutions which need to be developed or obtained from a third party (whether a vendor or an open source development consortium).

The roadmap will be a top-level solution, giving strategic information. The process which went into developing the roadmap, which may include a detailed identity management audit, will have produced more detailed analysis that should make it possible to turn the general requirements which can be seen in the roadmap into a collection of detailed requirements, as would be appropriate for an Invitation to Tender (ITT) document or project plan.

Identity management and access management solution capabilities

An identity and access management solution will most certainly include the following components:

- **a central repository of identities and related identity information**
- **synchronization mechanisms to various applications** – to make sure that different applications are able to 'talk' to each other to enable the gathering and publishing of identity information
- **account provisioning/de-provisioning abilities** – to control access for individuals within connected IT systems by provisioning/de-provisioning accounts within these systems and by managing those accounts' rights based on identity information
- **an authentication technology** – to verify the user's identity or which organization the user comes from
- **a directory** – a software application for organizing information about a computer network's users and resources; the organization's IT directory service supplies attributes (e.g. specific details about a user) used to determine whether the user is allowed access (the process known as authorization)
- **a federated identity provider** for organizations that use federated access management (see Chapter 8) – to enable authentication and authorization to remote services via federated means
- **an authorization system** – to determine what the identified and authenticated user is allowed to access and what operations he/she is allowed to carry out.
- **auditing facilities** – to provide accounting information
- **group management** – to enable automated and/or manual placement of users into groups (useful for authorization decisions).

There may also be other components, such as:

- **an identity reconciliation facility** – to provide an automated and/or manual mechanism for taking existing accounts from multiple IT systems and identifying, to a certain degree of probability, that those accounts belong to a single individual and linking them within the central identity repository
- **password management** – to enable password synchronization between IT systems, enforce global password policy across these systems, etc.

- **a shared authentication service** – to allow seamless access to a variety of systems with a single credential.

With so many components on offer, it is important that the organization is clear about what it is trying to achieve, both in the short and the long term, before setting out to procure new IT solutions that may prove ineffective and/or costly.

Establishing requirements with suppliers
Assessing capabilities of identity and access management products

After the organization has identified some potential technologies and/or services that may be suitable, the next step will be to assess the chosen products against a pre-defined set of criteria to make sure that they fit the organization's specific needs. This is very important, as even though the shortlisted products may offer the same core functionality, they may do it in many different ways. The *Identity Management Toolkit* outlines a series of technical tasks that each available product may or may not be able to perform. To assess the suitability of a particular product for a specific organization, the importance of each of these tasks should be assessed by the organization, and then each shortlisted product should be evaluated in terms of its ability to perform these tasks and the importance assigned by the organization to those tasks. The product that can achieve the largest majority of these has a good chance of being the most suited to that particular organization. The list below doesn't include the full list of possible options covered by the Toolkit, but should give a good idea of the high-level tasks that a suitable product should cover:

- **data connectivity** – e.g. ability to connect to databases, directories, files, and/or web services using well defined protocols for data flows in and out
- **data synchronization** – ability to fit with the synchronization models of each of the various existing systems which will share data with the product
- **model (or topology)** – e.g. ability to work in point-to-point mode with no persistent data storage except data source and destination
- **data matching/de-duplication** – e.g. support for record merges
- **data transformation** – e.g. ability to apply data rules, using a rules engine

- **audit** – ability to audit and store details of all activity
- **governance** – ability to integrate with the management systems of existing software services within the organization.

General identity and access management software considerations

There are also other things that need to be considered during the selection process, such as the following.

Technical appropriateness

Different identity and/or access management products have different technical capabilities and would be best suited to a particular environment. For example, academic institutions have different requirements from commercial organizations, so if a product in question is largely used by the commercial sector, it may not be suitable for the academic sector and vice versa. It is also important to consider future technical and organizational needs of your organization or library in order to assess whether a product is suitable.

Cost

The cost of an identity and/or access management product can vary widely, including ongoing and future costs. The potential growth of the customer base needs to be considered to make sure the product will remain cost-effective if the number of users increases. The costing model used needs to be based on per-seat (or per-user) licensing, rather than per-server licensing.

Flexibility

Any organization has a variety of IT systems and products in operation, so it is important to ensure that the organization's individual requirements are catered for, and that it will be possible to connect all these systems together. Again, it is worth considering both short- and long-term organizational goals.

Maturity

A wide variety of identity and access management products are currently on offer. Some of this software has been available for a number of years and may be a safer bet when choosing a new product to implement, while more recent developments may offer new functionality but have not had the benefit of time to determine their capabilities and stability.

Scalability

For organizations that can see significant future growth, such as an academic institution or a dynamic business, the question of scalability is also very important. Choosing a product that will scale well to cope with an increase in both users and systems will ensure that scalability doesn't become an issue a few years down the line.

Security

This is particularly important for an identity management system which sits at the core of the organization's IT infrastructure and must be highly secure, with comprehensive access controls.

Data storage (and the Cloud)

Several vendors are introducing Cloud storage for user data into their products. This is likely to provide convenience and lessens reliance on the security knowledge of the in-house IT team, but introduces other concerns. For example, storage of data in the Cloud may mean that it is not in the same legal jurisdiction as the institution, and care must be taken with relevant legal differences (e.g. those between EU and US privacy regimes). Intermittent connectivity issues may prevent access to the data, impairing the functionality of the system. The organization will need to place a great deal of trust in the vendor's security and privacy systems. Therefore, careful consideration needs to be made before taking the step of moving to the Cloud, and the issues need to be discussed in detail with the vendor before going ahead.

Outsourced/third-party identity management (Identity as a Service)

There are now companies which will carry out some aspects of identity management on the organization's behalf. Outsourced identity management providers offer authentication (typically using a federated architecture) and provisioning. Many of them are oriented to the commercial market, and effectively aim to link users to multiple Software as a Service (SaaS) providers.

The usual means by which IdM is offered by third parties, known as Identity as a Service (IdAAS), is through the Cloud, so the considerations above on use of the Cloud also apply here. The additional potential benefits here are that outsourcing the work of installing, managing, and maintaining an identity management system frees up resources at the organization, saving time and money. The institution will still need to be responsible for managing the relationship with the supplier of their identity management services, and will need to be especially careful in this regard because of the sensitivity of identity management.

Open-source identity management systems

Many components of an identity management system (e.g. directories, single-sign-on software) can be realized with open-source software. Some vendors of identity management software also make open-source versions of their products available, typically with reduced functionality. Open-source software is particularly suited to an ad hoc, piecemeal approach to identity management, as components can easily be added when needed. With sufficient in-house technical expertise, open source can also be easier and cheaper to integrate with other systems already in use. Full-scale open-source IdM systems are also now available.

However, the potential issues with open source software are also well known. There is often no guaranteed support (though informal support from user communities and developers is often usually very quick and helpful). There is no guarantee that the developers will continue to work on the product (though this is also a problem with commercial products, where the vendor could go out of business or change its focus). Its use can be difficult to sell to senior management, who expect software to be obtained through a traditional customer-vendor relationship, particularly with the expectation that an ITT is produced and answered by interested vendors. Internal technical expertise is needed for installation, configuration and management, which offsets the zero cost of the software itself (though there can be other benefits to the institution from having such expertise available).

Choosing a vendor

Choosing a reputable and reliable vendor is a serious matter. There are several factors that may influence this process. For example:

- **Existing customer base** Does the vendor specialize in a particular area of business (e.g. banking)? Does it have a good understanding of the organization's sector? Does the vendor have implementation experience in a similar organization? Can we deliver on time and on budget? It is a good idea to request some customer references from potential vendors to get a better feel for what they can offer.
- **Partners** Since any new systems and/or products will have to interoperate with a number of other systems, it is good if the potential new vendor has proven partnerships with vendors of the systems already in place.
- **Vendor stability and support** Identity and access management systems are key systems within an organization, so a vendor with a proven track record of financial stability is more likely to be able to offer support and development in the future.

Selection strategies

This section makes it clear that choosing a suitable identity and/or access management system that fits the organization's technical and organizational requirements, and is flexible, cost-effective, reliable and secure, is not easy. Sources such as Gartner (2011) can make this process easier. JISC InfoNet (2012) has some good general advice on working with commercial suppliers. For organizations that don't have sufficient experience in identity and access management, hiring a consultant or outsourcing to a third party might be a good option.

Asserting library requirements in a wider-scale system procurement

It is obvious that library IT systems do not exist in isolation but are part of the wider organizational set-up. It is important to get a detailed view of the organizational IT set-up, including IT system procurement plans, prior to investing in new library systems (for example). In particular, it is unlikely that many libraries will today be taking a lead technical role in the specification and management of large-scale institutional IdM technology.

However, the library has an important role to play, as both a consumer and originator of identity management information, and should therefore expect to be (and push towards being) heavily involved in consultation about the IdM systems within the institution, whether these involve technical solutions such as the ones discussed above or whether it is management of the human processes which are involved in identity management, such as student registration.

Library requirements as an originator of identity data

There are a relatively small number of people whose identities in an organization will be created because they are involved with the library: these are basically the visitors, whose management is discussed in Chapter 10. It is now the case that most university and college libraries will require registration for visitors before they are permitted to use the library facilities, for a variety of reasons, including management of repeat visits, the use of electronic resources, the gathering and analysis of usage statistics and the need for the acceptance of library rules.

In many organizations, the library will remain the manager of data concerning visitors, and this is typically done either in the library management system or in a database designed and managed in-house. In the future, it is likely that more of the management of these individuals in the longer term will be passed to the central IT departments of the institution, especially if an organization-wide IdM solution has been adopted. The registration of such users will still remain the responsibility of the library, and it is important that any special requirements the library has for their management (e.g. special flags to indicate each type of library visitor) are met by the central system.

In addition, the library may wish to originate data concerning individuals who are part of the organization-wide IdM already. This used to be more prevalent than it is today, when libraries would often issue separate library cards in addition to any identifying tokens which were given to users by the organization as a whole. It is, however, now the case that modern commercial library management systems should be capable of integration with cards issued by other systems, which means that the same tokens can be used in the library as throughout the remainder of the institution.

Finally, the library will manage the licences it purchases, and will therefore be the only part of the organization which can know who is entitled to access what. This information must be fed into the appropriate parts of the institution-wide IdM, especially if the library does not itself control institutional identity providers used for FAM-based access to electronic resources. This means that there needs to be interaction and, hopefully, integration between the library's licence management system and the institutional IdM.

Library requirements as a consumer of data

The library also has important roles as consumers of data produced by IdM in the rest of the organization; these are more straightforward, but will probably account for more data use than the systems where the library is the originator of personal data. The principal technical system in the library is of course the library management system, and this, and several other systems such as door and turnstile control mechanisms, will consume data relating to students and staff (in the university/college context). Libraries also contain computers and laptop points which need to be connected to the appropriate systems, though this is less of an IdM concern for the library (as network credentials will be set organization-wide). Other data will be needed for functions which are common to any department of the organization, including human resources needs, which in the library will include the scheduling of the time spent on customer-facing roles such as manning the issue and help desks.

In order to ensure the library's needs are met by institution-wide systems, it is important for library management to have some understanding of the requirements within the library which an organization-wide technical solution to manage IdM would need to meet, to feed into the development of an invitation to tender.

Implementation options

Implementation phases

There are many possible ways in which an identity and/or access management system can be implemented, depending on the organization's specific situation and available time and budget.

There are two basic implementation phases:

- **Phase 1** The first phase involves drawing up a detailed specification of the hardware and software required, and a detailed implementation plan.

- **Phase 2** The second phase is the actual implementation work detailed in the implementation plan, which includes testing, documentation and migration of existing data.

Implementation approaches

There are different options for organizing and then carrying out the implementation work detailed above. If an organization has adequate resources and expertise, it may decide to carry out both phases internally. The obvious advantages of this approach are saving costs on external consultancy fees, and in-house detailed knowledge of the systems once implemented. However, this approach relies on having significant experience in and knowledge of the solutions involved, and is likely to require significant resources and time.

Another possible approach is to implement the first phase internally and the second phase externally. With this option, an organization would carry all the preparation work internally, including preparing a detailed technology specification and an implementation plan. The second phase would be carried out by issuing an ITT for the actual implementation. This approach has the same advantages as the previous one but requires significant experience in the solutions on offer to be able to choose the most appropriate products for the job, and have the in-house detailed knowledge of the overall design of the implemented systems.

Alternatively, an organization may feel that it would benefit from some external expertise to make sure that the most appropriate technologies are chosen and opt for outsourcing all or some of the first-phase implementation to a third party.

Of course, some organizations may choose to outsource both phases to a third party, either as a single project or two separate projects. The advantage of this approach is that the organization can benefit from external expertise and save time and effort. The disadvantage is that there is less control over the implementation process, and possibly the end product too. Also, depending on the contract, there may or may not be opportunities for staff to gain the knowledge and skills required for long-term support development of the new systems. There are significant costs, both short- and long-term (e.g. annual support fees) that need to be considered with this approach.

The range of access and identity management products

There are many commercial products available on the market which offer the core functionality of an identity management and/or access management system, as well as additional features. Many larger vendors (e.g. Microsoft, Novell, Oracle, CA, Avatier) offer a set of applications that can form a complete solution, should one be needed. There are also smaller vendors (e.g. Ping Identity) that offer identity and access management solutions. Increasingly, vendors offer Cloud-based solutions (e.g. Ping Identity, Cryptocard).

A number of vendors offer third-party support for organizations that would like to implement an identity and access management solution but wish to outsource some or all of the system support and/or management. For example, an organization may wish to implement an open-source system but outsource system support. Another scenario would be an organization that wishes to subscribe to an outsourced identity provider (e.g. OpenAthens by Eduserv) to act on the organization's behalf. In 2008 the Joint Information Systems Committee published a briefing to help UK institutions that wish to implement federated access management with third-party support and gives a list of possible options (JISC, 2008).

It is not possible to give recommendations on the product to be chosen, as all products on offer have relative strengths and weaknesses, and the final choice will depend on the organization's particular circumstances.

Conclusions

To summarize, the procurement and implementation of a commercial identity and/or access management system solution is a complex undertaking. It is crucial to do thorough preparation work before deciding to procure and implement a new system to avoid problems later on. The preparation work will help ensure that the chosen set of products and service will fit the current and future needs of the organization and, in particular, the library, and that the chosen vendor will be able to provide the support required for both the initial implementation and future support and development. This means that it is of vital importance that the library understands its needs from such a system, and that library management work to ensure that these needs are reflected in the procurement process.

References

Gartner (2011) *Gartner Technology Research Centre,*
www.gartner.com/technology/home.jsp.
Joint Information Systems Committee (2008) *Third Party Providers of Federated Access Management Solutions: guide for institutions,*
www.jisc.ac.uk/publications/briefingpapers/2008/bpidentityprovidersv3.aspx.
Joint Information Systems Committee (2012) *Identity Management Toolkit. Selecting Supplier Solutions for Identity Management* (updated version),
www.identity-project.org.
JISC InfoNet (2012) *Working with Commercial Suppliers,*
www.jiscinfonet.ac.uk/infokits/commercial-suppliers/index_html.

10

Internet access provided by (or in) libraries

Increasingly, an important function served by public libraries (and university or other libraries that offer access to the public) is that of 'internet café'. Users are not drawn by any information resources that are physically within the library, but by the availability of access (often free of charge) to the internet. What should libraries be aware of when providing internet access, and what technologies can they use to manage such access appropriately?

Introduction

History of library-based internet access

There have been libraries offering online services since before the internet became a global phenomenon; the author of this chapter had his first introduction to the online world through the MIST MUD role-playing game (better known as Essex MUD), accessible from Essex University through a terminal hooked up to a modem in a tiny room in an Oxford college library via the earliest JANET service in early 1988, a service available free between 2 a.m. and 8 a.m. (Laurie, 2003).

However, the availability of such services through libraries remained sporadic in the UK for some time, essentially being offered in academic libraries and only to institutional members. This began to change at the end of the 1990s, as the internet itself became part of mainstream culture. 'In

1997, only 5 per cent of libraries had internet access. By 1999, this had risen to 41 per cent; in 2004, it was 67 per cent' (reported at www.politics.co.uk/reference/public-libraries, source unknown); 100% for static (as opposed to mobile) service points was reached by 2008, with an overall level of 6 terminals available per 10,000 of the UK population (Department of Culture, Media and Sport, 2008, 6) and over 95 million internet accesses taking place from public libraries in 2011 (CIPFA, 2011).

Online access from academic libraries is also an important part of higher education culture. In 2011, electronic resources accounted for 26% of library expenditure by member libraries of SCONUL (see Glossary), in addition to spending on internet access and computer equipment by institutions as a whole; there were 288 terminals available per 10,000 FTE students, and 38% of library seats offered laptop access (SCONUL, 2011).

Range of services offered in UK public libraries

The range of services offered by UK public libraries is now fairly standard. It has developed over time, though the major change since 2001, when UKOLN (see Glossary) produced an issue paper on library internet services (Harrison and Ormes, 2001), has been the increasing availability of wireless access and the lending of e-books. Typical services include the following:

- Wired network services available free to library members (though some authorities do charge, especially for lengthy sessions); booking may be required. Some libraries also offer sessions to non-members.
- Wireless access for users' own laptops, which is less common although the proportion of libraries offering it is increasing. Access is often through shared passwords, which are made available on signature of terms and conditions accompanied by proof of identity.
- Use of common software, such as word processors on provided terminals, but the range available is likely to be limited (especially for entertainment software such as games).
- Use of printers (at extra cost per page printed).
- Access to the internet generally, with a filter for child protection.
- Access to a range of subscription-only internet sites, some of which may also be available remotely to members.
- Access to library catalogue and associated member services (reservations, renewals, etc.).

(This list was developed by the author of this chapter through a survey of the relevant sections of UK local authority websites in early October 2012.) Some libraries offer courses in computer/internet use, though in many cases these are available through local authority adult education services.

Many of these services will require access and identity management, of varying kinds, to be detailed below. The mechanism used to fulfil this requirement is a major distinction between the internet services offered by a library and by commercial providers of access such as internet cafés.

Range of services offered to the public in UK academic libraries

Academic libraries will generally offer the same services as public libraries. The major differences are:

- there are likely to be far more terminals available, with space for wireless use (and often network terminals to plug laptops into the wired network)
- the range of subscription-only internet sites is far wider
- financial provision per user is likely to be higher (and the expectations of users correspondingly so)
- some services will be wider in scope than the library (e.g. the campus network)
- the pervasive service philosophy is likely to be less amenable to commercial solutions, especially in larger institutions.

The practical differences are thus those of resourcing and scale, but the philosophical difference will make a difference to the solutions selected, which in turn will lead to differences in the access management requirements for their management and use.

Library internet access outside the UK

The United Nations has declared that access to the internet is a human right (La Rue, 2011), meaning both that there should be freedom from censorship online and that states should aim to have universal access. There are still, however, much lower levels of access to the internet in developing states as opposed to developed states (26.3 compared to 73.8 users per 100 inhabitants in 2011, figures taken from International Telecommunications Union (2013), and La Rue reports a tendency for access availability to be concentrated in urban areas and restricted to socio-economic elites.

Attempts to broaden access in several nations include the establishment of access points, which are generally not linked to an existing public library service. The reason for this is the paucity of public library provision outside North America and Europe (Ignatow, 2011); a public library is often seen as a symbol of cultural imperialism (e.g. Odi, 1991, and others quoted by Ignatow). Instead of using the small number of existing libraries, access points are set up from scratch. The largest such access point network consists of the 125,000+ Common Services Centres (CSCs) set up by the government of India since 2006 (http://csc.gov.in). The 'e-Kiosks' provided by this scheme are in fact quite similar in terms of content offered to the forms of internet access from UK public libraries: the aim 'is to develop a platform that can enable Government, private and social sector organizations to align their social and commercial goals for the benefit of the rural population in the remotest corners of the country through a combination of IT-based as well as non-IT-based services' (India Development Gateway, 2012). The tone is perhaps less entertainment-focused than UK library services' descriptions of internet access (which tend to emphasize being able to keep in touch with family and friends), with CSC newsletters focusing on issues such as literacy schemes and skills development (e.g. CSC E-Governance Services India, 2012).

In North America and Europe, however, public library internet access is similar to that in the UK. Two randomly chosen library services, that of Victoria, British Columbia in Canada (www.gvpl.ca) and Banja Luko, Bosnia (www.nub.rs) act as examples: both offer free wired access to the internet (apparently unfiltered in each case), with subscription-only materials. The former also offers free wireless access to its members. The USA has had a long lead in terms of internet access in libraries, as described in Ormes and McClure (1996).

In academic libraries, the situation is also similar globally, with the state of development of online access reflecting the wealth of the country. In Malawi, ranked among the poorest countries in terms of GDP per capita (see http://en.wikipedia.org/wiki/List_of_countries_by_GDP_(nominal)_per_capita), the University of Malawi does not currently have terminals in its library, but is seeking to install enough to have 20 computers per 100 students by 2015, with a new fibre-based internet connection for the university providing cheaper connectivity than presently available (University of Malawi, 2011); this is approximately equivalent to the move to the next stage from the early JANET connectivity described in the first paragraph of this chapter. In Algeria, a country about halfway down the GDP listings, the

University of Algiers library offers subscription resources and general internet access (sites outside the university domain requiring authentication to obtain access) and appears to be approximately equivalent to the UK academic library of today (Université d'Alger, 2012).

Wired access

'Wired' network access refers to the case when a computer is directly attached to the network with a cable, nowadays usually using the Ethernet network protocol, over which internet protocols can be run to obtain access to online resources. This was, for most of the history of computer networking, the only method of connection, and still remains the mechanism of choice for public access terminals, physically housed within a library. This section will concentrate on the policy and technical decisions related to the management of a wired access service in a library which will require identity management on the part of the library (or contractors).

Library-managed terminals

While it is possible to set up a terminal in such a way that internet access is always available, it is likely that some form of authentication is going to be required. In an academic library, the most simple authentication is to use the same network user credentials as apply to the rest of the campus network, though this is not the only option (see the discussion of public access below). In public libraries, registered users will generally have a token (almost always a card with a barcode on it) which can be used to provide a user ID with which a password or PIN can be associated. (Many academic libraries will also provide such a card and PIN, and this is usually used to access personal library account services, such as loan renewals.) Such an access scheme is usually managed through the library management system.

Once logged in, decisions about access may still need to be made. If there is a booking system for terminals, it will be necessary to ensure that the user who has authenticated is the same as the user who booked the session. A number of public library websites indicate that their internet access offers different levels of filtering depending on the age of the user, and the decision as to which filter is to be applied will be dependent on information stored about the user. Both of these processes may be carried out manually, with the librarian checking the identity or age of the user before permitting physical access to the machine. Public library services also may require management of payments, either for the whole session, or after an initial free period, and measures will need to be taken to ensure that access is granted or denied when payment is made or fails to be made, as appropriate.

The other issue is obtaining user assent to terms and conditions which govern internet use. In UK academic libraries, these will almost certainly be based on the standard JANET Acceptable Use Policy (JANET, 2011a). Public library services will have formulated their own policies, which may also be derived from policies imposed on the libraries by their internet service provider. The policy can be signed on registration for membership (of an academic institution or library service), on booking a session (for the first time, or every time), or when actually starting the session. Some specific clauses of the policy (including filtering and any monitoring) should probably be brought to the attention of the user on a per-session basis.

Users' own laptops

Much of the above discussion will apply to a user's laptop which is plugged into the network (wireless access is covered separately, below). Some differences may arise:

- The library does not control the software installed on the laptop in the same way that it will do for a computer terminal permanently installed in the library. A system may be in place to register the user's hardware before it is permitted to be plugged into the network, and measures may be in place to try to prevent a laptop which is infected with malware, or which has software which can be used for malicious purposes, being connected to the network.
- Measures to ensure that terms and conditions are accepted, that sessions are terminated at the end of a booking period or when payment lapses, and to filter access to the internet, cannot be reliant on software installed on the laptop but must be set up on the network.

Wireless access
Wireless network authentication

In the modern world, laptops, tablet computers and potentially other personal devices are more likely to be used wirelessly, with the network accessed using a variety of protocols which can have different authentication and authorization regimes (the Wikipedia article on Wireless Security, http://en.wikipedia.org/wiki/Wireless_security, provides a fairly accessible introduction for those interested in more detail). The technical details of these protocols are not really relevant here, and the main decisions from the management point of view are about how to present the network authentication to the user. There are three commonly used methods to do this:

1 **Authentication before access using individual credentials arranged previously** This commonly uses credentials which have been obtained on registration as a member of a public library service or of an academic institution, but it may be necessary in some instances to register separately for wireless internet access. This has the advantage that the credentials to be used are managed for other purposes and are 'owned' and have value to the user, which helps to prevent insecure activities such as sharing with friends.

2 **Authentication before access using shared credentials arranged previously** This mechanism often uses a username and password which is changed frequently to avoid reuse, and the username and password is given to a user at the start of the session (often when the user signs terms and conditions of use). It is used by some public libraries, especially where access is available to non-members, and is common in commercial premises which offer free Wi-Fi to customers. Its main advantage is that it is easy for the organization offering the Wi-Fi service to administer.

3 **Limited free access with the option of signing in for greater privileges** Typically, access is given to a very limited range of websites, in many cases simply a site which accepts payment for the wireless session. This mechanism is common in commercial settings, including services, such as BT wifi (formerly BT OpenZone) (www.btwifi.co.uk) in the UK, which are available across large parts of the UK. It is also used in some public libraries, and has been used by academic wireless services, though in this sector it is tending to be phased out in favour of the first option above. The advantage of this mechanism is that the steps which a user has to go through before obtaining full access are completely customisable, and so can easily include online terms and conditions or payment. There have also been various schemes for free Wi-Fi access (Jefferies, 2011).

eduroam

eduroam is a service developed since 2003 to allow members of academic institutions to have wireless internet access from other institutions, authenticating directly using credentials supplied by their home institution, or, in other words, using federated authentication. The service is available across the UK, where it is administered by JANET; organizations which support eduroam are listed on the JANET website (www.ja.net/products-services/janet-connect/eduroam/eduroam-participating). For a user to access eduroam, both their home organization and the place that he or she is visiting need to be registered as participating organizations. (It is also possible to register solely as a home or visited organization.) eduroam is also available internationally, though for details of individual organizations you will need to check their websites or use a list of individual member organizations and administering organizations, such as the one found at the Wikipedia page on eduroam (http://en.wikipedia.org/wiki/Eduroam). eduroam can be accessed from a wide variety of devices, including some mobile phones, and is usable from most modern operating systems.

eduroam's federated authentication is based on wireless security protocols, rather than on web single sign-on as used by Shibboleth (discussed in Chapter 8), for example. Users are assigned usernames and passwords, with the usernames containing a suffix (usually the domain name of their home institution) that is used to redirect the authentication to the appropriate authority. Another difference from Shibboleth is that no attributes are passed to establish different levels of access; once authenticated, access is granted dependent on settings from the home institution, which is usually unrestricted web access.

eduroam originally supported the third option for authentication above, the use of a web page which challenges for authentication credentials, but this is now deprecated in favour of authentication before access is requested.

Material in this section was originally developed for the JISC Identity Toolkit blog (McLeish, 2012).

Paid services

As has already been mentioned, some public libraries offer paid internet access. Academic libraries are generally free of charge for access to their premises, including by members of the public, but that will not necessarily cover internet access or the reading of subscription-only journals. All libraries already make some charges for a variety of purposes, including the traditional overdue fines and charging for printing consumables.

Where public library internet services are paid for in the UK, this is usually required for non-members of the local library service or for lengthy sessions (i.e. the first half-hour or hour is free).

Public library user access to many services subscribed to by UK public libraries is based on library card numbers, without further credentials (i.e. no associated password). This is known as 'barcode authentication', and is supported by vendors such as Proquest and Thompson Gale, among others (Proquest, 2011; Thompson Gale, 2003). Checking of the barcode is based on matching to the patterns used by a library service's barcode generation process (e.g. length, valid characters, check sums, and so on), and is not therefore able to distinguish between currently active and de-activated library cards, though a barcode number is probably hard to guess if the user doesn't have access to a relevant card number.

For academic library users, access is based on a variety of possible methods, which include IP (location)-based access without authentication, federated access management, and individual or shared credentials (the last two having become very uncommon by 2012). Each of these is discussed in detail elsewhere in this book.

Coverage

The informal survey of library service websites mentioned above showed that in 2012 around 30% of public library services advertised that they offered some form of wireless internet access; coverage in academic libraries was nearly 100%. Not all public library branches will have wireless access points available, even if the service is offered in others controlled by the same local authority. It is more likely to be available in larger library branches than in smaller or rural ones.

Public access issues

Where non-members of a library (known as 'walk-in users') are able to use some of the services provided by the library, whether public or academic, there are some access management issues which need to be sorted out. The policy side of this deals with which services such individuals are entitled to use, while the technical side relates to the mechanisms by which access can be provided to these services. The considerations for policy will be the same for libraries in both sectors, while the technical solutions will be different for a variety of reasons (historical, resourcing and financial).

Public library authorities will have, as mentioned, their own requirements which non-members will need to satisfy to obtain access to the internet. The situation in an academic library will be governed by the policies laid down by JANET as provider of internet access, as described in JANET's guest and public network access factsheet (JANET, n.d.). According to this, users are divided into three categories, two of which ('guests' and 'visitors') being among those covered by this chapter. The difference is that guests are non-members whose reason for being at the institution is due to the institution's remit in education and research, so would include attendees at academic conferences, for example, while attendees at commercial conferences would be classed as visitors.

The JANET eligibility criteria (JANET, 2011b, paragraph 15) only allow the organization to permit access to JANET services if they are members or guests, so other methods for doing so, such as the use of a commercial internet service provider, would need to be used to provide internet access to visitors should this be desired. Institutions considering the provision of internet access to visitors as opposed to guests should make sure they understand the legal implications of such a move, which are summarized in JANET (n.d.) and could involve the fulfilment of onerous procedural requirements that are not needed for members or guests.

Access to subscribed services

Access to subscribed services for walk-in users is legally dependent on the terms of the licence purchased for each service by the library in which they are situated, just as it is for subscribers to the library, whether academic or public.

The issues surrounding walk-in users apply more in the academic library case than the public library case, as anyone living in the UK with a postal address can become a member of at least one public library service, and can therefore use their home library credentials to obtain access to subscribed services in any other public library, once they have internet access. Academic libraries, on the other hand, only offer full membership to members of the institutions they serve, with eduroam access for members of other academic institutions, which means that those who are not members will have to be catered for specially.

Policies and responsibilities

In the case of access to subscribed journals, the policies and responsibilities of the subscribing organization are set out in the licence agreement. This basically means that access can be offered to services which have licence agreements that allow this, and prohibited for those that do not. Whether or not such access is provided at all, and who has which library usage right, is basically for the library to decide, though there may be factors which require it to be offered, such as conditions associated with grants or bequests, or historically linked with specific collections. Walk-in users and other users who are not themselves members of academic libraries can be divided into the following groups (based on the useful list at www.nottingham. ac.uk/is/libraries/visitors/visitors.aspx):

- staff and students from other universities, who may well be able to use eduroam to access online material, or who have access rights defined by agreements from library consortia such as SCONUL Access (www.sconul.ac.uk/sconul-access)
- members of non-commercial organizations which have an association with the institution that may provide access rights as a result, e.g. NHS trusts (the bodies which manage local public health care in the UK), colleges with shared courses, overseas institutions, etc.
- members of commercial organizations which have taken out 'commercial membership' for a fee (typically less per person than the external borrowers below)
- school groups and others taking part in outreach or business/community engagement (BCE) activities, who may well have access rights as a result of the schemes involved – for more details see the EAM2BCE guide (JISC Collections, 2011)
- alumni and former staff, who may have some library usage rights, but are likely to need to register and pay a fee (less than that for non-alumni, usually) for fuller access
- members of the public, who may be able to register for schemes which give enhanced access rights for a membership fee ('external borrowers'), but who often have some library usage rights without doing so. This often includes access to a limited range of electronic subscribed services, as well as reference access to the physical collection of the library.

There are thus two issues: preventing walk-in users from having access to subscribed services which normally use IP authentication but which do not permit them to have access; and the provision of access to subscribed services which do permit them to have access. In both cases, the technical problems which arise are a consequence of the way that academic library access management 'piggybacks on established university IT systems and safeguards which have not always been specifically designed to support the licence restrictions of publishers' (Robinson et al., 2012). While eduroam allows many walk-in users to access material through their home institution subscriptions, there are still many others who do not have access to this service.

The general perception of the best way to manage walk-in users is to require registration before access is granted, through a single point of access (e.g. a registration desk near the library entrance) (UCISA, 2007). This provides the opportunity to ask for signature of terms and conditions, and allows the assignment of credentials to the user (including both library cards and usernames/passwords). In some cases, the credentials assigned will be associated with institution-wide services (though with lesser rights than those assigned to members), while in others the credentials will be associated with library-managed databases (often those which are part of the library catalogue software). These credentials and the access they give need to be carefully managed, and thought needs to be given to the length of time for which credentials for walk-in users can be valid.

The next step is to understand the rights which are granted to walk-in users by each of the licences which the library has paid for, and ensure that the terms from new licences are recorded. The record for a resource will also need to include information from subsequent discussions with publishers, clarifying or amending existing terms. This can be done with a purchased electronic resource management system or an open-source alternative, or by using smaller-scale or more generic solutions (such as a wiki or shared spreadsheet or document). A wiki-based solution is described in a recent article in the Ariadne journal (Robinson et al., 2012).

Once the ways in which user credentials and licence conditions are to be managed have been implemented, it is possible to consider how to arrange access to the appropriate resources for walk-in users. The recommended solution to this issue, for users who do not have access through their own institutional federated access or eduroam connection, is to use dedicated kiosks (UCISA, 2007). The authors of the Ariadne article outline a practical method to set these up, using the OpenKiosk extension to the Firefox web browser (https://addons.mozilla.org/en-US/firefox/addon/open-kiosk/) – but note that this extension is not compatible with recent releases of the browser software.

Summary

Access to online resources through libraries was available almost as soon as anywhere had access, and the provision of services has become almost universally available across Europe and North America in both academic and public libraries. In the rest of the world there are fewer public libraries and public access is being provided in other institutions, while academic libraries are catching up rapidly with the West. Wireless is now widely available, in academic libraries usually through eduroam, to visitors from other institutions. Issues continue to affect access to resources for walk-in users, however.

References

CIPFA (2011) *Trends from CIPFA Public Library Statistics*, Chartered Institute of Public Finance and Accountancy.

CSC E-Governance Services India (2012), *CSC Nav Jeevan newsletter*, February, http://csc.gov.in/images/csc_newsletters/csc_nav%20Jeevan_february%2012.pdf.

Department of Culture, Media and Sport (2008) *Public Library Service Standards*, 3rd rev. edn, http://webarchive.nationalarchives.gov.uk/+/http://www. culture.gov.uk/images/publications/PublicLibraryServicesApril08.pdf.

Harrison, J. and Ormes, S. (2001) *Internet Services: the range available to library users*, issue paper from the Networked Services Policy Taskgroup, UKOLN, Bath, www.ukoln.ac.uk/public/earl/issuepapers/range.html.

Ignatow, G. (2011) What Has Globalization Done to Developing Countries' Public Libraries?, *International Sociology*, November, **26** (6), 746–68.

India Development Gateway (2012) *Common Services Centres*, www.indg.in/ e-governance/cscscheme/common-service-centres-scheme.

International Telecommunications Union (2013) *Key Global Telecom Indicators for the World Telecommunications Service*, www.itu.int/en/ITU-D/Statistics/Pages/publications/wtid.aspx.

JANET (n.d.) *Guest and Public Network Access Factsheet*, https://community.ja.net/ library/advisory-services/guest-and-public-network-access.

JANET (2011a) *Acceptable Use Policy*, Version 11, May 2011, https://community.ja.net/library/acceptable-use-policy.

JANET (2011b) *Eligibility Policy*, Issue 1.0, May 2011, https://community.ja.net/library/janet-policies/eligibility-policy.

Jefferies, D. (2011) Should Councils be Investing in Free Public Wi-Fi Networks?, *Guardian*, 5 December, www.guardian.co.uk/local-government-network/2011/ dec/05/councils-free-public-wifi-networks.

JISC Collections (2011) *Access for Engagement: extending access management to business community engagement in universities and colleges*, JISC, https://www.jisc-collections.ac.uk/Our-projects/EAM2BCE.

La Rue, F. (2011) *Report of the Special Rapporteur on the Promotion and Protection of the Right to Freedom of Opinion and Expression*, Human Rights Council, Seventeenth Session, distributed 16 May, http://documents.latimes.com/un-report-internet-rights.

Laurie, M. (2003) *Escape from the Dungeon*, http://arch-wizard.com/history.html.

McLeish, S. (2012) eduroam, The Identity Toolkit blog, 27 September, http://theidentitytoolkit.wordpress.com/2012/09/27/eduroam.

Odi, A. (1991) The Colonial Origins of Library Development in Africa – some reflections on their significance, *Libraries & Culture* **26** (4), Fall, 594–604.

Ormes, S. and McClure, C. (1996) *A comparison of public library internet connectivity in the USA and UK*, UKOLN, Bath, www.ukoln.ac.uk/publib/USAUK1.htm.

Proquest (2011) *Instructions on How to Set up Barcode Access to ProQuest*, http://support.proquest.com/?articleid=2272.

Robinson, K., Jennings, L. and Lockton, L. (2012) Walk-in Access to e-Resources at the University of Bath, *Ariadne*, **69**, August, www.ariadne.ac.uk/issue69.

SCONUL (2011) *Annual Library Statistics 2010–2011*.

Thompson Gale (2003) *Frequently Asked Questions – Authentication*, http://access.gale.com/authentication/authentication_faq.html#FAQ Barcode.

UCISA (2007) HAERVI: *HE Access to e-Resources in Visited Institutions Best Practice Guide*, www.ucisa.ac.uk/publications/haervi_guide.aspx.

Université d'Alger (2012) *Utilisation d'Internet*, Bibliothèque Universitaire, Université d'Alger, http://bu.univ-alger.dz/index.php/services/utilisation-dinternet.

University of Malawi (2011) *University of Malawi Strategic Plan, 2012–2017*, www.unima.mw/wp-content/uploads/2012/07/2012-2017-UNIMA-Strategic-Plan-30-March-2012.pdf.

11

Library statistics

Licensed electronic content accounts for a significant proportion of many libraries' budgets. It is therefore important that libraries are able to collect and analyse reliable and meaningful e-resource usage data in order to guide their future decision making. This chapter looks at why and how libraries collect usage data, and some important developments designed to make the process easier.

Why libraries collect electronic resource usage statistics

For many libraries around the world licensed electronic resources account for a significant proportion of the library budget. In order for libraries to be able to make informed decisions about how that budget is spent, they need to have a good idea of how much their e-resources are being used and what user groups are making use of them (Lynch, 1998, 10). This is equally true of resources licensed to a single library or a resource-sharing consortium.

Some libraries have devolved budgets, where if a particular resource is only used by one department, that department has to pay for the resource even though it is provided by the library. Resources that are used across many departments are paid for centrally. So it's important for libraries to know which resources they should be paying for and which should be paid for by another department. Academic libraries are often funded as a top slice of the institution's budget, before it is divided up between departments, so centrally paid-for resources take a proportion of the budget of every department, even though some departments may not actually be making use of these resources; not to mention that some resources may, in fact, be of interest to multiple departments but are only being used by one department due to poor resource promotion by the library.

Just as with print resources, librarians need quality usage data for e-resources to guide their collection decision making. E-resource usage statistics offer great potential. In the past, librarians had to guess how much an index or journal (both types of material which are important e-resources today) might be used, or undertake a slow and time-consuming shelving study in order to obtain journal usage data (Duy and Vaughan, 2003, 16). With electronic resources, usage data can often be obtained automatically and offer much more detailed information about how a resource or product is being used, when and by whom. There are different measures that can be used to assess usage, such as the number of searches performed over a certain period in an electronic database, or the number of full-text downloads from an electronic journal (Pesch 2007, 207).

Challenges in collecting electronic resource usage data

Despite the advantages offered by e-resource usage statistics, librarians often find the task of getting a clear picture of the use of an electronic collection a 'difficult and tedious process' (Cooper, 2007, 172). These are just some of the reasons why collecting meaningful, reliable and timely electronic resource usage data can be difficult:

- **Lack of standards and inconsistency in vendor-supplied electronic usage data** A lot of literature on electronic resource use statistics produced after the introduction of electronic journals in 1998 identified the lack of standards amongst publishers for the production and reporting of usage data as the most significant barrier to obtaining quality resource usage data (Luther, 2000; Blecic et al., 2001; Duy and Vaughan, 2003; Baker and Read, 2008; Cooper, 2007). However, some vendors, particularly smaller ones, don't provide any usage data at all (Duy and Vaughan, 2003, 16). There may also be technical issues that make usage data temporarily unavailable or unreliable.
- **Marketing** There is also a question of whether libraries can trust statistics produced by vendors. Vendors are concerned that low usage

data may mean the cancellation of their product and reduced revenue, so some vendors may attempt to inflate usage figures in order to remain in business (Luther, 2000; Duy and Vaughan, 2003, 17).

- **Increasing list of content vendors** It is not just the quality of usage data that may be a problem but the actual quantity of it, as the number of electronic resource providers continues to grow (Pesch, 2007, 207).
- **Print v. electronic subscriptions** A library may have an electronic subscription to a journal as well as a print copy, so both print and electronic access data has to be evaluated in order to get a good idea of the journal's usage (Cooper, 2007, 172).
- **Consortia subscriptions** Another challenging aspect of collecting usage data involves consortia subscriptions, as the consortium may collect its own usage data (often minimal), which may be available in addition to or sometimes instead of vendor-supplied data (Blecic et al., 2001, 43).
- **Sensitive data** Some usage data collected by both libraries and vendors might be of sensitive nature (e.g. demographic data or individual level data), so there are legal and data protection issues that need to be tackled by both vendors, single licensing organizations and library consortia (Lynch, 1998, 10; Merk, Scholze and Windisch, 2008, 158).
- **Advances in search technology** Continued developments in search technology, e.g. Open URL linking technology and RSS feeds, change the way users access electronic resources and will affect the way use statistics need to be collected and analysed (Blecic et al., 2001, 42).
- **Technical difficulties** There might be some technical difficulties in extracting usage data, as demonstrated by the challenges faced by the new federated access management technologies such as Shibboleth. More on this can be found in the next section of this chapter, on the RAPTOR project.

This list can be continued but should provide an insight into the challenges faced by serials librarians who wish to collect and make sense of electronic resource usage data.

To date, the motives for and the problems of monitoring usage have been largely confined to serials and periodicals. However, other types of library resource, such as monographs, standard reference works and even fiction books, are increasingly being replaced by online alternatives. With the advantages in stock management that this may bring to libraries there usually comes pressure from suppliers to adopt a subscription model more like that established for serials and, therefore, many of the same arguments for monitoring and analysing usage data, and making business decisions based on this, for an even wider range of the library's resources.

How libraries collect usage data
COUNTER project

In 1998, the International Coalition of Library Consortia (ICOLC) released *Guidelines for Statistical Measures of Usage of Web-based Indexed, Abstracted, and Full Text Resources* (International Coalition of Library Consortia, 1998). Some of the data elements recommended by ICOLC were later used by the COUNTER (Counting Online Usage of Networked Electronic Resources) project (Counting Online Usage of Networked Electronic Resources, 2011). COUNTER's first code of practice became available in 2003 and provided a much needed standard for recording and reporting electronic resource statistics. The 2003 code of practice was followed by Release 2 (2005) and Release 3 (2008). Release 3 of the code of practice requires the implementation of the SUSHI protocol (SUSHI 2011). The Standardized Usage Statistics Harvesting Initiative (SUSHI) is a SOAP-based (Simple Object Access Protocol) web service for harvesting COUNTER-compliant statistics developed by NISO (National Information Standards Organization, 2011). Although there are still some inconsistencies in the way vendors provide usage statistics and not all vendors are COUNTER-compliant, COUNTER and SUSHI have made the process of collecting usage data much easier.

Studies show that a large proportion of usage statistics currently gathered by libraries are provided by vendors (e.g. through the publisher website or through COUNTER) but that is not the only source of usage data available to libraries (Baker and Read, 2008, 54; Greer and Smart, 2010, 3).

E-resource management systems

Many commercial library systems offer usage data gathering capabilities, e.g. the Millennium Electronic Resource Management module (Innovative, 2011), WebFeat's SMART Usage Tracker (no longer available) and Serials Solutions' Management Services (Serials Solutions, 2011). Commercial electronic resource management systems (ERMs), such as EBSCONET ERM Essentials (Ebsco, 2011), have also become an important tool for tracking e-resource usage. Some libraries have invested in home-grown e-resource management systems which have a use data component (Schulz, 2001, 454).

Third-party statistics gathering services

A number of third-party use statistics services are now available, most notably ScholarlyStats – an online portal for library usage statistics (ScholarlyStats, 2011), Google Analytics – an online web analytics service by Google (Google Analytics, 2011), and Journal Use Reports – a research assessment and collections management tool by Thomson Scientific and the University of Melbourne, Australia (Thomson Scientific, 2011).

In the UK, the Joint Information Systems Committee (JISC) has developed an Online Usage Statistics Portal (JUSP), in collaboration with Mimas Data Centre, Cranfield University and Birmingham City University (JISC Collections, 2013). The portal provides a 'one-stop shop' for libraries to view, download and analyse their usage reports from NESLi2 publishers (a UK national licensing initiative).

Authentication information

Authentication information can also be used for gathering details about user transactions that take place, i.e. an entry for every time a user logs into a service. Authentication systems, such as Shibboleth, can be used for this purpose. More detailed information about user activity once the user has logged into a service can be obtained from analysing log files of a web server that hosts a resource (typically done by the resource provider), linking servers or proxy software, such as EZproxy (which can be done by the library).

A log file is a file that contains a list of events, which have been 'logged' by a computer. Log files can come in different formats, such as the popular Common Logfile Format (CLF). The CLF was developed in 1995 and is a standardized ASCII text file format typically used by web servers for logging user access (Luotonen, 1995). There are a number of parsing engines available for harvesting log file data, such as Log Parser from Microsoft (Microsoft, 2010) and Java XML Log Analyser (Nioto, 2010). The SUSHI project discussed earlier is an example of a communication protocol used for harvesting log file data. Reading raw statistical data from log files is hard, so there are also several log file reporting systems to choose from, such as open-source AWStats (Sourceforge.net, 2010) and commercial XpoLog Log Management (XPLG, 2010). Many libraries put a lot of effort into harvesting and analysing log file statistics, as demonstrated by the University of Sussex Library in the UK, which wrote a special script for collecting EZproxy log file statistics.

One of the benefits of using fine-grain log data, at whatever point in the supply-chain it is collected, to monitor usage of e-resources is the opportunity it provides to understand the behaviour of individual library users, and use that understanding to improve the services a library offers to its users. But once data is disaggregated in the ways that current access management technologies allow, there is a fine line between monitoring the usage of a resource, and 'snooping' on the reading behaviour of an individual user. However altruistic the intentions of the librarian, there will be users who may have valid reasons for concern and objection to this.

Arguably, businesses that use the internet for purely commercial relationships with their customers (users) have stronger motives (increased sales, turnover and profit) than those of most libraries for analysing the behaviour of users and tailoring (sometimes without human intervention) the design of the online services they provide to user behaviour. Much of the success of Amazon as a retailer, initially of books but latterly of almost any imaginable retail consumer product, has been attributed (Anderson, 2004) to their pioneering of 'smart' recommendation services ('Customers who bought this item also bought . . .'). The majority of consumers in general have accepted this without question and perceived it as a pure benefit, but probably with little appreciation of the volumes of detailed personal data being collected. However, there are signs of growing concern among users about the use of personal data collected by online services. Anonymizing collected data and closely following the data protection legislation will help protect library users from any privacy breaches.

There are some interesting developments in the world of authentication statistics. For example, the Joint Information Systems Committee (JISC) in the UK has recently commissioned a project to provide a tool for harvesting event-based log information from a organization's authentication and authorization infrastructure (particularly the Shibboleth identity provider, EZproxy, and OpenAthens LA services) and presenting a statistical analysis of the resulting information in a non-technical, easy-to-understand manner. The project is called RAPTOR (Cardiff University, 2012). Notably, the designers of RAPTOR recognize that, at least for UK academic libraries, a large proportion of online usage is converging through the two channels of federated access direct to vendor services, and access via library-managed proxy servers (often also protected by the same federated access authentication service to provide a more consistent 'seamless' entry point for users). Their objective is that RAPTOR will combine usage data from (at least) these two significant points in the supply chain, to include a larger proportion of all the e-resources available via a library (Smith, 2011). It is important to note that RAPTOR will not show access statistics of accesses permitted because of the user's IP address without further authentication (i.e. neither via federated access or proxy-based access). The only way to get IP-based access statistics is direct from the vendor/service itself (e.g. through COUNTER). There is more discussion on RAPTOR in Chapter 8.

A similar project is under way in Switzerland. The AMMAIS (Accounting and Monitoring of Authentication and Authorization Infrastructure) project aims to provide a statistical tool for the members of the Swiss access management federation run by the Swiss Education & Research Network (SWITCH). AMMAIS builds on the earlier work by SWITCH (Schnellmann and Redard, 2006).

The AMAAIS and RAPTOR projects are working together on developing a common information model for event-based information, and are beginning to develop open standards for the exchange of such information.

In Finland, the AAIEye monitoring and reporting tool is available to the members of the Finnish access management federation (HAKA). The tool is designed to provide a centralized server for collecting usage statistics submitted by service providers and identity providers (HAKA, 2010).

Another example is the work being undertaken by Eduserv in the UK. Eduserv operates OpenAthens – a proprietary federated access and identity management system (Eduserv, 2011). MyAthens, the OpenAthens e-resource management module, allows libraries to extract some simple usage statistics for OpenAthens-enabled resources. Eduserv is currently working on Project Monteverde – the OpenAthens usage collector module, which aims to provide a complete in-depth statistics-reporting platform for OpenAthens users (Orrell, 2010).

Institutional repositories

Another area where libraries need electronic resource usage statistics is institutional repositories. A growing number of libraries, particularly academic ones, manage an online institutional repository. Institutional repository statistics is a fast-developing field and there are a number of projects that have been conducted recently or are currently under way.

In 2007 a collaborative European Union project undertook a comprehensive inventory study of the state of 114 digital repositories in the 27 countries of the European Union and provided a basis for contemplating the next steps in driving forward an interoperable infrastructure at a

European level (van der Graaf and van Eijndhoven, 2007). The Digital Repository Infrastructure Vision for European Research (DRIVER) project showed that about 70% of those repositories logged download and access data but only 30% offered item-level statistics in 2006. About half of the repositories that offered item-level statistics were based in the UK and about a quarter were planning to implement such a service (Merk, Scholze and Windisch, 2008, 152).

A similar project Australian project, titled the Australian Benchmark Statistics Service (BEST), was conducted in 2007 by the Australian Partnership for Sustainable Repositories (APSR) in order to make recommendations for the introduction of item-level usage statistics in the Australian context (Australian Partnership for Sustainable Repositories, 2007).

In the UK, the Joint Information Systems Committee (JISC) sponsored the Publisher and Institutional Repository Usage Statistics Project (PIRUS). PIRUS I (2008–9) demonstrated that it is technically feasible to create, record and consolidate usage statistics for individual articles using data from repositories and publishers, despite the diversity of organizational and technical environments in which they operate (Joint Information Systems Committee, 2008). PIRUS 2 (2009–10) is to specify standards, protocols, an infrastructure and an economic model for the recording, reporting and consolidation of online usage of individual articles hosted by repositories, publishers and other entities (Cranfield University, 2010).

Another UK project, Interoperable Repository Statistics (IRStats), developed a pilot usage statistics module for repositories that use DSpace or Eprints software (University of Southampton, 2009).

The open-source AWStats analytical tool, mentioned earlier, can be used for harvesting repositories statistics (AWStats, 2013).

Figure 11.1 illustrates a possible e-resources 'supply chain', the different points at which usage/traffic data can be collected, and how that data may be supplied to or accessed by the library.

Concluding thoughts

It is clear from this chapter that gathering and analysing electronic resource library statistics is not a straightforward affair and requires considerable effort from library staff. Many libraries have to analyse statistics from several sources, e.g. vendor-supplied, and/or institutional use data with data provided by link resolvers, web logs, and consortium reports in order to get

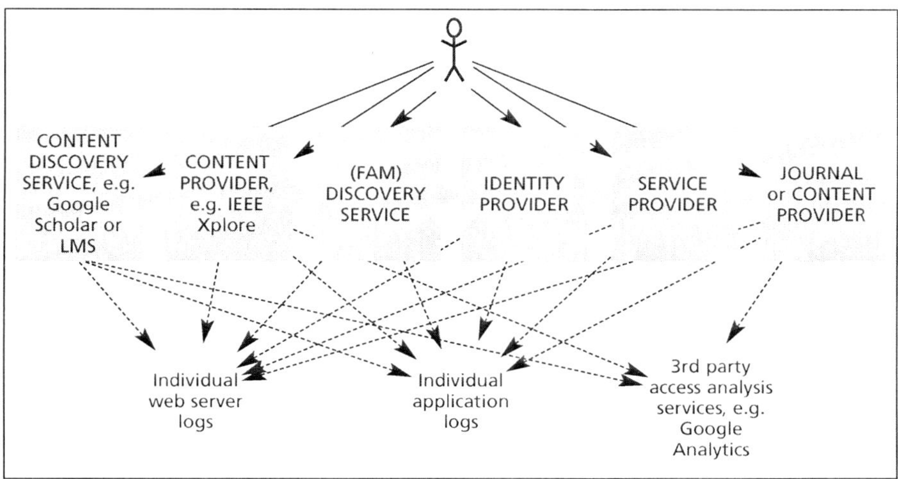

Figure 11.1 *E-resources 'supply chain'*

a clearer picture of resource use (Baker and Read, 2008, 52). On the positive side, some major research and development work has taken place in recent years in an attempt to make collecting and analysing usage statistics easier. Librarians can benefit from these initiatives and a range of training opportunities available from leading library governing bodies and vendors. It is unlikely that a magic solution can be found but steps are being taken in the right direction. It seems fitting to finish this chapter with a quote from Peter Drucker:

> Everything improved or new needs first to be tested on a small scale; that is, it needs to be piloted. The way to do this is to find somebody within the enterprise who really wants the new. Everything new gets into trouble. And then it needs a champion. It needs somebody who says, 'I am going to make this succeed,' and who then goes to work on it. . . . If the pilot test is successful – it finds the problems nobody anticipated but also finds the opportunities that nobody anticipated, whether in terms of design, or market, or service – the risk of change is usually quite small.
>
> Drucker (2004)

References and further reading

Anderson, C. (2004) The Long Tail, *Wired Magazine*, October, www.cubanxgiants. com/berry/329/spring11/readings/week7/longtail_anderson_wired.pdf.

Australian Partnership for Sustainable Repositories (APSR) (2007) Australian

Benchmark Statistics Service (BEST), http://apsr.edu.au/best/.

AWStats (2013) *AWStats: Free real-time logfile analyzer to get advanced statistics (GNU GPL)*, http://awstats.sourceforge.net/.

Baker, G. and Read, E. (2008) Vendor-supplied Usage Data for Electronic Resources: a survey of academic libraries, *Learned Publishing*, **21** (1), 48–57.

Blecic, D., Fiscella, J. and Wiberley, S. (2001) The Measurement of Use of Web-based Information Resources: an early look at vendor-supplied data, *College & Research Libraries*, **62**, 434–53.

Cardiff University (2012) *About RAPTOR*, http://iam.cf.ac.uk/trac/RAPTOR.

Cooper, M. (2007) The Importance of Print and Electronic Usage Data: getting a clear picture, *Serials Review*, **33** (3), 172–74.

Counting Online Usage of Networked Electronic Resources (2011) *About COUNTER*, www.projectcounter.org.

Cranfield University (2010) *About PIRUS 2*, www.cranfieldlibrary.cranfield.ac.uk/pirus2/tiki-index.php?page=pirus2.

Drucker, P. (2004) *The Daily Drucker: 366 days of insight and motivation for getting the right things done*, Harper Business, New York.

Duy, J. and Vaughan, L. (2003) Usage Data for Electronic Resources: a comparison between locally collected and vendor-provided statistics, *Journal of Academic Librarianship*, **29** (1), 16–22.

Ebsco (2011) *EBSCONET ERM Essentials*, www2.ebsco.com/en-us/ProductsServices/ERM/Pages/index.aspx.

Eduserv (2011) *Access and Identity Management*, www.eduserv.org.uk/aim.

Google Analytics (2011) *Welcome to Google Analytics*, www.google.com/analytics.

Greer, V. and Smart, P. (2010) *RAPTOR User Requirements, RAPTOR Project*, http://iam.cf.ac.uk/trac/RAPTOR/attachment/wiki/ProjectDocumentation/ RAPTOR_User_Requirements.pdf.

HAKA (2010) *About AAIEye Monitoring & Reporting*, www.csc.fi/english/institutions/haka/instructions/services-tech/aaieye.

Innovative (2011) *About Millennium ILS*, www.iii.com/products/millennium_ils.shtml.

International Coalition of Library Consortia (1998) *Guidelines for Statistical Measures of Usage of Web-based Indexed, Abstracted, and Full Text Resources*, http://legacy.icolc.net/webstats.html.

JISC Collections (2013) *About the Journal Statistics Portal*, http://jusp.mimas.ac.uk/about.html.

Joint Information Systems Committee (2008) *Publisher and Institutional Repository Usage Statistics (PIRUS)*, www.jisc.ac.uk/whatwedo/programmes/pals3/pirus.aspx.

Luotonen, A. (1995) *The Common Logfile Format*,
www.w3.org/Daemon/User/Config/Logging.html.

Luther, J. (2000) *White Paper on Electronic Journal Usage Statistics*, Council on Library
and Information Resources, www.clir.org/pubs/reports/pub94/contents.html.

Lynch, C. (ed.) (1998) *A White Paper on Authentication and Access Management Issues
in Cross-Organizational Use of Networked Information Resources*, Coalition for
Networked Information,
www.cni.org/about-cni/staff/clifford-a-lynch/publications.

Merk, C., Scholze, F. and Windisch, N. (2008) Item-level Statistics: a review of
current practices and recommendations for normalisation and exchange, *Library
Hi Tech*, December, 151–62.

Microsoft (2010) *Log Parser 2.1*, www.microsoft.com/downloads/en/details.aspx.

Miller, R. (2002) Shaping Digital Library Content, *Journal of Academic Librarianship*,
28 (3), 97–103.

National Information Standards Organization (2011) *About SUSHI*,
www.niso.org/workrooms/sushi.

Nioto (2010) *Java XML Log Analyser*, http://sourceforge.net/projects/jxla.

Orrell, D. (2010) *OpenAthens Roadmap to 2011 Presentation*,
www.slideshare.net/eduserv/openathens-roadmap-to-2011.

Pesch, O. (2007) Usage Statistics: about COUNTER and SUSHI, *Information Services
and Use*, **27**, 207–13.

Schnellmann, P. and Redard, A. (2006) *Accounting for the Authentication and
Authorization Infrastructure (AAI), Pilot Study*, Swiss Education & Research
Network (SWITCH),
https://www.switch.ch/aai/docs/AAI_Accounting_Pilot_Study.pdf.

ScholarlyStats (2011) *Welcome to ScholarlyStats*,
www.scholarlystats.com/sstats/default.htm.

Schulz, N. (2001) E-journal Databases: a long-term solution?, *Library Collections,
Acquisitions and Technical Services*, **25**, 449–59.

Serials Solutions (2011) *About Serials Solutions*, www.serialssolutions.com.

Smith, R. (2011) RAPTOR project, e-mail, 26 May.

Sourceforge.net (2010) *What is AWStats?*, http://awstats.sourceforge.net.

Thomson Scientific (2011) *About Journal Use Reports*,
www.researchinformation.info/products/product_details.php?product_id=21.

University of Southampton (2009) *About Interoperable Repository Statistics (IRStats)
Project*, www.irstats.com/main.php.

van der Graaf, M. and van Eijndhoven, K. (2007) *The DRIVER inventory study*,
www.driver-support.eu/linkspubs/inventorystudy.html.

12

The business case for libraries

Implementing a library access management system requires close co-operation between the library and IT services, as well as support from senior management. This chapter looks at the wider benefits of access management within the host organization, opportunities for further development and how to use this information to produce a successful business case.

Introduction

Today, academic libraries are less likely to adopt their own authentication and access solutions than to make use of the existing identity management carried out by the institution of which they are part, which should now be mature enough to support many of a library's requirements. After all, the same consideration which suggested the FAM model in the first place, that resource providers do not wish to carry out IdM and will not be as good at it as the organizations which already need to do it, applies in a modified form to the relationship between library services and the main IdM systems of the institution: the library does not have a good reason to duplicate any of the institution-wide processes which are already carried out. This is essentially the reason that libraries can now be classified principally as consumers of IdM, as discussed in Chapter 9.

This does not mean that there is no role for the library in the institutional management of its identity services. At the very least, the library has a large number of requirements which follow from the way it wishes to use identity data. The library will need to monitor developments in IdM, and ensure that its current needs are still being met, with accurate data in the form needed for efficient library services, whether this is for user access to the library management system or for FAM-based authentication and authorization to electronic resources.

The library is likely to be setting up new services, or new versions of services, and these might well have IdM requirements which are not necessarily being met by existing institutional systems. For example, many institutions in the UK are currently working on implementing research data archives. These have access management needs that may include a requirement for virtual organizations, for researchers at other institutions who are collaborating on projects with local colleagues to be able to access shared material, before, during, and after archiving. A research data archive is likely to be closely linked to a current research information system (CRIS), which may also be run by the library. This needs to store data concerning research grants, research staff and students, publications, and research data so that it can make the links between them evident (so that, for example, it is possible to go from a publication listed in a repository to the relevant research grant information, or to the archived raw data which supports the publication) – and this system will be a consumer of identity and other data which may not previously have been consistently managed. Even if not run by the library, the CRIS will be a new source of identity data which needs to be accessed by the research data archive.

Even in the absence of a CRIS, research data management provides some complex access management issues. There are various ways in which research data can be classified, each of which have implications for access management. For example, there is data that is being stored at milestones during a research project, which is likely to be accessible only to the research team; in contrast, research funding bodies are increasingly encouraging or requiring the final data which forms the basis for published work to be public or semi-public (i.e. requiring that those who are allowed to access it are *bona fide* researchers). Teams involved in projects can be cross-institutional, or involve commercial partners (which means that some who should have access to the data are not part of the local access management systems); the work itself may be funded commercially, and concern sensitive data which the funders wish to use for financial gain and so wish to remain secret – but which still needs to be archived for future re-use. Without a

CRIS, management of the relationship between funders, researchers, papers, and data can become extremely complex, which may lead to incorrect access management decisions being made.

Another area of interest to libraries which generally has more simple access management considerations, the current growth in the 'big data' paradigm, can have at least one similarity to research data. While big data publications usually both are public access and do not require complex access management for the sources of data (unlike even open repositories of research papers), the records being made public often include sensitive personal data about individuals which needs to be redacted or 'sanitized' to preserve privacy, typically a complex and difficult process. When the material needing to be removed is not even always visible to the naïve reader (Kelly, 2008), it is clear that this is a major challenge.

Another possible source of new requirements for the library to pass to the institution could be a desire to slim down licence costs, by paying only for access by smaller groups of users who have an interest in a specific topic – staff from a specific faculty or department, and/or undergraduate students on a group of courses. Ignoring any difficulty there might be in persuading a publisher to negotiate such a lower-cost licence, the major issue is likely to be having a system which can provide accurate and up-to-date information about the membership of such groups. A variety of products exist to carry out this management task. It is a bit of a chicken and egg situation: without such a system, it is difficult to justify the utility of setting up access management rules which require it to be in place; but without the perceived need provided by complex access management rules, there is little impetus to install and configure a group management solution.

It is therefore important for the library to ensure that it has a voice in the planning of IdM in the institution. For this to happen, these three requirements need to be satisfied:

1 Library management needs to be convinced of the need for continued input from the library into IdM institution-wide.
2 A presence on important committees which discuss IdM needs to be maintained. It is important that such representation understands enough of the subject to contribute usefully to the work of the committees.
3 Changes to IdM need to be introduced properly into the library, as a key consumer of IdM in the institution.

To ensure that these requirements are satisfied, an important first step is to convince management of the key benefits to the library of well structured IdM. These will mainly match up with the benefits to the institution as a whole, but some will be more or less important, or have a different slant (legal and regulatory requirements, for example, would focus more strongly on licence agreement conditions).

Implementing a library access management system requires close co-operation between the library and IT services, as well as support from senior management. A good way of gaining this support is to produce a business case for the proposed changes which outlines the benefits of the new system and opportunities for further development. There is no single recipe for a business case, as organizational requirements and current positions will be very different. Often an organization has to carry out the changes out of necessity (as is often the case in the education sector), so a business case will be superfluous.

Where a business case can be used, it can provide a valuable tool to support successful outcomes and realization of benefits. According to Davies and Shreeve (2007, 9), the value of a properly written and managed business case stems from:

- presenting and communicating the rationale for the project
- presenting the big picture to the rest of the organization within a single point of reference
- permitting performance management by setting out benefits and envisaged outcomes
- providing an auditable trail for accountability.

This chapter looks at the wider benefits of access management within the host organization, opportunities for further development and how to use this information to produce a successful business case, should one be required. It does not aim to cover other aspects of project management, as this is covered by many books, articles and training courses. Organizations may have specific guidelines and policies in regard to project management (e.g. the use of frameworks based on PRINCE2 or other formal methodologies) which cannot be covered by this chapter.

This chapter will provide general guidance that can be applied to access and/or identity management projects of any size, from small-scale changes to data formats in an identity repository to the implementation of a central identity management system. This chapter will, therefore, suggest some generic components which can be used to produce a business case for an access management project. It is assumed that an organization has carried out an audit or equivalent exercises to provide a gap analysis, so that there will be an individual or group of individuals with a good sense of where the gaps lie and what could be done about them.

Managing change to business processes is often a difficult task, and when producing a business case for doing so, the author needs to be aware of potential difficulties that will be encountered. These tend to be political issues which are usually difficult to quantify in advance. Those who run processes may feel that they 'own' them, and resent or fear changes made to them, and consciously or unconsciously sabotage projects which seek to alter the processes. Managers do not want to see crucial information moving out of the control of their team, particularly if their understanding of the replacement processes is kept vague. Those being assigned new processes may feel that they will now have too much work. These kinds of issues can only be solved by involving those who will be affected by change before the project begins: at the business case development stage, and by ensuring that all affected staff will be kept informed and/or involved throughout the proposed project.

This chapter draws heavily on Chapter 9 of the JISC *Identity Management Toolkit*, revised in 2012 (Joint Information Systems Committee, 2012). Another very useful reference source is the JISC *Business Case Toolkit for Federated Access Management* (Davies and Shreeve, 2007).

Key benefits of quality identity management

Key benefits from designing and managing internal projects to close some known gaps in existing access management processes will include improvements in security, conformity with legal restraints and efficiency.

Improved security

Well designed, well understood, well documented and properly carried out access management processes protect assets belonging to the organization.

Organizations in general and libraries in particular have a duty to their members (e.g. staff, users) to manage data about them competently. This data itself has value, both to the members themselves and to the organization, and it can contain very sensitive information (such as bank account details). Unauthorized access to, or loss of, or inaccuracies in, part of this data are all potential causes of problems with any process which uses this part. So it is vital that safeguards are in place to protect user data, both technical (e.g. the use of secure HTTP for authentication to web applications, such as virtual learning environments) and managerial (e.g. a procedure governing what information is permitted to be stored in mobile devices, which may be stolen or mislaid off the organization premises).

In addition to value in itself, user information is used to allow authorized access to other resources of value to the institution. This means that information made available to a third party could be used to gain unauthorized access. Even where the actual credentials needed for access are not obtained by these third parties, the user attributes can often be used to obtain them (e.g. by providing information which can be used to guess poorly chosen passwords, or to persuade others to provide access when the third party poses as an individual who has lost their credentials, a type of social engineering). Security breaches of this type will damage the reputation of the organization and may have legal consequences, as well as the direct losses which can be incurred when access is gained to physical and electronic resources (e.g. exam papers in preparation in an education institution). Protecting sensitive user data is thus a form of insurance against potentially very serious security breaches.

Improved conformity with legal restraints

Effective access and/or identity management processes will help prevent breaches of the data protection legislation and of licence agreements signed by the organization.

Institutions increasingly have legal constraints which regulate aspects of identity management. These are likely to include general legislative requirements, such as data protection legislation, and requirements derived from agreements the institution has entered into, such as resource licences, federation membership agreements or partnerships. Clearly, it is essential for organizations to use their best efforts to comply with these constraints, and any work which is intended to improve identity management must look into what effect compliance will have on the desired outcome of a project. This should in turn mean that it is a priority to make sure that information on legal matters is available to those who might be designing and implementing identity management solutions. In some cases, such as with the multitude of resource licences that a library is likely to be a party to, this can be quite difficult in itself. It is likely to be useful to make an attempt to compile and maintain a list of known restrictions and access conditions which arise from sources such as resource licences, to help ensure compliance.

Improved efficiency

Well organized identity and/or access management processes will prevent duplication of effort, and speed up processes such as user registration to minimize user frustration (e.g. with new staff members taking weeks to obtain working access to e-mail). Well documented processes are easier to hand over to new staff, or to work with where the normal process management is unavailable. Well designed and properly implemented policies will ensure that management at all levels is able to obtain a good understanding of what the processes are and how they work. Inefficient, poorly documented and duplicated business processes will be an unnecessary financial cost to the organization. Duplication of processes leads to wasted time and an increased potential for security problems. The latter is particularly likely to be the case if one of the processes is unofficial, and is carried out by someone lacking training in relevant subjects such as maintaining a data store securely.

Designing an IdM project

The following stages, most of which are going to be common to projects in any large organization, may need to be considered:

- identifying the people to be involved in planning
- identifying the aims and scope of the project
- deciding on the approach to use
- integrating with non-IdM work (if considered desirable)
- putting together a project plan and budget
- putting together a business case.

This list is not necessarily chronological; indeed, the first four need to be at least considered more or less together as each will impact on the other three. The sensible way to approach this is to iterate through the first four until all those involved have common understanding of the basic project ideas, and then proceed to the business case, project plan and budget.

Where there is an institutional roadmap for identity management, it is important that any IdM projects or project components are designed to fit in with the overall requirements of the roadmap; this will impact every one of these stages.

Identifying the people to be involved in planning

The list of common gaps in the gap analysis associates each gap with a set of stakeholders within the organization. In many cases, this should immediately suggest the people to approach to be involved in the planning. Generally, it is likely to be essential to involve representatives from the departments involved in central IdM administration (e.g. IT services, student registry, human resources, etc.). The seniority of the individuals that need to be involved will naturally depend somewhat on the institutional culture and the scale of the proposed project. This list is different from the list of those who will actually carry out the project, or who are needed at some stage of the project to provide input, feedback, or evaluation.

Identifying the aims and scope of the project

There are several questions which need to be answered here.

Are there other known IdM issues which are closely related to the one(s) which prompted the project proposal which could sensibly be integrated?

It is important to balance seizing the opportunity to kill two birds with one stone against the danger of weakening the focus of the project, which can lead to a lack of direction among project staff, as they work to different ends.

How far should the proposed project go?

It might make sense to only partially fill the gap(s) in some cases, e.g. where existing tools can be easily modified or new ones purchased to fix the majority of processes which fall in the gap, but other cases will be difficult to solve for practical or political reasons. Small-scale quick wins are better than lengthy, convoluted projects which take a long time and may never produce the outputs expected of them.

Is the project going to be policy-led or practice-led?

It is often useful to produce a published policy document for the proposed change. One approach is to draft the policy where there is a gap first, and then adopt practice which fulfils the policy. (This runs the risk of impracticality.) The other approach would be to sort out the practice where there is a gap, and then draft a policy which describes the new practice. (This runs the risk that the policy never gets written as time on the project is spent fine-tuning the process.)

Will political difficulties need to be overcome or the institutional culture changed?

Projects which need to do this are likely to be far more difficult to manage, and run a heightened risk of failure. Allowance must be made for this in planning the project, and it is important to discuss the strategy for achieving such goals as early as possible in the process. It is also likely that the culture, especially the resistance to change, will differ between different departments, and this will need to be taken into account when considering this aspect of the project planning.

Deciding on the approach to use

The approaches for an identity and/or access management project might include the following, in approximate order of the scale of change involved:

- installing a central identity management system and using this to replace or amend all existing IdM practices and bring them up to standard
- outsourcing all or part of identity management to an external organization
- making ad hoc changes to existing systems to plug gaps
- deciding that a gap is too insignificant/too expensive to fill and leaving the processes alone.

Each of these has advantages and disadvantages, which are summarized briefly on the next page (Table 12.1). It is likely that any institution is likely to apply several of them, either to different processes or over differing timescales. Whatever approach is chosen, it is important that an institution

Table 12.1 *Pros and cons of different approaches to AIM*

Method	Advantages	Disadvantages
Central identity management system	Makes tracking of identity management processes simple; There should be reasonable documentation/training available to ensure that processes are independent of (e.g.) staff retention; Problems may well have been ironed out by earlier users of the system	Expense; Integration with other systems (such as email, networking, etc.) may not be simple; The process of putting together an invitation to tender and evaluating responses to it may need to be extremely complex; Involves a major upheaval to existing systems and will not immediately be familiar to identity managers
Outsourcing identity management	It is no longer a problem that needs to concern the institution	Expense; Ensuring privacy when records are handled by individuals who have no direct contractual link with the institution (and may even be in different legal jurisdictions which have different views on privacy etc.); The process of putting together an invitation to tender and evaluating responses to it may need to be extremely complex
Ad hoc changes	Can be made over as long a period of time as necessary; Cheap; Gradual change means that most identity managers will be able to adapt easily	Political issues may inhibit necessary change (e.g. removal of autonomy from one department's identity management); New processes will need to be designed in-house and will not have been tested by others
Making no change	Zero immediate cost; No requirements to change familiar work practices	Hidden costs of unfixed problems may become very real in the future; Areas of legal non-compliance will not be fixed

creates a policy/strategy for identity management, and aims to converge to it over a set period of time.

It should be noted that making no change is only recommendable for minor gaps. The disadvantages of doing nothing are likely to greatly outweigh the advantages for other issues with IdM.

For an individual project, it is useful to score possible approaches for the following properties:

- **Difficulty:** difficulty of achieving target (as defined previously)
- **Risk:** level of risk of not doing anything
- **Measurability:** how easy it is to measure success; use of metrics (such as the change in the time spent enrolling new users and setting up their accounts) is likely to be particularly important.

Integrating with non-identity management work

Carrying out an access or identity management project may require non-access management work to be carried out. In other cases, other work might well benefit from being tackled in the same project as fixing a gap. For example, extending single sign-on to a virtual learning environment (VLE) might fit in well with a planned upgrade to the VLE software. Many institutions have rigid timetables for changing mission-critical software, in order to minimize disruption, so any access management work on such tools may need to be scheduled to fit these timetables. Changing business processes is also likely to cause disruption and should be approached with similar care.

Additionally, the same staff are likely to be involved in both access management and non-access management aspects of the work planned, as they will understand such matters as the existing software installation and configuration. This makes a single project that involves both strands more cost-effective than two projects that are working on them separately. Trying to work on multiple projects can lead to problems with time management for those involved, and the relationships between the work involved are unclear. To take the VLE example again, the addition of single sign-on may require the installation of software patches, which in turn require particular versions of underlying systems such as the web server, and this may be incompatible with the non-upgraded VLE software in unexpected ways.

Putting together a project plan and budget

If the project manager is not experienced at working within the institution, it will be useful for them to talk through their plans with someone who is experienced at running internal projects, as they are likely to have useful structural, political, and financial insights, such as suggestions for useful people to involve in planning, potential sources of funding, etc.

Thought should be given as to who will fund the work. Access management gaps may well involve several departments from different divisions of the institution, e.g. IT services, human resources and the library. It may be possible to tie in some or all of the work with a related external funding opportunity, particularly if it can be argued that the work to be done is innovative.

Many access management projects will benefit from the inclusion of users to provide feedback from those who will be affected by the proposed changes. The term 'users', in this case, is not necessarily those who would be end-users of access management, such as students and teaching staff, but would include administrators of systems which are to be changed or whose mode of operation will be changed as an outcome to the project. (And where this happens, integration of such changes needs to be considered as part of the project task list.) For example, changes to the user attributes stored in a repository are likely to affect other systems that consume these attributes and therefore will need to make changes to configuration or, more seriously, to the processes and software involved. (See also the discussion about stakeholders below).

The planners need to decide how the project is to be structured. This includes how it should be divided into phases, a basic idea of how the work could be divided up between stakeholders, what the exit strategy should be for the project (e.g. who will maintain software installed during the project after it is completed?), whether and how users need to be involved, etc. Where there are political obstacles to overcome, a well documented pilot/testing phase with a friendly guinea pig group is likely to be advisable.

Some institutions will have structural requirements for project proposals which are to be funded internally; this will also be true of any external funding bodies involved. Budget holders and senior managers who will be stakeholders in the planned project may also have (extra) requirements.

Putting together a business case

The discussion in this section is based on the summary of business case structure provided by the Office of Government Commerce (OGC) (no longer available).

Strategic fit

It is important that any proposed change fits in with the overall objectives of the organization. There are several aspects that need to be considered.

Business need

The business need for high quality access and identity management – and thus to projects which will fill gaps in access and identity management provision – can be based on the three key benefits associated with good access and identity management discussed earlier, and are likely to apply to some extent to any project aimed at increasing IdM quality.

Contribution to key objectives

The business case for an IdM project needs to point to the business targets/objectives outlined in the organization's IT/estates strategies which it will help to achieve.

Stakeholders

IT managers, library staff, staff in MIS, human resources and similar administrative departments, and senior management are likely to be stakeholders in most important IdM processes in any organization. When putting together the business case, the author needs to consider whether other groups in the organization should also be included

Scope

The options for reduced scope or larger-scale versions of a project will be dependent on the precise nature of the work being considered. It should be clear what the issues relating to each option are; in particular, it is sensible to note where options could sensibly be delayed to a follow-on project.

Constraints

Again, this will depend on the individual organization and the specific project but is something that needs to be considered very seriously, as the consequences of not doing so can be severe.

Dependencies

There are likely to be dependencies which are not IdM-related and which would affect any business project, such as the availability (or recruitment) of staff. More specifically, IdM projects might require the completion of IT systems projects (e.g. updating software in use in the institution to a particular version), or planned changes to other aspects of the institution (e.g. work on physical security systems by the estates department). There are no general dependencies for work on IdM processes.

Strategic benefits

These will largely depend on the business needs and should be considered at both local and strategic levels. It might be useful to make a reference to the organization's key strategic documents, such as IT service or library strategic plans.

Strategic risks

It is not possible to give an exhaustive list of general risks for IdM projects (for example, there may be specific risks associated with the fulfilment of IT requirements that are part of the project which are best evaluated by local experts). Where IdM change is a part of a larger project, there will also be risks which are not specific to IdM (and which may not even be related to IdM).

Critical success factors

The success of IdM projects is to be measured in the adoption and use of the new systems and processes by the individuals within the institution for whom they are intended; there may also be opportunities to make specific measurements which would indicate success (e.g. a reduction in the number of IT helpdesk queries relating to the IdM process involved). It is likely to be useful to include in the project recommendations that satisfaction with the new systems continues to be measured directly for a couple of years after the conclusion of the project as a whole.

Options appraisal

Clearly, the available options will depend heavily on the particular project. However, the IdM aspects are likely to have options related to those discussed in the gap analysis: make no change, make ad hoc changes (which should be spelled out for the specific IdM work under consideration), outsource, integrate with existing central IdM systems. Clearly, not all of these will be appropriate options to consider in every case, but it should be possible to adapt at least some of these into options to appraise with a SWOT analysis (Wikipedia, 2012). Options appraisal may include the various elements, as suggested below.

Opportunities for innovation and/or collaboration with others

These will be determined by the precise nature of the project and will to a large extent depend on the institutional culture.

Service delivery options – who will deliver the project?

Options worth considering here include in-house management and delivery; the use of consultants; external suppliers; working with other organizations. Where systems need to be maintained following the completion of the project, it is useful to indicate whether those who deliver these systems will continue to maintain them or whether this will become the responsibility of others (and if so how the transfer of control is to be handled); and how this requirement can be costed in the longer term.

The JISC *Toolkit for Federated Access Management* has a useful options appraisal chart (Joint Information Systems Committee, 2012, 51) that can be used to aid the planning process.

Affordability

Budget costs will naturally be determined by the project as a whole but any proposed project needs to be affordable and the budget needs to be agreed. Where a range of stakeholders is involved, multiple budgets may need to be agreed before a project can be initiated.

Achievability

The final consideration when planning a business case is whether the chosen option is 'achievable', i.e. whether it can actually be implemented. If a major change is proposed, it is worth considering whether the organization is ready for it before embarking on the project. It is always useful to see whether there are any other organizations that have carried out similar work, as many of them would gladly share their experience. Where business process changes are being made, it is sensible to seek involvement from as many stakeholders as possible to minimize the risks associated with politically motivated obstruction. Thinking about a realistic contingency plan would also help make the project more realistic.

Conclusions

Producing an effective business case for IdM (and indeed any business case) requires careful preparation and effective communication between all the interested parties. There are tangible benefits to achieving high-quality IdM, so that the time and effort put into improving it is well spent. Sometimes it takes time to fully appreciate the impact of the change once it is carried out, and this needs to be taken into account when planning for project appraisal.

References and further reading

Davies, C. and Shreeve, M. (2007) *Federated Access Management: institutional business case toolkit*, Curtis & Cartwright Consulting Limited (commissioned by the Joint Information Systems Committee, UK), www.jisc.ac.uk/media/documents/themes/accessmanagement/cc297d001-1.0%20business%20case%20toolkit.pdf.

Joint Information Systems Committee (2012) *Revised Identity Management Toolkit,* www.identity-project.org.

Kelly, S. (2008) How Tracked Changes Have Made Businesses and Government Look Foolish, *Making the Most of Word in Your Business* blog, www.shaunakelly.com/word/sharing/publicexamplesoftrackchanges.html.

Wikipedia (2012) 'SWOT analysis', http://en.wikipedia.org/wiki/SWOT_analysis.

Afterword

The purpose of this book has been to describe how recent developments in access management technologies have affected the world of the library. The case studies which follow are concrete examples of how libraries around the world have adopted access management concepts and adapted them to fit their own situations, whether academic or public, large or small.

In the world in which we now live, in which even the most famous libraries have to compete for scarce resources, is it possible to still make a case for investment in identity management? The authors believe that it is, and not only that, but that it is essential to do so: for ease of management, for risk amelioration, and to ease the path for the library user to access the resource which they want to use.

It is impossible to predict the future accurately. Even science fiction writer Isaac Asimov, famed for his ability to suggest the implications of new science for society, wrote a short story which he later described (Asimov, 1975) in the following terms: 'I predicted that Mount Everest would never be climbed, five months after it was climbed'. Even bearing this and other examples in mind, however, we would like to present some final thoughts about the future of access management in libraries.

Access management is not going to go away in the short term. Some individuals have suggested that copyright will or should become a thing of the past (e.g. Richmond, 2011) – along with privacy (Mark Zuckerberg, quoted in Johnson, 2010), and the physical book (e.g. Coover, 1992). But it seems more likely that individuals and, probably more importantly, corporate entities, will continue to wish to restrict access to at least some of the items they produce. Indeed, the introduction of 'paywalls' restricting access to paying subscribers by several formerly free newspaper websites in recent years (BBC News, 2013) is one indication that this desire is becoming more acute to some. Any such information necessitates some form of access management, to keep out those who have no right to access, while making it as easy as possible for those who should be able to access it to do so.

Libraries are undergoing a process of rapid change in the internet age. And yet, whatever form they take and by whatever name they call themselves, there will be organizations which arrange access to their individual members (who again may not be so named) to collections of restricted data, whether on shelves or online. These organizations will need to practise identity management for their members in order to prove to the data collections that they are entitled to access.

Federated access is the model which is most widely touted as the means by which this can be done in the future. As we described, it offers distinct advantages by separating out the identity management from the access management. It is, however, expensive and complex to set up and maintain, with associated usability issues, in comparison to less ambitious (and often less secure) alternatives. Its future is perhaps, then, less secure than that of access management itself. However, it is certainly still a youthful technological idea, and, as such, is likely to become easier to manage and use as time passes. Current use ignores much of its potential sophistication for micro-management of subscriptions to those members who are identified as belonging to specific groups; although various attempts have been made to make use of this ability, a 'killer app' for it has yet to be discovered. So we believe that it is still a likely candidate for future access management strategies to adopt.

We hope, but cannot be entirely confident, that open standards will continue to drive innovation in access management, and that the competing standards currently being touted by various groups will continue to grow closer and more easily interoperable.

Above all, we expect that user choice will be key in determining the future of access management. Technologies which have been used to make it hard for users to gain the access to which they feel entitled have generally failed to gain widespread acceptance (see e.g. http://en.wikipedia.org/wiki/Digital_rights_management). At the same time, security and privacy concerns have failed to dent the popularity of social networking; many users claim to be concerned about their privacy and security, but do not act to protect themselves in practice (see e.g. Pitkänen, 2009). So it is unclear exactly how access control, privacy and security will shape the online world of the future. But shape it they will.

References

Asimov, I. (1975) Afterword to the short story *Everest*, in the collection *Buy Jupiter*, Doubleday.

BBC News (2013) The Sun Newspaper to Introduce Online Paywall, 27 March, www.bbc.co.uk/news/entertainment-arts-21951753.

Coover, R. (1992) The End of Books, *New York Times*, 21 June, www.nytimes.com/books/98/09/27/specials/coover-end.html.

Johnson, B. (2010) Privacy No Longer a Social Norm, Says Facebook Founder, *Guardian*, 11 January, www.guardian.co.uk/technology/2010/jan/11/facebook-privacy.

Pitkänen, O. (2009) Users' Awareness of Privacy on Online Social Networking Sites – Case Facebook. In *BLED 2009 Proceedings*, Association for Information Systems, www.academia.edu/501576/Users_Awareness_of_Privacy_on_Online_Social_Net working_Sites_Case_Facebook.

Richmond, S. (2011) An Outdated Law That Puts a Cap on Creativity, *Telegraph*, 3 August, www.telegraph.co.uk/technology/news/8679633/An-outdated-law-that-puts-a-cap-on-creativity.html.

Appendix 1

Case studies

A number of case studies have been collected for this book. Below is some guidance on the relevance of each to a specific chapter of the book. However, in many cases the same case study is relevant to more than one chapter. The authors are particularly grateful to all contributors to the case studies for documenting their real-world experiences for readers.

Case study list

- Extending access management to business and community engagement activities at Kidderminster College, UK – Chapter 10
- Moving from Athens to Shibboleth at University College London, UK – Chapter 8
- Online reciprocal borrowing registration for Western Australian University Libraries – Chapter 10
- Library and IT collaboration: driving strategic improvements to identity and access management practices and capabilities – Chapter 8
- Managing affiliated users with federated identity management at UNC-Chapel Hill, USA – Chapter 12
- Tilburg University and the SURFfederatie, the Netherlands – Chapter 8
- Delivering access to resources in a joint academic and public library building, UK – Chapter 10
- Single sign-on across the USMAI Consortium, USA – Chapter 8.

Extending access management to business and community engagement activities at Kidderminster College, UK

Main author/contributor: Graham Mason, Overt Software; Rebecca Williams, Project Officer, Kidderminster College
Name of institution: Kidderminster College Training, UK

Background

Kidderminster College Training (KCT) offers apprenticeships for students aged between 16 and 24. The students spend four days per week in the workplace and one day per week in college. Students study towards National Vocational Qualifications (NVQs) in various areas and can be on the programme between one and four years.

Access management issues

Kidderminster College would like to enable the employers of the college students to have access to Moodle, the Kidderminster College virtual learning environment (VLE), so that employers can access reports and monitor data on their employees' progress and attendance. It could be used as a quick link portal to information relating to the student.

The students can already access the VLE, as they are registered students, but the college would like them to have their own course on the VLE (currently no course set up for NVQs). It would be useful for them to have access to e-resources associated with their NVQ that they can reflect and apply in their work placement. This would also bring improvements in employer engagement and enhanced efficiency in liaising with employers regarding monitoring. With regard to commercial e-resource licences, the licences would need to be extended to cover 'third-party access', so that the employers (who aren't actually enrolled as part of the college) could gain access.

Kidderminster College uses a system called PICS to register its students and their employers. The system is also used for data compliance, financial reconciliation, reporting, tracking and standards audits. The PICS operators are responsible for registering the student/employer, updating records and eventually removing records from the system once the student has completed and left the scheme. At the time of writing there were around 60 employers (although this changes from year to year) and between 20 and 100 students who would need to be set up manually as guest users with ID and password and would also have to be manually removed. Linking the VLE directly to the PICS system would generate an automatic process for registering/removing students and employers from the VLE.

Identity-managing the employers

Students are enrolled on the apprenticeship programme; to be enrolled they must be 'employed'. When the students are on the apprenticeship programme they are in the workplace for four days per week. When in the workplace they report to their supervisor. Currently the college liaises with the employer/supervisor through reviews (which occur every 10–12 weeks) and they also receive a report from college each term. It is hoped that by extending the licence to enable the employers to access the VLE (including e-library) the college will be able to expand on the relationship between the employer and the college, improve on the supervisor's knowledge of what the apprentice is learning and also enable the supervisor to monitor the apprentice's progress on a weekly basis.

At the time of writing the employers are input to the college's PICS system but are not 'enrolled', so they have no access to the VLE. For various technical reasons, it is not currently possible to enter the employers into the customer information system (CIS). The college is also unable to give employers full access to the VLE (including e-library) due to licensing restrictions. The college is unable to cover the costs of extending the licences, so until these problems are overcome the employers will be using a restricted access profile.

To create the supervisors' identity management records a report will be run using the PICS system; this report is then modified to suit the bulk upload option in the VLE. The usernames and passwords have to be input manually, however, a generic password can be used, as the user will change this when they first log in.

A new area on the VLE has been specifically created for apprenticeships and work-based learning. By creating this separate VLE the college can manage exactly what the employers can and can't access. Within the KCT VLE, each subject area has been password-protected, to protect documents and resources. As the licence for the e-library at present does not extend to employers, the college is unable to give them full access.

After creating the employer log-ins the college will send a letter notifying the supervisor that their log-in has been created, with their username and password, and advising that they should change their password when they first log in to the system, for security reasons. The letter will also include contact details for the VLE administrator.

Barriers to progress

It would be best to enter the employers into CIS, so that the employers could use the federated access management portal to log in. However, in order to achieve this, employers would need to be included in the college Active Directory environment, as this is the sole data feed into the identity provider used to gain access to the college virtual learning environment.

This raises several issues for the network team that maintains the Active Directory environment within the college. If employers were added to this environment they would in theory have all the associated permissions of being a student/member of staff in the college, i.e. access to any of the computers within the college buildings, e-mail accounts and space on local servers to store documents. Aside from this, they would also have access to the college VLE and associated learning resources stored on the VLE, and more questionable access to the online e-library. This poses several concerns over licensing issues with the e-library, the main concern being that the current licensing for the e-library stipulates that only registered learners can have access to the materials online. If employers were included in the AD environment then it would be a possible breach of e-library licensing if they were to access and use these materials.

A possible solution to this problem would be the creation of a separate parallel enterprise directory, which could include all kinds of non-official user accounts which could feed into the identity provider. However, this is currently not practised within Kidderminster College.

Future recommendations

1 Ebrary to be promoted further to tutors/students and also a direct link off the front page of the VLE to facilitate easier use.
2 A user guide to be included at the induction stage for both student and employer on the use of the VLE.
3 Consider ways of extending the ebrary licence to cover work-based learning employers/supervisors.
4 Ebrary resources to be brought up to date and additional resources included.

Moving from Athens to Shibboleth at University College London, UK

Main author: Margaret Stone, IT Services Development Officer, UCL Library Services
Institution: University College London (UCL), UK

Background

Founded in 1826, UCL is London's leading multidisciplinary university, with 8000 staff and 22,000 students. UCL has strengths in subjects ranging from biomedicine, science and engineering and the built environment to laws, social sciences, arts and humanities. Research and teaching are carried out by more than 4000 academic and research staff based in 72 academic departments. UCL, therefore, has a substantial number of identity holders, requiring access to a highly diverse portfolio of systems and services.

Library and IT services

UCL Library Services subscribes to over 12,000 electronic journals, more than 300 electronic databases and an increasing number of electronic books, covering the 60 or so subjects which are taught in the institution. Access is mediated through various systems, including the Aleph library catalogue, the SFX link resolver and the MetaLib library gateway and cross-searching tool.

Prior to the implementation of federated access management, the library had moved from Athens to Athens DA (See Chapter 8), which devolved the authentication to local systems. This was used alongside IP address authentication for on-campus users, coupled with the IP proxy server, EZProxy. These mechanisms provided maximum flexibility of access for users both on and off campus.

UCL Library Services works closely with the UCL Information Services Division (ISD) on matters such as server management and authentication, although the two services are not operationally merged at UCL.

Access management issues

An earlier issue in access management, the costly administration of separate usernames and passwords for Athens access, was resolved at UCL by the introduction of Athens DA. Another issue was the number of electronic resources which were not available off-campus via Athens. To mitigate this,

UCL introduced the IP-based proxying software, EZProxy. This required users to access resources through links controlled by the library. Users who navigated to UCL's subscription resources off-campus through a non-UCL route would need to recognize that the 'Athens log-in' was applicable, and identify themselves to Athens as a UCL member in order to use the devolved authentication system.

The next problem to arise was the move of Athens from a free to a subscription service in 2006. UCL sought to investigate the available alternatives.

Approach

UCL had already become an early adopter of the Shibboleth technology through involvement in the ShibboLEAP project (www.angel.ac.uk/ShibboLEAP). The project was funded by the Joint Information Systems Committee (JISC), the main public body that oversees IT developments in the UK education sector. Staff received training and peer support for this through JISC. The technology then became JISC's recommendation for federated access management (FAM), so UCL investigated it as a replacement for the subscription OpenAthens service. Shibboleth had the obvious advantage of being in place at UCL already and of being a natural successor to the existing devolved authentication.

The remaining arguments for Shibboleth were that: it was based on open standards; it could be used for other applications across the institution, not just in the library, giving a wide-ranging single-sign-on experience; and it had the potential to offer more fine-grained authorization than Athens.

The adoption was a joint project between Library Services and Information Systems (now ISD), and formed part of the technical implementation of UCL's information strategy. The cost to UCL was not very high, particularly as the technology had already been proven during the JISC project. The cost of implementation was approximately 0.3FTE (full-time equivalents) in staff time over 2 years, including the JISC project. The cost of hardware was negligible compared to staff time, and was drawn from existing institutional capacity, for a number of parallel authentication projects. The savings to UCL would eventually be the equivalent of the OpenAthens annual subscription, as the staff time for maintenance is not much more for Shibboleth than for Athens DA.

UCL first installed and load-balanced a second Shibboleth identity provider server, then joined the UK Access Management Federation and contacted publishers to set up the log-in mechanism. Testing and trouble-shooting continued until the 31 July 2008 deadline for the end of free access to Athens. Originally, UCL intended to move as many resources from Athens to Shibboleth as possible, and to use the Shibboleth–Athens gateway (a temporary solution that provided interoperability between Shibboleth-supported and Athens-supported resources) for those resources which were only available via Athens. However, the eventual cost of the gateway was equivalent to retaining OpenAthens. Since many publishers had not completed the move to federated access management by July, UCL reluctantly decided to subscribe to OpenAthens for a one-year transition period.

UCL used this period to continue testing federated access management by soft-launching the new mechanism for all resources as they became available. Users were able to see the new log-in alongside the Athens log-in, and many started using it, but no publicity was released. Interestingly, despite fairly high usage of the new mechanism, no support enquiries were received in the library. UCL then went live with federated access management at the end of the OpenAthens subscription on 31 July 2009.

Towards the end of the transition period, a programme of training sessions was arranged for library staff, together with documentation for end-users. The overall message would be to encourage users to follow library-mediated links to resources, but information would also be provided about the new log-in.

There were one or two risks in the above approach. Switching to full local responsibility for authentication, including the technical infrastructure, was managed by a gradual roll-out with a long testing period. As early adopters, UCL had limited peer support, but sufficient networks were built, and this occurred mostly during the earlier JISC project.

A significant problem was the slow take-up of federated access management by publishers, which threatened the service for end-users. This was eventually mitigated by the significant cost of buying a subscription to OpenAthens to smooth the transition, in conjunction with increased dependence on EZProxy.

The other major problem concerned marketing for end-users. The terminology of federated access management was found to be very confusing for users, because publishers did not adopt a standard. Although potentially more meaningful to the uninitiated than 'Athens log-in', the sheer variety of log-in labels such as 'Institutional Login', 'UK Federation Login' and 'Shibboleth Login' required a robust approach to internal publicity, coupled with lobbying of service providers for an improvement.

Benefits

Through the implementation of federated access management, UCL realized the benefits of wide-ranging single sign-on using a standards-based technology. Increased local control and transferable expertise were gained, and the ongoing cost of a subscription authentication service was avoided. The approach resulted in a good network of peer support to aid future development.

One unexpected benefit was that a number of library resources which had not previously used Athens authentication implemented Shibboleth. This resulted in further flexibility for UCL users, who gained a log-in mechanism for more resources reached through non-UCL routes.

Future plans

UCL plans to continue extending federated access to library resources, as more service providers adopt the technology. It may also be necessary to take advantage of Shibboleth's attribute release to meet more granular access control requirements for some resources. In addition, more advanced user personalization options may be available from some service providers, subject to appropriate attribute release policies.

In parallel, UCL is adopting Shibboleth authentication for other institutional systems. It is already in use for internal library systems, such as MetaLib and EZProxy, and UCL's digital collections service (DigiTool), research publications service (Symplectic) and the locally developed research portal, the Primo discovery system, as well as UCL's online recruitment system (WCN) and event management system (Columba). Further integrations are developed on an ongoing basis including, at the time of writing, plans for the Moodle virtual learning environment, the Serco Facility CMIS timetable system and the OSHENS health and safety system. Beyond UCL, other collaborations and federations can also be explored.

Advice to other institutions

Although the route taken by UCL (early adoption) is no longer available, UCL would recommend using the Shibboleth technology with a local identity provider, for maximum flexibility and control. Where this is not possible, a third-party solution may be preferred, but the peer support networks and UK-based training are substantial and helpful.

UCL benefited from having a robust user directory and identity management in place already, and from the experience of local authentication under Athens. In addition, it was crucial to have good teamwork across library and information systems departments, marrying the necessary technical knowledge with a thorough understanding of service providers, licence terms and user practices. This gave a firm foundation for future partnerships and developments.

Online reciprocal borrowing registration for Western Australian University Libraries

Main authors: Peter Austin, IT Infrastructure Architect, Edith Cowan University IT Services Centre. Lynne Vautier, Associate Director, Curtin University Library. Daniel Piczak, Systems Analyst, Curtin University Library.
Name of institution: Edith Cowan University and Curtin University on behalf of the West Australian Group of University Libraries (WAGUL), Australia.

Background

The West Australian Group of University Libraries (WAGUL) was created in 1992 by the then members: Edith Cowan University (ECU), Curtin University (Curtin), the University of Western Australia (UWA) and Murdoch University (Murdoch). Notre Dame University joined the group in 1999.

WAGUL exists to enhance and expand access to information by staff and students of the member institutions. The WAGUL Online Reciprocal Borrowing Registration service is an important way in which that aim is fostered.

Western Australian University Libraries operate under the University Library Australia (ULA) national borrowing scheme, which aims to provide free borrowing to students and staff of universities that are members of the representative body Universities Australia.

Figure CS1 gives an indication of the number of students who directly benefited from the automation of registration and authentication project.

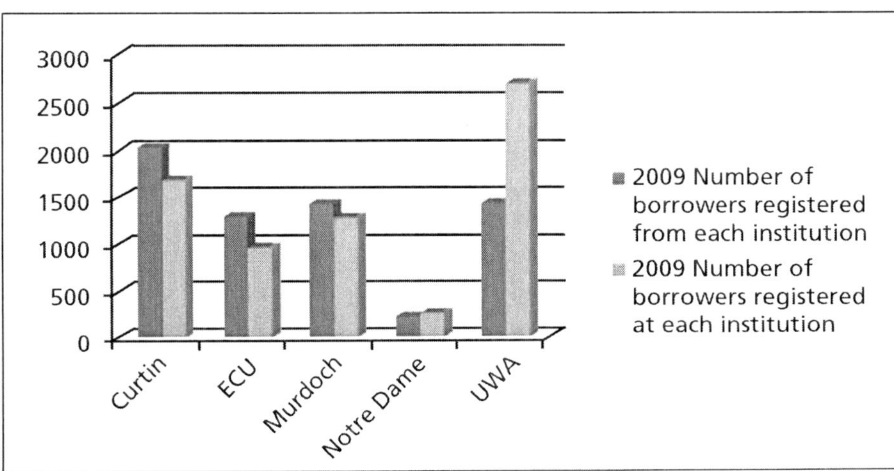

Figure CS1 *Number of students who benefited from the project*

Library and IT services

Each library in the group varies in both population and the age and size of their physical and digital collections. Reciprocal access across WAGUL provides all current students and staff of Curtin, ECU, Murdoch and UWA with access to all the physical collection resources held across the group. (Notre Dame does not currently participate in the online service.)

Access management issues

Prior to online reciprocal borrowing registration, staff and students had to present themselves in person at each library they wished to use, show proof of ID and current enrolment or employment and then, at busy times such as the start of semester, wait at least 24 hours before returning to borrow the resources.

Library desk staff would then need to manually enter the client's details into the library management system, which was both time-consuming and sometimes inaccurate due to keying errors, etc.

Approach

The advent of the Meta Access Management System (MAMS) Testbed Federation, a prototype access federation infrastructure for Australian universities based upon Shibboleth version 1 technology, provided an opportunity to implement an online reciprocal borrower registration service. A business case, showing how the access management issues described above could be alleviated via the use of Shibboleth technology, was presented to the MAMS project team and funding obtained to develop the application. When the MAMS Testbed Federation was replaced by the Australian Access Federation (AAF, www.aaf.edu.au), a production access federation infrastructure for universities and research institutions both within Australia and overseas, the service was migrated to Shibboleth version 2 technologies.

Technical deployment

Initial development work was undertaken by IT services at ECU with final configuration and deployment undertaken by Library Services at Curtin.

The service is implemented as a collection of Perl CGI scripts hosted at Curtin, and protected by Shibboleth service provider (SP) software. The service is registered with the AAF and represented in AAF metadata. Access to the service is limited, via business rules, to staff and students from a subset of the

AAF identity providers (IdPs): that is, WAGUL member institutions.
The attributes obtained from the IdP are:

- staff/student number (represented by the LDAP uid attribute)
- display name (represented by the LDAP displayName attribute)
- e-mail address (represented by the LDAP mail attribute).

Additional attributes, required to be entered by the client, are:

- title
- library barcode
- address details
- contact phone number
- libraries that the client is requesting access to (excluding the client's own institution's library).

The screenshot in Figure CS2 illustrates an example of the online form, showing information provided by the IdP.

When the form is submitted, the client data is e-mailed to each of the requested libraries.

Figure CS2 *Screenshot of the information provided by the IdP*

Institutional roll-out

WAGUL rolled out the service in the middle of 2008, with the change over to
the AAF occurring at the end of 2009. The web address of the service is
http://wagul.curtin.edu.au/reciprocal_registration.html.

Operational management of the system

A set of business rules governs the way the system works in operation. These
include the following:

- Clients can select more than one library to register with at a time.
- Client's details are sent to the libraries selected via an e-mail to a generic
  e-mail address at each institution.
- Membership is personal, and not transferable.
- Reciprocal borrowing rights are valid for the current academic year and
  expire on 28 February of the year following registration.
- While using another university library, clients are bound by the rules and
  regulations of the host university.
- If clients are experiencing problems with the registration process they are
  directed to contact their home institution.
- Loan limits, borrowing lengths, fines and collection access vary across the
  institutions.

Costs

There were costs in terms of staff time at each institution in implementing and
testing the service. However, the major development and implementation cost
was covered by a MAMS grant.

Problems/risks

There were some concerns about the privacy of client data when exchanging
this with another institution. However, this concern has been substantially
mitigated by adherence to the privacy requirements of AAF membership.

One further issue is problem solving. It has proved challenging at times to
isolate the cause of the problem on the infrequent occasions when the system
'breaks'. Problems sometimes bounce back and forth between individual
libraries and Curtin before the problem is diagnosed and solved.

Another challenge is the testing that needed to be done prior to implementation and occasionally even now. Contacts at each university change and people are busy and have other priorities.

Benefits

The benefits of the online reciprocal borrowing registration service are enjoyed by both the participating libraries and the clients.

Clients can now register in advance and arrive in the library knowing their record has been created and they are ready to borrow. In addition, library staff can simply copy and paste client data into their respective library management systems using accurate data.

Future plans

In future WAGUL would like to be able to upload the client data directly into the library management system of each library. This would completely do away with the present copy-and-paste approach. Unfortunately, not all the partner libraries in WAGUL use the same library management system (UWA, Murdoch and ECU use Innovative Millennium and Curtin uses Ex Libris ALEPH) and there is no common interface.

In addition, there would be advantages in extending the range of attributes released from the IdP to include some of the eduPerson and auEduPerson attributes. This would allow for finer-grained allocation of reciprocal borrowing rights.

Since the service is registered with the AAF, it would be possible to extend access to other members of Universities Australia who are also members of the AAF. This would remove the current manual process in place for clients from these universities.

Advice to other institutions

We strongly recommend the adoption of an online reciprocal borrower registration service for any situations where this is presently being done manually. WAGUL has demonstrated it can be implemented with minimal resources, provided there is access to a federated authentication.

Library and IT collaboration: driving strategic improvements to identity and access management practices and capabilities

Main author: Tod A. Olson, Systems Librarian, University of Chicago
Name of institution: University of Chicago, USA

Background

Established in 1890, the University of Chicago is a research and educational institution with over 5000 undergraduates,10,000 graduate, professional, and other students and 2200 faculty and other academic personnel. In addition, the university libraries also support the 9500 employees of the University of Chicago Medical Center. The University and the Medical Center are well known for intensive research activity, especially in physics, economics, law and economics, medicine, sociology, and other fields.

Library and IT Services

In addition to a physical collection of some 8.5 million items, the University of Chicago Library maintains access to a number of licensed electronic resources, including over 57,000 individual electronic journal titles and over a million e-books. The library uses a number of online systems, including the Horizon integrated library system (SirsiDynix), SFX and Metalib for OpenURL resolving and database cross-searching (Ex Libris), ILLiad, Ares and Aeon for interlibrary loan, electronic course reserves, and special collections retrieval and management (Atlas Systems), and the AquaBrowser discovery tool (Serials Solutions). Access to protected services and materials is provided primarily through IP-based authentication, Shibboleth, and in a few cases account-specific IDs and passwords.

Shibboleth is used throughout the university to broker access to a variety of systems ranging from regular web access (campus portal, medical course materials, etc.) to administrative processes and research computing resources.

LDAP and Active Directory are also used for access to some applications and for workstation or server access both in the library and across the university. RADIUS is used to manage network-level access, particularly for wireless, both through the captive web sign-on and for eduroam.

IT services (ITS) is responsible for maintaining the Shibboleth identity provider, the campus LDAP and Active Directory domains, RADIUS, and the central identity and access management database which feeds them. The library and ITS have a long history of collaborating in many areas, including access to licensed resources, identity management, and general operations.

Access management issues

The library is obligated to regulate access to licensed resources and services. Typically, the library negotiates licences so that electronic resources are available to faculty, students, staff, and anyone who is physically present in a library location. Many content suppliers accept on-campus IP addresses for authentication, and a proxy server allows for off-campus access. Some content providers require individual log-ins and passwords for users, and a very few issue a group password for all users, which the library must somehow protect. More recently, many of the major suppliers have also begun to accept Shibboleth authentication. In the library-negotiated licences, the content suppliers tend to speak broadly in terms of authorized users and expect the library to regulate access to their materials and ensure that only authorized users are able to access the licensed resources. The library's ability to regulate access is, therefore, linked to campus identity management; limits and changes to identity management on campus affect the library's ability to regulate access according to its contractual obligations.

Additionally, the library has consortial and reciprocal agreements with other institutions for access to various resources, services, and applications. Issuing credentials across organizational boundaries puts an additional password management burden on users and creates identities in the library's system for which it has no reliable updates, e.g., when the individual leaves his or her home institution.

The need to regulate access to resources and services and the desire not to proliferate passwords are felt not only at the library, but also across campus. The university approaches this problem in part by enabling users to use a single account to access an increasing number of services, coupled with improving our ability to manage what each user can access with that account.

Past practices

In 2004, access management for the library, and identity management for the whole of the university, were very different than they are today. There was (and still is) an expectation that an individual physically on campus with access to a workstation or the campus network should not be inconvenienced with additional authentication to use licensed library resources. The library offered public access workstations for walk-up use without authentication to anyone with building access, and other departments similarly had unauthenticated workstations available for their own reasons of convenience.

For off-campus access, users would configure their browsers to use the library Squid proxy server. Authentication to that proxy server was provided by two separate directory servers, one for the university, the other run by the Medical Center for its particular and separate authentication needs. The proxy server and other applications on campus had been customized to authenticate against the two separate directories. Some uses of these directories had potential for password exposure. Fragmented workflows for maintaining these directories meant that an individual's attributes in them were frequently out of date, individuals with appointments in both organizations (e.g., most physicians) had separate identities in each directory, and there was little ability to co-ordinate between the two. Building central resources, such as a university telephone book, involved manual integration of multiple identity resources.

There are many keepers of identity information on campus. Human resources, the registrar, the library, the alumni office, the Laboratory School (providing primary and secondary education) and other departments have separate systems for maintaining identities, all of which complicate reconciling authoritative identity information.

A unified directory was desired. It would be maintained through co-ordinated workflows and be the authoritative source of current affiliation and other attributes for individuals. Greater accuracy and substantial cost savings could result from a unified directory that would encompass the whole of the university community. But this would introduce populations into the directory, such as alumni, who are not covered by the library's licences to e-resources, breaking with the old assumption that authentication against the directory was equivalent to authorization for use of a licensed resource.

A more flexible way to manage authorization was clearly needed. The key was that authorization could be determined based on user attributes from the directory, but only a few are needed by any single service. For example, a user's affiliation, such as 'faculty' or 'student,' determines whether they are authorized to use many library-licensed resources. For other services at the university, department or individual ID may be the relevant attributes. In addition, the need for authorization across fluid organizational boundaries was increasing. Not only did library suppliers need to authorize users, but similar needs were arising with other external organizations, such as government entities and other academic institutions.

A better way forward

Shibboleth solves these problems. It allows the library to release to a service provider only those attributes needed by that service provider to determine authorization, protecting more sensitive user attributes from unnecessary dissemination. And as a federated system, Shibboleth provides both authentication and attributes for authorization as a service that an external organization can call upon. The user types his/her log-in and password at the university log-in page, and the external organization receives reliable authorization information.

Co-ordination among the university's many sources of campus identity remains a challenge, in part due to legacy systems and a history of decentralized operations. Nevertheless, duplicated identities are less frequent and easier to resolve, attributes are more current, and having one authoritative source for authentication and authorization information makes it easier to provide each user with access to the services they need, and to manage change to that access as the user's role at the university changes.

Providing unauthenticated workstations had to come to an end because of pressure across higher education to be more accountable for activities taking place on their networks (illegal file sharing being a notable example). So that specific network activity can be traced to individuals, all access to networked workstations now requires a log-in for use. All library patrons now have to log in to public access workstations, and walk-in users are granted temporary IDs that are integrated into the campus authentication infrastructure. This was a large change for users at the time, but is now accepted.

Another effect of this increased accountability is dealing more severely with compromised machines: machines to which an unauthorized user has gained access and/or control. When compromised machines are detected, they are blocked from the campus network until IT services is assured the machine is malware-free. Typically, this means wiping the machine and reinstalling from scratch. This has proven effective motivation for departments to keep their machines up to date with current security patches.

One of the more common forms of abuse involved systematic downloads of content. For example, compromised workstations on the campus network have been employed by remote, unauthorized users to systematically download content from content providers. When content providers notice such download abuse they may disable access from an individual host if it can be identified (and this may be the proxy server), or all of campus, until the library and/or IT services take corrective action locally. This illustrates the problem with IP-based authentication: if any machine on the network is compromised, it has complete and unquestioned access to IP-protected resources.

Nowadays, abuse and its detection is a little different. IT services takes measures to proactively monitor the network for mal-activity and to detect compromised accounts. The library gets involved when library resources are specifically involved. Content providers have informed us of users redistributing an article to large numbers of colleagues, of workstations having left open a back-door proxy, and of massive or systematic downloads. Taking the excessive downloads as an example: while there have been exceptions, the majority of cases brought to our attention in recent years have involved an authorized user engaged in a research project. Thanks to tighter auditing of network log-ins and activity, that user can be easily identified and educated.

Approach

Implementation of federated access management was tightly coupled to a new architecture for identity management. The current campus identity management architecture, designed and implemented by IT services, revolves around the Master Constituency Database (MCDB), which accepts updates from a variety of core business systems as well as dozens of 'trusted agents', people entrusted by deans and directors. The MCDB then propagates changes to the LDAP and Active Directory domains for the campus and integrates with the identity management system that populates the Active Directory used by the Medical Center. LDAP in turn provides authentication and the various attributes used by the university's Shibboleth web single sign-on (SSO). The University of Chicago RADIUS implementation, needed for our eduroam participation, also relies on LDAP for authentication and attributes. See Figure CS3 for a representation of this architecture. There remain multiple sources of identity across campus: the registrar, library, human resource services, etc. Duplicate identities can still occur, but are relatively easy to resolve when detected. Meanwhile, applications only need to check one directory for authentication and authorization credentials.

When IT services discovered the consequences that adding new user groups to the campus identity management system would have for authentication with the campus proxy, it approached the library with these issues. Working with the library to solve these access issues would be a first step to addressing the increasingly complex authorization needs across the university. IT services proposed Shibboleth as the preferred authorization method and EZproxy as the new proxy server. It was decided to use a hybrid approach of direct Shibboleth interaction with service providers who support it, and a proxy

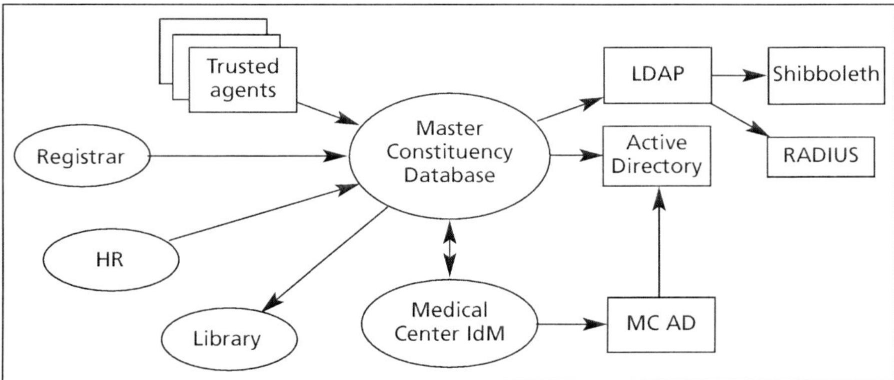

Figure CS3 *University of Chicago identity management architecture*

server for those who do not. Development of a Shibboleth-aware version of EZproxy had recently been announced, and it would be the first use of a campus-located service for Shibboleth. A Shibboleth-aware EZproxy would allow the university to use attribute-based authorization with non-Shibboleth-aware service providers, and service providers can be migrated away from EZproxy as they adopt Shibboleth support. The InCommon Federation's Library Collaboration now has recommendations for the hybrid Shibboleth/EZproxy environment, for implementation suggestions and best practices: see www.incommonfederation.org/library.

Initially, the proxy server was configured to perform LDAP-based authentication via PubCookie, a web SSO technology. The temporary use of PubCookie let the library quickly bring up a web single sign-on environment that multiple applications could use, and allowed IT services to gain experience running EZproxy in production while simultaneously bringing up a production Shibboleth identity provider. After a few months, EZproxy was configured to authenticate using the Shibboleth web SSO, backed by the LDAP directory, which is pre-fed by the MCDB.

At that time, the LDAP directory still contained only individuals who were entitled to use restricted resources through the library's licensing; the university had not yet had a real test of splitting authentication from authorization. However, as the university moved to fully integrate the campus ID namespace and include the Medical Center, Laboratory School, and alumni in campus authentication services, the equivalence of authentication and authorization would be broken. The library had planned with this in mind, and EZproxy was configured to check the Shibboleth-provided user attributes against the requested resource, and allow or disallow access accordingly. This made EZproxy the successful first test of the new infrastructure, and in particular of the ability to determine entitlements based on released attributes.

The transition to EZproxy and Shibboleth was done in stages, with the library and IT services working together to manage this transition. First, there was a co-ordinated roll-out of EZproxy. All catalogue interfaces and other databases were configured to route links to protected resources through EZproxy. URLs on library web pages and in the campus course management system were updated. A 'ProxyIt'! bookmarklet was created to help users send arbitrary URLs to EZproxy. There was a publicity campaign. The library knew that old bookmarks and old browser configurations would linger, so after several months the library replaced Squid with a redirect page which provided a proxied URL and advised users to update bookmarks or contact the maintainer of the referring page.

The move to EZproxy meant a visible change to the URLs for licensed resources. Where Squid relied on custom configuration of each user's browser, EZproxy relies on the URL to direct the browser to the proxy server. Library-controlled services, such as the catalogue, AquaBrowser, SFX and Metalib, are all configured to rewrite URLs so that access to all resources routes through the proxy server. Because EZproxy re-writes URLs, researchers can no longer blindly copy URLs from our content providers and use them unedited in citations or send them to colleagues, as the URLs often route through our EZproxy.

For user convenience, EZproxy is configured to automatically proxy users coming from on campus. For off-campus users, the proxy requires authentication with the Shibboleth web SSO and checks the user's attributes to see whether they are authorized for a particular resource. As the library moves resources to Shibboleth, it is expected that EZproxy will also step out of the loop, and not proxy access to Shibboleth-aware resources. Not all resources require authorization, so if a resource is not in EZproxy's configuration file, the proxy server will forward the browser directly to the remote service, stepping out of the interaction entirely.

Many of the library service providers require something in the URL to indicate that Shibboleth authentication and authorization are to be used. Many library service providers also support a 'session initiator', a special parameter in the URL that indicates which identity provider to use, short-cutting the need for the user to select their home institution as a step in the log-in process. In the university's EZproxy hybrid environment, links to, say, EBSCOhost or JSTOR can be rewritten to automatically include these parameters and EZproxy can then step out of the loop. It is, however, somewhat difficult to direct a user's web browsing into the local EZproxy/Shibboleth environment if the user starts elsewhere. For example, if a user finds an article in Google Scholar from a resource that the library licenses, the direct link to the resource will probably request that the user pays to download the article. On the other hand, the same link through the library's OpenURL resolver will send the user through the proxy and, therefore, into the university's federated access environment. However, from off campus there is no direct way to assert that the user is covered by the library licences. The ProxyIt! bookmarklet was created for this sort of circumstance, but is only a partial solution. So challenges remain in directing users into the university's hybrid EZproxy/Shibboleth environment from the myriad places in which they may be on the web.

More recently, the university has implemented Grouper, a group management toolkit from Internet2, to manage user membership in groups. Attributes related to group membership can be released to Shibboleth service providers and are also made available to applications through LDAP, Active Directory, RADIUS, and directly from Grouper. This makes some aspects of attribute management much simpler, and allows the university to move some role management out of some applications and into the identity infrastructure.

Benefits

The Shibboleth adoption has brought several benefits, one of which is web single sign-on. As more services move towards participating, there are fewer times when the library users must authenticate themselves as they move between services, and users have fewer log-in/password combinations to keep track of.

The federated nature of Shibboleth means that users can authenticate with their campus credentials when dealing with outside services. For the library, this means licensed resources and services. For other departments, this simplifies user log-ins with government agencies, grid computing, and similar. The user's campus credentials gain them access, but since they authenticate to the campus Shibboleth identity provider, their password never goes through the remote system, which is good from a security perspective.

Even within campus, there are benefits to a single authentication and selective revealing of attributes. Applications can reduce the amount of account management and user information, and rely on the released attributes, which reduces multiple versions of the data around campus and ensures the application is working with up-to-date, authoritative user information.

Attribute-based control is another benefit. While simple entitlement is all that is needed for many resources, service providers can map attributes to levels of privilege, allowing different abilities, based on a user's affiliation or other information. For example, HathiTrust is developing a download service targeted at visually impaired users. Eligibility will be indicated by an attribute available in a member institution's Shibboleth identity provider and released specifically to that service.

Because EZproxy can now determine entitlements to specific services based on an individual's attributes, even those library content providers (and applications used elsewhere on campus) which are not Shibboleth-aware benefit both from the single sign-on environment and attribute-based authorization.

An important part of the university's strategy is participation in the InCommon Federation, a higher education access management federation operated by Internet2. Members agree to common rules and behaviours about authentication and authorization, to act in good faith, as both identity and service providers.

The larger project to revise campus identity management brought about much better co-ordination of campus identities, most notably for those with clinical practices in the Medical Center and foundational scientific research programs in the university.

The selective authorization for services can make it easier to manage the changes in an individual's entitlements and their relationship to the university changes over time, whether arriving at or leaving the university, or changing roles while remaining. It is also possible to temporarily disable an individual's entitlements to specific services, for example to manage a security incident, without disabling their access to other services.

Future plans

Shibboleth service providers continue to be added to the campus Shibboleth identity provider configuration, as Shibboleth is now a preferred means of authentication and authorization. There are at this writing some 79 University of Chicago-only service providers registered with the university Shibboleth identity provider (including test systems), and the university has set up custom attribute release policies for 25 InCommon members; 43 applications are registered with the university's Grouper installation. The use cases are quite diverse and include both academic and administrative uses.

There are plans to allow on-campus service providers to register with the university Shibboleth identity provider without requiring ITS intervention, so that it is easier for campus entities to protect their resources.

Users will be given more control over how their attributes are released. InCommon is encouraging identity providers to support uApprove and service provider metadata related to attribute requirements. This would allow the service provider to state which attributes it would like to receive and why, and allow the user to approve or deny the release of any of these attributes to that service provider. Users will then have more say in balancing personalization and privacy.

Wider campus deployment of Grouper will allow different administrative sections to manage their own group-based membership and attributes. For some campus applications, this gives the potential for moving role management entirely into the identity management infrastructure, so that the application does not require a shadow database of identity and authorization information.

The university continues to allow IP authentication for on-campus locations because of a desire, once a user has authenticated to a workstation or the campus wireless network, to ease access to licensed information and avoid requiring another log-in when a licence does not require it. The issue is that the university does not yet have a true single sign-on that encompasses both campus network and web SSO. With recent changes to both the university identity architecture and campus network architecture, there is potential to leverage authentication credentials for a workstation or network log-in for initializing Shibboleth authentication. In this foreseeable future, the network and identity management infrastructures could negotiate credentials with each other, with the result that IP authentication could be disabled and the user would not be inconvenienced by a second log-in.

Advice to other institutions

Federated access management has many benefits, and is enhanced by strong local identity management. Library and broader university needs in these areas are closely aligned. Implementation can be done in measured steps, each one with its own demonstrable value while building toward a long-term goal of better infrastructure and integration.

Tod Olson would like to thank Tom Barton and Arin Komins of University of Chicago's IT Services for their input on this case study.

Managing affiliated users with federated identity management at UNC-Chapel Hill, USA

Main author: Andy Ingham, Assistant Head of Library Systems, UNC-Chapel Hill

Institution: University of North Carolina (UNC)-Chapel Hill, USA

Background

UNC-Chapel Hill is the oldest public university in the USA and currently enrols roughly 29,000 students (18,000 undergraduates). Degree programs include law, social work, medicine, dentistry, information and library science, business and pharmacy.

Library and IT services

Electronic holdings at UNC-Chapel Hill include e-journals, e-books and other electronic research tools. The library leverages a traditional online catalogue system along with the Endeca software for facet browsing of collections. Additionally, SerialsSolutions is used as the portal for access to e-journals. An EZproxy server is utilized to control access to licensed external resources. Access is provided to university students, faculty and staff, primarily via their central university identity (ONYEN). For certain users, access is instead provided via their PID (person ID) or via what is known as the AHEC ID (for certain health affairs professionals).

Many specialized IT services for library staff and patrons (such as the EZproxy service) are provided by a group of IT professionals employed within the university library. Many others (such as the central identity management infrastructure) are provided by staff at the university's information technology services department, which provides general IT support for all of campus.

Access management issues

Many of the access issues the library has faced centre around the fact that certain populations of users, most notably UNC Hospitals users, generally do not hold accounts within the campus's main central user database. This account, called the ONYEN (see https://onyen.unc.edu), is available to any user affiliated with the university but many users do not actually have such an account. While the library could have required such an account in order for those users to access library electronic resources, such a requirement was not enforced in certain cases. The likely reason for that was that the ONYEN was a relatively new concept (when the proxy service was introduced in late 1999) and the library (as a service organization at its core) felt that such a requirement was too cumbersome. Regardless of the reason, this legacy remains, and is one of the primary reasons why the library must maintain multiple options for user authentication to our EZproxy service.

Approach

The decision to use federated identity management for access to library resources evolved out of two separate concurrent happenings. The first was the implementation at the campus level of an ERP project to replace aging administrative systems at the university, of which a strong central identity management component was essential. The second was the library's involvement in a statewide initiative to implement a shared discovery and request interface that included all constituent UNC institutions and was based on the WorldCat Local platform. Initial indications were that in order to support the interlibrary loan/borrowing functionality of that system, the library would need to have a Shibboleth-based mechanism available to authenticate users. That project evolved in such a way that it no longer required the Shibboleth component, but by that time the library had seen the benefits of leveraging the new campus identity provider (IdP) for other purposes.

Several compelling arguments can be made for the business case of pursuing federated identity management. Managing identities for affiliates of the university in a central way makes sense for fiscal, efficiency, privacy, and security reasons – any time that more systems can be replaced by fewer, it will reduce the associated costs as well as the number of places where data could be compromised. The Shibboleth architecture furthers this privacy-preservation by completely separating the authentication and authorization steps, keeping sensitive information about users local to the institution and expecting the service provider (SP) to make the authorization decision based upon a minimal set of attributes about each user. The move at UNC-Chapel Hill to implement a Shibboleth option for individual electronic resource vendors also has the dual advantages of:

- making direct (un-library-mediated) access to remote vendors for remote users a real possibility (compared to the impossibility of such unmediated access in the current proxy environment), and

- removing the overhead and complexity of having to route traffic through a proxy server, an improvement that is increasingly critical as requirements for new electronic resources evolve.

Once the university decided to support a Shibboleth identity provider, it was decided that the library would leverage that implementation. Specific decisions about how to implement Shibboleth and what architectural components were needed for its success came from the author's involvement in the InCommon-sponsored library working group (https://spaces.internet2.edu/display/inclibrary/InC-Library). Involvement with that group provided the on-the-job training for how to proceed.

The InC-Library group came up with best practices for how libraries (and resource providers) should set up their architectures. Those best practices are available at https://spaces.internet2.edu/display/inclibrary/Best+Practices. Working with campus ID management staff, the library set up the mechanisms within the institutional directory to provide the appropriate individuals' accounts with the requisite eduPersonEntitlement attribute (assigned a value of 'common-lib-terms'). (Again, the library entered the process after the university had set up the identity provider infrastructure as well as joined the InCommon federation). At that point, the library was able to shift the EZproxy authorization mechanism (for those individuals who ONYEN-authenticate) from a check of the integrated library system's user database to a check for the proper eduPersonEntitlement attribute and value, as returned by the identity provider after successful authentication. Next, the library worked on configuring the EZproxy installation so that it would properly direct traffic for both Shibboleth and non-Shibboleth authenticated users to both Shibboleth and non-Shibboleth enabled resources (handing the session off for Shibboleth users connecting to Shibboleth resources and continuing to proxy the rest of the variations). This left the library, then, at the point of simply having to enable Shibboleth for additional remote resources (one by one) and configuring EZproxy to know how to handle each one (again, one by one).

Costs

Since the library is utilizing an identity provider that the university set up (and the library had already licensed EZproxy), the costs have been exclusively personnel costs, which are somewhat hard to quantify. Because the author was coming at the problem area relatively unfamiliar with Shibboleth, the initial time commitment was directed at becoming familiar with the general concepts.

For other campuses to take advantage of the work that the InC-Library group has done should require only a modest amount of time. The single biggest task is one of negotiation, initially with campus identity management staff around the issue of setting up and managing the eduPersonEntitlement and then subsequently with remote resource providers around the issue of their support for the technology. If a hybrid Shibboleth-EZproxy set-up (as explained in the best practices site described above) is set up, the amount of ongoing work required will vary significantly from institution to institution, based on such factors as the number of ways people are allowed to authenticate and how the EZproxy configuration file is maintained. That being said, there will be a certain amount of staff time that would be spent on maintaining authenticated proxy access, regardless of whether Shibboleth is involved or not.

As with any relatively new technology, the risk involved is primarily around the level of adoption among peer institutions and relevant service providers. The library is comfortable with this unknown, based on the growth in the number of InCommon member institutions and the steady increase in adoption of Shibboleth in Europe, North America, and elsewhere. The author's suspicion is that adoption would be faster if the architecture wasn't so complex; this is definitely a barrier, especially for smaller institutions.

Benefits

Most of the benefits of federated identity management are still the very long-term (and to some degree yet unrealized) promises of single sign-on that includes personalization services across a wide range of resources and of simple (to the user) and secure interinstitutional collaboration. The benefits that are already realized, however, include raised awareness of the importance of streamlined user management, of preserving user privacy, and of securing user credentials. The other big promise of Shibboleth with electronic resources (that it will obviate the need for any proxy service at all) is understood to be something that will take a long time to realize, due to the number of electronic resource vendors that must join InCommon and make their products Shibboleth-capable. The major vendors, for both UNC-Chapel Hill and other institutions, will likely be Shibboleth-capable in the short term (often because they have experience in markets outside the USA); their smaller and less well financed brethren may take many years to become Shibboleth-capable.

Future plans

At UNC-Chapel Hill, future plans include continuing to configure additional remote e-resources to use Shibboleth. Furthermore, there will probably be opportunities to spread out in new directions, using Shibboleth to authenticate users to other types of services, such as interlibrary loan or to do truly interinstitutional authorization to locally hosted applications or resources.

The author would whole-heartedly encourage other institutions to begin implementing federated access management, starting off with information available from the InC-Library group's work (at the URL above). There is a non-trivial amount of effort involved in gaining the basic understanding of the architecture and setting up the environment, but the potential benefits are immense.

Tilburg University and the SURFfederatie, the Netherlands

Main author/contributor: Teun Nijssen, IT consultant and Security Officer, Thomas Place, Innovation Manager Academic
Name of institution: Tilburg University, the Netherlands

Background

Tilburg University is a specialist university that is ranked the best in the Netherlands. The research and education is in economics, business administration, law, social and behavioural sciences, humanities and theology. In many of these fields, the university belongs to the top institutes in Europe.

In 1927 the university started with 28 economics students. Today there are 13,000 students and 1,000 FTE academic staff.

Library and IT services

Tilburg University runs a merged service called library and IT services (LIS).

The e-library consists of nearly 22,000 e-journals and more than 3000 e-books.

LBS of OCLC is used as the integrated library system. The online catalogue is part of an integrated search solution called Get It! that is run locally. Get It! integrates catalogue records and the metadata of articles and open access publications. Get It! replaced the iPort library portal, which is based on federated search.

Access management issues

Since the early 90s, all students have been using the same password for all IT and library services. Academics and support staff have two passwords: one for web services via LDAP and one for network services, such as file storage, mail and printing. At the time of writing (December 2010), the university is implementing an Exchange server. This will provide users with a single password for all university services. The LDAP service and its passwords are used for single sign-on in university applications, such as the student portal that integrates Blackboard, as well as a number of other web services. A subset of the attributes that contain data about people in the LDAP services is passed to the university Shibboleth identity provider for use in remote contexts. This identity provider can pass attributes to other Shibboleth identity providers or service providers.

VPN is used for off-campus access to external databases that rely on IP address checks. As an alternative to VPN the university offers federated access. For this the university depends on the SURFfederation and the service providers that are members of the federation. Historically, the first information providers that joined the SURFfederation were Elsevier and Ebsco.Swets. Legal Intelligence and Muse followed later and now run live services. There are also a number of services that are at the test stage. Google and Microsoft joined in 2010 (concentrating on Google Apps and Microsoft Live), which was a real breakthrough for the SURFfederation. A much smaller but interesting information provider is OCLC Leiden, which offers a transaction-based service: interlibrary loan (ILL). Tilburg University was the first university in the Netherlands to make use of interlibrary loan via the federation. Transaction-based services require the exchange of different attributes from those of a 'read-only' service. (Attribute control is covered in more depth in the Approach section below.)

For single sign-on, the university uses A-Select. A-Select is an open-source system for authenticating users of web services. The main funder of the A-Select development was SURFnet, the organization that is responsible for the Dutch academic network. SURFnet decided to stop the support of A-Select in 2011. Some universities will migrate to Open A-Select (the unsupported service) but Tilburg University will replace A-Select by a combination of CAS and ADFS. Some of the challenges of this approach are covered in the next section.

Approach

This section covers the following issues:

- multiprotocol support: multiprotocol exchange between the identity provider and the federation, and between the federation and the service provider
- attribute transfer between the federation, Tilburg University and a service provider (e.g. Elsevier v. OCLC – interlibrary loan)
- . Microsoft Active Directory and Unix (CAS) integration.

Multiprotocol SURFfederation

SURFfederation uses PingFederate software as its central component where identity providers and service providers interoperate. At the time of writing the number of identity providers connected to the federation was 64. Not all of these identity providers run the same protocols: many of them still run A-Select but there are also a large number of Microsoft sites with ADFS, as well as Shibboleth sites. The protocol exchange is governed by the annually reviewed Federation Scheme, the joint willingness to migrate to true SAML 2.0 in the near future and a simple legal contract. Until the time when native SAML is run by all sites, the multiprotocol plug-ins into PingFederate tie the identity provider side of the federation together, while simultaneously supporting a wide variety of service provider protocols.

Local attribute transfer control

Dutch privacy law regulates how organizations can handle any information that can identify a specific person. By their very nature, identity providers are prime examples of processes that deal with names of people and with attributes that describe their roles or entitlements. Hence, privacy law does apply here.

   The SURFfederation solves this problem by exposing no data from an identity provider to any other part of the federation, without explicitly configuring it. An identity provider is always authoritative about data that needs to be released. The identity provider or, indeed, any user can log in to a special service provider of the federation itself that shows what attributes are in principle made available to the federation. Typically this is a small subset of the data that is known at the identity provider of the organization, or even of the identity provider LDAP attribute scheme. Even if attributes are in principle released to the federation, this does not imply that all service providers get the data when a user accesses their services. The identity provider decides what attributes are given to each service provider. For multivalued attributes, even subsets of possible values can be released or masked.

A couple of examples are Elsevier Science Direct, versus OCLC Interlibrary Loan versus SURFspot. After a log-in by a user, Elsevier only gets two pieces of information about the user: the fact that he has already successfully logged in and one value of his eduPersonEntitlement called urn:mace:dir:entitlement:common-lib-terms. The presence of this Common-Library-Terms value is a statement that the identity provider makes about a user: the user is someone who is eligible to access services as a student or staff member, or a walk-in user as specified in the contract between the publisher and library. If Elsevier wishes to know an e-mail address or a common name of the user to provide him with personalized services, Elsevier may ask for these items and it is the user's choice to either supply the data or refuse. The organization, however, always acts in accordance with the privacy law.

For interlibrary loan, Tilburg University releases two attributes: a username and the surname of the user from its identity provider to the OCLC service provider. These attributes are required for the service. OCLC has a list of usernames that are allowed to use ILL and the remaining balance these users have (ILL is a paid-for service). The surname of the user is required when sending the loaned material to the local library from a remote location: it is convenient if the receiving library knows who will come and pick up the ordered book.

Another example is SURFspot, where students and staff can order software (e.g. Microsoft Office) for home use. The usual hardware like USB sticks or MacBooks is also for sale. Although SURFspot is part of the SURF family of services and, just like SURFnet, under the umbrella of SURF Foundation, it is actually an internet shop. People pay and bought material is delivered to their homes, without any involvement of their university. In this context, privacy law allows more identifying information to be released from the identity provider to the shop in order to avoid fraud. SURFspot gets the surname, given name and the e-mail address attributes at user log-in.

Active Directory and CAS integration

Tilburg University wishes to migrate from the A-Select software to a new environment that implements both its local single sign-on and its SURFconext identity provider. A-Select, no longer supported from 2011, is neither mainstream nor SAML 2.0-compliant. Several universities in the Netherlands are planning to migrate to Open A-Select, but Tilburg is likely to follow a different path.

At Tilburg University a very large university project replaced Novell Netware with Microsoft Windows 2008 Server R2 and a lot of associated services by the end of 2011. Many of these services offer single sign-on to the majority of the end-users, as they are authenticated by the Active Directory log-in. The exceptions are services that are run in a Linux context and users that run Ubuntu or Apple Macs without logging in to Active Directory.

Tilburg University has now reverse-engineered Microsoft version of Kerberos authentication that underlies Active Directory log-in and ticket granting in the Microsoft Domain environment. Also LDAP V3 and SAML are now understood to the level that one realizes that typical A-Select-like protocols can be implemented using a few pages of Perl and SimpleSAMLphp. The protocols and data structures themselves do not suffice: you also need the plug-ins in common server software, such as Apache, Blackboard, Oracle or LAMP stacks. Many of these have a CAS plug-in. Tilburg University investigates if an Active Directory log-in plus CAS front-ends locally, and ADFS with a few claim transforms for federation use might do the job. But it is too early to make decisions.

Tilburg University now runs production with the following software solution: the interface to SURFconext runs SAML, the interface to CAS servers runs the CAS protocol, a few remaining servers that use the A-Select protocol are approached using this protocol, and users who employ an Active Directory login simply no longer notice that its credentials suffice to access all these services.

Advice to other institutions

An attempt to integrate Active Directory log-ins with non-Microsoft services is not for the faint-hearted. Unless you have extensive programming capabilities, it would be better to use ADFS with Shibboleth, depending on the platforms used locally. The Tilburg environment strongly depends on a multiprotocol federation and skilful staff. This will vary from institution to institution.

Delivering access to resources in a joint academic and public library building, UK

Main author/contributor: Paul Williams, eLibrary Manager, City Birmingham University, UK
Name of institution: University of Worcester/Worcestershire County Council

Background

The University of Worcester (UW) has a population of roughly 10,000 students, the majority of whom study on an undergraduate course, and 700 staff. As an organization, the university started life as an Emergency Teacher Training College in 1946, becoming a college of higher education in the 1970s, and finally gaining full university status in 2005. With a wide portfolio, the university has gained an excellent reputation in areas such as teaching, nursing and sport. It is also home to the National Pollen and Aerobiology Research Unit and Association for Dementia Studies. The Hive is the first fully integrated university and public library in Europe, and was officially opened by Queen Elizabeth II in July 2012.

Library and IT services

The university uses the Capita LMS, presenting online resources to library members using a combination of Capita's Prism catalogue and Serials Solutions' Summon platform. Managed by the 360 Resource Manager tool, the university provides access to roughly 240 databases, covering nearly 40,000 unique journal titles and a range of e-books selected from platforms such as Dawsonera.

   For authentication to e-resources, the university is currently utilizing OpenAthens LA (Local Authentication) linked to the internal user directory delivered through Microsoft Forefront UAG (Unified Access Gateway), providing users with secure single-sign-on (SSO) access to both internal and external web-based resources.

   Before the Hive launch, public access to local libraries was governed purely by their library account, with PC use governed by the Netloan booking system and printing/copying using a staff-mediated service.

   In the Hive set-up, responsibilities for both library and IT services are shared, with the strategic lead being taken by one party or the other in accordance with the partnership agreement. The Hive has a jointly appointed Library Manager, with services delivered by both the university and county council library staff. First-line ICT support for Hive users is provided by university technicians, with further support available from both the university's ICT teams and the county council IT provider.

Access management issues

The Hive presented a number of interesting access management questions, due to a range of service decisions. First, the project would deliver a combined LMS, shared and managed between the two partners. Secondly, university members and the public would both require access to PCs across the building, where their experience should be consistent with that in other buildings across each service (university facilities and public library branches). Thirdly, while access to online library resources should be open to all users where possible, and turnaways were undesirable, resource licence restrictions had to be followed.

Approach

For a solution to each of these issues, plans were passed through the Hive's service development board during the overall project implementation stage. This meant full backing from both organizational partners, and the commitment of resources.

For the question of the combined LMS, the approach was joint procurement of hardware and some very clear decision-making around areas of responsibility for both partners. In practice, the system was to be implemented by a cross-organizational project team, led by a member of university staff. Consultation was the key here, working out where complete integration was required (for example integrated stock and catalogue), and where this was undesirable (funding streams). For access management, this led to a development of the library catalogue, which carries a mix of authentication methods, dependent on the user. Public members can access services using their PIN number, while the same interface also allows for LDAP authentication with student users, a service to which they were already accustomed. It does make choice of wording challenging within the interface itself, to avoid prompting groups for the wrong credentials.

An interesting outcome of this project was the need to 'de-duplicate' borrower records, where an individual was previously a member of the public library and also a student or member of staff. The approach here was to make their university account (with its increased allocation) the master account, and to bring all loans, fines, etc., across, while maintaining the old account in the background. The challenges are still being worked through, with the question of access management for student accounts in other county branch libraries a key area of work.

For public users, library membership dictates access to PCs, whereas student members have access due to their university membership. Again, this presented a challenge, with the project team deciding on a dual approach of Capita's

Keystone product for delivering public account data into the Hive's Active Directory (the Microsoft LDAP directory), and student data going directly from university registry systems. The end result is the same for the user, although it does require a very clear understanding of the architecture in case of issues. This separation of accounts and identity is also important in delivering key service concerns as we move forward, such as specific desktop environments for groups or changes to the web filtering approach for students and the public.

In the case of library online resources, those which are provided under a JISC licence are made available for walk-in users in the Hive, so necessarily IP-authenticated. To allow UW members to access them beyond the walls of the Hive, they are placed behind a proxy server, managed by the student's single-sign-on account. With little cost for the proxy server, the main resource required here was concentrated on liaising with JISC and the database providers.

Beyond the usual hardware, software and licensing costs, there are potential savings to be made in sharing an LMS, as well as the contingency provided by pooled staffing. One set of hardware requires a mutual trust in each other's capabilities, and access management for a diverse set of users, with different historical and wider context issues requires the ability to extend staff knowledge of authentication methods.

Benefits

The benefit for a complex facility like the Hive has to lie in the flexibility of any approach. Identity is key, whether this is within Active Directory or the library management system (which of these is the case is determined by the borrower type). As the systems were launched on the opening day of the Hive, there was a lot of potential for service decisions to change over time, as the organizations and users started to understand the facility as a live building. Therefore, as systems developers, it was essential for staff to be mindful of the need to disentangle services based around identity. This was achieved, and has been utilized well within the first year, as services have evolved.

Future plans

Currently, the priority is to ensure the consistency of access across sites, be they university or public branch libraries. The main issue is access to self-service facilities, and the sharing of data between systems necessary to enable this, particularly where branch libraries do not share the same suite of access management tools. There is a reliance here on some third-party suppliers, but this is starting to lessen.

Advice to other institutions

The key, as with most projects, is to really understand from stakeholders what they need. With a project like the Hive, hundreds of service decisions are being made simultaneously, so a robust method for mapping and reflecting these in systems (particularly with regard to access) is vital. The actual tools used, Capita's LMS, Prism and Keystone products, Active Directory, MyPC and others have all been robust and flexible enough for our approach, with good support in all areas.

Single sign-on across the USMAI Consortium, USA

Main author: David Kennedy, Head of Library Systems, Johns Hopkins University
Name of institution: University System of Maryland and Affiliated Institutions (USMAI), USA

Background

Formally established in 1999, the University System of Maryland and Affiliated Institutions (USMAI) is a consortium of higher education libraries in the State of Maryland, USA. The consortium consists of 16 administratively distinct libraries across 14 universities throughout the state. The USMAI office is centrally located at the University of Maryland, College Park, the flagship university for the State of Maryland.

When taken as a whole, the consortium is home to over 125,000 FTE students. The consortium, which licenses access to over 800 databases, ranges from small liberal arts colleges to large research universities, and includes two law schools, a medical school and four historically black colleges.

Library and IT services

The USMAI consortium is built upon a history of shared borrowing across the separate institutions and collective purchasing of access to licensed e-resources, and has developed a set of core shared library services. Shared services across the 16 institutions include a shared catalogue, a metasearch interface, an OpenURL resolver, interlibrary loan software, and electronic resource management software. Access to library services, as well as licensed resources, are governed through a single-sign-on infrastructure based on the Shibboleth and EZproxy technologies.

Organizationally, there is an IT office in the University of Maryland library that hosts, supports, develops and maintains the shared library services for the consortium. This IT office supports all 16 libraries, and, therefore, works with the central IT offices across the 14 institutions.

Access management issues

Prior to the current single-sign-on infrastructure at USMAI, there were a handful of issues that were difficult, if not impossible, to solve in the previous software environment, circa 2004/2005. The most relevant of these issues are briefly defined below.

The first issue was that there was not a single sign-on across all shared library services in the consortium. Even though the shared services were centrally located and interacted with each other, they each managed sign-on internally, meaning they each had their own separate log-in process. For the end-user, the library user, this meant signing on more than once when navigating between library services and also to licensed e-resources.

The second issue concerned integration between library services and other campus services, such as portals for students and learning management systems. Since USMAI is a consortium of libraries, each institution within the consortium has a central IT office which manages the overall IT environment for its respective university. These central IT offices provided enterprise services, such as e-mail and learning management systems. The universities within USMAI were at varying stages of understanding and implementation of identity management solutions. Therefore the end-users had separate log-ins for accessing their campus applications and their library services.

The third main issue was to do with user credentials. As each institution was implementing its own identity management solutions, it was also making separate decisions related to issuing log-on credentials to members of its campus; some institutions used netIDs, others e-mail addresses and passwords. The library needed a single solution, and so used a library-issued barcode included in all student/faculty/staff ID cards across the consortium. By doing so, the library was asking its end-users for a different set of credentials for log-in from the one being asked for when logging into e-mail, or visiting their course home page.

These three main issues were all addressed as part of the implementation of the identity management and single-sign-on infrastructure outlined below.

Approach

The implementation of a single-sign-on infrastructure across the USMAI consortium was a phased approach. As already mentioned, the institutions within the consortium were at varying levels of identity management implementation, and organizationally distinct. Implementing a system-wide implementation of Shibboleth that involved all of the institutions' central IT offices agreeing to a solution would not have been feasible in a reasonable timeframe. Rather, the consortium was able to take advantage of some centrality already established between the libraries.

Therefore the implementation of a single-sign-on infrastructure across the consortium started in the libraries. One advantage that the libraries had was a central user database. The first phase in the implementation involved the libraries adopting a single-sign-on across the shared library services. Although Shibboleth was not widely deployed in the USA at the time, USMAI evaluated the architecture, deemed it an elegant solution and determined that it could be integrated with the shared library services. USMAI was also able to convince its key library software vendors to partner with them on the implementation.

The first phase involved implementing Shibboleth identity providers for each of the institutions within the consortium. It also involved making the consortium-wide shared services Shibboleth service providers that utilized the established identity providers. This first phase of services included authentication for the shared catalogue (Aleph), metasearch interface (Metalib), interlibrary loan software (ILLiad) and URL-rewriting proxy (EZproxy). This phase of the project started in 2005. At the time, Shibboleth was not widely adopted; USMAI was one of the first, if not the first, library consortium to implement it. In addition, for some of the third-party software that was Shibboleth-enabled during this deployment, such as ILLiad and Metalib, USMAI was the first customer to work with them on a Shibboleth integration. This first phase of the project addressed the first issue outlined above: no single-sign-on across shared library services. This phase was implemented completely within the libraries, without co-ordination with central IT at any of the member institutions. In order to address the second and third issues, the libraries needed participation from the respective central IT organizations.

With an identity management infrastructure already established across the consortium, including production library services, the libraries approached the central IT groups and presented them with three participation options, for which each institution could make their own decision:

1   They could do nothing; users would still have single sign-on across library services, using a library barcode.
2   They could allow the library-hosted Shibboleth identity provider to access an institutional LDAP (Lightweight Directory Access Protocol) server as the authoritative source for user data; users would have single sign-on across library services, using familiar institutional log-in credentials.
3   They could implement an institutional Shibboleth identity provider that would work with library services and campus services; users would be able to have single sign-on across all campus and library services.

At the time of writing, four of the member institutions have implemented an institutional Shibboleth identity provider and have joined the InCommon federation – InCommon is the US equivalent of the UK Access Management Federation. One of the institutions, the University of Maryland, implemented Shibboleth and integrated the institutional Shibboleth identity provider with the library services.

From the library perspective, the costs associated with this implementation were all personnel costs. The technology stack used to implement the single sign-on infrastructure in the libraries was based solely on open-source software and the test and production instances of the infrastructure were deployed on existing hardware. The library personnel involved with the first phase of the implementation were roughly 3 to 4 person-months.

Costs for the second phase are not included, because those costs were mostly outside the library, and harder for the author to gauge.

Benefits

The most direct benefit from this project was a true single-sign-on solution. Not only was this a benefit to library users, but it also brought IT management benefits. The single-sign-on infrastructure externalized authentication from each application. This was a more modular, service-oriented approach than previous efforts at single sign-on. It allowed for separation of concerns between software, which simplified software changes, such as upgrades.

Another benefit from this implementation was the ability to provide fine-grained access control to licensed resources. One of the libraries in the consortium is a medical library, with varying restrictive licensing agreements with different resource providers. USMAI was able to enforce these licensing agreements by combining Shibboleth and EZproxy software.

Future plans

The Shibboleth infrastructure at USMAI was based on Shibboleth version 1.2.1. This version has not been supported for a few years, and is in need of an upgrade. There are currently no future plans for changes to the single-sign-on infrastructure currently in place.

Advice to other institutions

At USMAI, the investment in single-sign-on technology has more than paid for itself in terms of the benefits to the organization. Today, the Shibboleth software is a lot more mature than it was in 2005, and is also integrated into a lot more relevant library software. The InCommon community has developed roadmaps and best practices to help institutions with implementations. If an institution has not yet implemented a federated access solution, Shibboleth should certainly be a consideration.

In terms of lessons learned at USMAI, technology is not the most challenging aspect of identity management. Often, the most challenging aspect is communication and co-ordination between departments within an organization. At the University of Maryland, as well as at other universities, one of the most difficult of these challenges to co-ordinate is how to deal with 'special people'. 'Special people' can be friends of the library, university affiliates, alumni or trustees. In many cases where an identity management solution has developed over time, there exists a difference between the campus community that is represented in the enterprise directory and that which is represented in the library user database. Resolving these differences, especially the 'special people', and developing a workflow for managing their identities among the organization's systems of record, is usually a process. One thing that has worked for the author of this case study at multiple institutions in the last decade is to start the conversation early on campus, and continue to push the conversation forward around the management of identities for 'special people'.

USMAI Institutions

Bowie State University
Center for Environmental Science
Coppin State University
Frostburg State University
Morgan State University
Salisbury University
St. Mary's College of Maryland
Towson University
University of Baltimore
University of Baltimore Law Library
University of Maryland
University of Maryland, Baltimore County
University of Maryland, Eastern Shore
University of Maryland Health Sciences and Human Services Library
University of Maryland Law Library
University of Maryland University College

Appendix 2

A White Paper on Authentication and Access Management Issues in Cross-organizational Use of Networked Information Resources

www.cni.org/about-cni/staff/clifford-a-lynch/publications

Clifford Lynch, editor (cliff@cni.org)
Coalition for Networked Information
Revised Discussion Draft of April 14, 1998

About this paper

A first draft of this paper was released for review by members of the CNI Access Management list on March 28, 1998 and generated a great deal of electronic discussion within the closed CNI-AUTHENTICATE mailing list. This was followed by a meeting in Washington DC on April 5, 1998 to review and discuss the draft paper and comments generated on the list up to that date. The revision has also benefited from discussions at a Digital Library Federation/National Science Foundation Workshop held in Washington on April 6, 1998 on closely related issues. My thanks to all who contributed.

This version, which incorporates many of the ideas from this process, is being prepared for distribution at the Spring CNI Task Force meeting in Washington DC, April 14-15; it is also being placed on the CNI website (www.cni.org) for wider dissemination. Note that in some places time did not permit me to fully incorporate earlier comments or to research questions that were identified, and I have tried to indicate where changes will be made prior to the preparation of the final version. The paper also still needs some considerable editorial work, and I ask readers to be forgiving of editorial problems. Comments are invited and should be sent to cliff@cni.org. About 10 May, 1998, I will prepare a final version of the white paper which will be placed on the CNI website.

1.0 Introduction

As institutions implement networked information strategies which call for sharing and licensing access to information resources in the networked environment, authentication and access management have emerged as major issues which threaten to impede progress. While considerable work has been done over the last two decades on authentication within institutions and, more recently, in support of consumer-oriented electronic commerce on the internet, a series of new technical and policy issues emerge in the cross-organizational authentication and access management context. This white paper, which is being prepared by the Coalition for Networked Information in conjunction with a large group of volunteer reviewers and contributors, is intended to serve several purposes:

- To identify and scope the new issues that emerge in the cross-organizational setting and to provide a framework for analysing them.
- To map out the various best-practice approaches to solving these problems using existing and emerging technology so that institutions and information providers can make informed choices among the alternatives and consider how these choices relate to institutional authentication and access management strategies.
- To provide a common vocabulary and framework to assist in the development of licensing and resource-sharing agreements, and to highlight technical and policy considerations that need to be addressed as part of these business negotiations.
- To lay the foundation for possible follow-on formal or de facto community standards development in access management. If large scale use of networked information resources is to flourish, we need to move away from the specialized case-by-case access management systems in use today and towards a small number of general approaches which will let institutionally based access management infrastructures interoperate with arbitrary resources.

2.0 Defining the Cross-organizational Access Management Problem

The basic cross-organizational access management problem is exemplified by most licensing agreements for networked information resources today; it also arises in situations where institutions agree to share limited-access resources with other institutions as part of consortia or other resource sharing collaborations. In such an agreement, an institution – a university, a school, a public library, a corporation – defines a user community which has access to some network resource. This community is typically large, numbering perhaps in the tens of thousands of individuals, and membership may be volatile over time, reflecting for example the characteristics of a student body. The operator of the network resource, which may be a website, or a resource reached by other protocols such as Telnet terminal emulation or the Z39.50 information retrieval protocol needs to decide whether users seeking access to the resource are actually members of the user community that the licensee institution defined as part of the license agreement.

Note that the issue here is not how the licensee defines the user community – for example how a university might define students, staff members and faculty (all of the problems about alumni, part-time and extension students, adjunct faculty, affiliated medical staff and the like); it is assumed that the institution and the resource operator have reached some satisfactory resolution on this question. Rather, the issue is one of testing or verifying that individuals are really a member of this community according to pre-agreed criteria, of having the institution vouch for or credential the individuals in some way that the resource operator can understand. Such arrangements are often called 'site' licenses, but this term is really inaccurate; while physical presence at a specific site may be one criteria for having access, a better term is 'group' license or 'community' license, emphasizing that the key consideration is membership in some community, and that physical location is often not the key membership criteria.

Progress in interorganizational access management will benefit everyone. To the extent that resource operators and licensing institutions can agree on common methods for performing this authentication and access management function, it greatly facilitates both licensing and resource sharing by making it quick, easy and inexpensive to implement business arrangements. It benefits users by making their navigation through a network of resources provided by different operators more seamless and less cumbersome. The central challenge of cross-institutional access management is not to set up barriers to access; it is to facilitate access in a responsible fashion, recognizing the needs of all parties involved in the access arrangements.

While this white paper will give some particular emphasis to issues that arise in the higher education and library communities (particularly at the policy level) the problem under consideration here is very general, and in fact occurs in general corporate licensing of networked information services, or co-operation among business partners.

As we will see in the next section, not only are there questions about how best to accomplish this technically, there are also a series of intertwined policy and management considerations which need to be considered.

The focus here is on group licenses that may be subject to some additional constraints (for example concurrent user limits) rather than on transactional models where individual users may take actions to incur specific incremental costs back to the licensing institution over and above base community licensing costs. Any incremental cost transactional model will need to incorporate at least two additional features: a set of user constraints that become part of the attributes for each authenticated user and which are made available to the resource operator, and a means by which the resource operator can obtain permission for transactions by passing a query back to the licensing institution. This involves a much more complex trust, liability and business relationship between resource operator and licensing institution, as well as consideration of financial controls and a careful assessment of security threats. It will not be considered further here.

Note that there are several other cross-organizational authentication, authorization and access management issues which are beyond the scope of this paper, including the authentication of service providers and verifying the integrity and provenance of information retrieved from networked resources.

2.1 Terminology and Definitions

Throughout the rest of this paper we'll use the general terms 'resource operator' to cover publishers, website operators, and other content providers (including libraries and universities in their roles as providers of content), and 'licensee institution' to cover organizations such as universities or public libraries that arrange for access to resources on behalf of their user communities.

Authentication and authorization actually have very specific meanings, though the two processes are often confounded, and in practice are often not clearly distinguished. We will use the term 'access management' to describe broader systems that may make use of both authentication and authorization services in order to control use of a networked resource.

Authentication is the process where a network user establishes a right to an identity – in essence, the right to use a name. There are a large number of techniques that may be used to authenticate a user – passwords, biometric techniques, smart cards, certificates. Note that names need not correspond to the usual names of individuals in the physical world. A user may have the rights to use more than one name: we view this as a central philosophical assumption in the cross-organizational environment. There is a scope or authority problem associated with names; in essence, when a user is authorized to use an identity this is a statement that some organization has accepted the user's right to that name. For authorization *within* an institution this issue often isn't important, and in some schemes a user may only have a single identity; for cross-organizational applications such as those of interest here, this relativistic character of identity is of critical importance. A user may have rights to use identities established by multiple organizations (such as universities and scholarly societies) and more than one identity may figure in an access management decision. Users may have to decide what identity to present to a resource: they may have access because they are a member of a specific university's community, or a member of a specific scholarly society, for example. Making these choices will be a considerable burden on users, much like trying to shop for the best discount rate on a service that offers varying discounts to different membership and affinity groups (corporate rate, senior citizen rate, weekly rate, government rate, etc.).

A single, network-wide (not merely institution wide) access management authority would simplify many processes by allowing rights assigned to an individual by different organizations to become attributes of a master name rather than having them embodied in different names authorized by different organizations; yet such a centralized identity system probably represents an unacceptable concentration of power, as well as being technically impractical at the scale we will ultimately need. It should be noted that within the UK Athens project we can see a model of a rather centralized authorization system which has been scaled successfully to quite a large number of users, and which by virtue of its centralized nature has allowed rapid progress in wide access to networked information. The Athens experience and the factors – technical, social, cultural, and legal – that have enabled it to work in the UK call for very careful study as we consider approaches for other nations such as the US.

A name or identity has attributes associated with it. These may be demographic in nature – for example, this identity signifying a faculty member in engineering, or signifying a student enrolled in a specific course – or they may capture permissions to use resources. Attributes may be bound closely to a name (for example, in a certificate payload) or they may be stored in a directory or other demographic database under a key corresponding to the name. Attributes may change over time; for example, from semester to semester the set of courses that a given identity is associated with may well change. Just because some system on a network has knowledge of a name does not necessarily imply that it has access to attributes associated with that name. There is a fine line between rights to names (authentication) and attributes; for some purposes, simply knowing that a user has a right to a name from a given authorizing authority may itself represent sufficient information (an implicit attribute, if one wishes) that can support access management decisions.

Authorization is the process of determining whether an identity (plus a set of attributes associated with that identity) is permitted to perform some action, such as accessing a resource. Note that permission to perform an action does not guarantee that the action can be performed; for example, a common practice in cross-organizational licensing is to further limit access to a maximum number of concurrent users from among an authorized user community.

Note that authentication and authorization decisions can be made at different points, by different organizations.

Some libraries are establishing consortia which involve reciprocal borrowing and user-initiated interlibrary loan services; in a real sense these consortia are developing what amounts to a union or distributed shared patron file. One can view this as moving beyond just common authentication and access management to a system of shared access to a common directory structure for user attributes, and a common definition of user attributes among the consortium members. This is an example of a situation where very rich attributes are available to each participant in the consortium as they make authorization decisions; interlibrary loan and reciprocal borrowing represent a much richer and more nuanced set of actions than would be typical of a networked information resource.

A subsection on models for access management, discussing the locus of authorization decisions and trust relationships between their resource operator and licensing institution, will probably be added here in the next revision.

3.0 Evaluation and Analysis Criteria

We will be examining a number of different proposed solutions to the access management problem. Before describing and analysing these proposed solutions, this section considers the various requirements that a viable solution needs to address. Obviously, there are trade-offs which will need to be made among the conflicting goals in the context of each specific resource access arrangement, and institutions will have to make policy choices about the relative importance of the various requirements.

3.1 Feasibility and Deployability

First and foremost, the authentication and access management solution needs to work at a practical level. From the user's perspective, it should facilitate access, minimizing redundant authentication interactions and providing a single-sign-on, user-friendly view of the array of available networked information resources. It needs to scale; it must be feasible for institutions to deploy and manage for large and dynamic populations of community members. It needs to be sufficiently robust and simple so that user support issues are tractable; for example, a forgotten password should not be an intractable problem. It needs to be affordable.

From the resource operator viewpoint, a viable access management system should not require a vast amount of ongoing production and maintenance. Configuration to add a new licensing institution should be simple, and ongoing maintenance of that configuration should not call for large amounts of information to be interchanged between resource operator and licensing institution on an ongoing basis (such as file updates). Software parameter changes – not new software – should be necessary to add additional institutions. There should be a clean, simple, and well defined (standard) interface between resource operator and licensing institution. A systems or network failure at one institution should not degrade a resource operator's service to other licensing institutions.

Practical solutions are inextricably linked to the installed base of software. Ideally, all of the software needed to implement an authentication and access management solution should be available either commercially or as free software. Good solutions will leverage off of the installed technology base, and also current investments in upgrading that technology base: they should not be specific to libraries or even to higher education if possible, at a mechanism level (though libraries or higher educational institutions may use these mechanisms in conjunction with policies that vary from those common in the corporate or consumer markets). Most importantly, the software support that end users require should be available in common packages – such as web browsers – that are already part of the installed base. Any solution that requires custom specialized software to be installed on every potential user's desktop machine starts with a severe handicap.

Similarly, any solution requiring specialized hardware, such as biometric systems or smart card readers, is certainly not going to be feasible on a cross-institutional basis, and while it might imaginably be workable within an institution's internal authentication system, some other technique would be needed to convey cross-organizational access management data. Few resource providers will be willing to limit access to users equipped with such specialized facilities.

Software isn't enough; there is also the question of whether the user knows how to configure and employ it. For example, current web browsers contain considerable support for client-side certificates and proxies, but few users know how to use these features. Education about an existing software base is easier than first replacing or upgrading an installed software base and *then* teaching users how to employ the new software, but it's still a substantial issue.

Kerberos is an interesting case study of the feasibility constraints. An institution could certainly make a successful decision to deploy Kerberos as a *local* authentication system by placing Kerberos support software on each user's workstation (perhaps via a site license to a vendor); however, inter-realm Kerberos is probably too intimate a connection between resource operators and licensee institutions to be viable, and most resource operators would also reject Kerberos as an interorganizational approach because of the requirements it places on end user systems at institutions that were not using Kerberos for local authentication. In the cases where Kerberos is being used for interorganizational resource sharing, I believe that one could argue that the participating institutions (typically consortium members) have made commitments to link their administrative and other support systems at a much more sophisticated level than one would find in the typical resource operator – licensing institution relationship and are coming more to resemble a single 'consortium institution' with an internal (local) authentication system.

Any solution also needs to reflect current realities; in particular, it must be able to recognize the need for a user community member to access a resource both independent of his or her physical location (for example, a user must be able to connect to the internet via a commercial ISP, a mobile IP link, or a cable television internet connection from home), and also the need for people to access resources by virtue of their location (for example, access may be granted to anyone who is physically present in a library, whether or not they are actually members of the licensee institutional community).

3.2 Authentication Strength

The solution needs to be reasonably secure. The resource operator needs confidence that an attacker can't forge a credential easily. All parties need confidence that credentials cannot easily be stolen by eavesdroppers on the net (for example, through sniffer attacks), and that they cannot be stolen easily from a user that exercises reasonable precautions. Also, systemic compromise is a concern: this is a very real difference between having an individual user's credentials compromised (in which case they can be canceled and new ones issued) and having the system as a whole compromised, which might call for reissuing credentials to everybody in the user community.

Authentication strength is a somewhat subjective question. For many of the approaches that we will discuss, strength comes from the details of cryptographic algorithms and key lengths used; but part lies also in overall system design and implementation and in the realities of user behavior, and this can often be the source of the largest number of vulnerabilities. Some level of reason is called for here; most of the resources being access controlled, while certainly valuable assets, do not represent immanent dangers to public safety or national security if access control is breached. An access management system needs to be complemented by monitoring and other controls on the part of the resource operator to limit the impact of a breach. Further, there are after-the-fact legal remedies which can be applied to limit the damage caused by such a breach.

The cryptographic technology underlying many access management systems is legally sensitive on an international export and import basis, and may also be constrained by various national laws (though within the US, cryptographic technology can be employed freely, at least today). This is important for several reasons: resource access may cross national boundaries, and also because members of an institution's user community may need to access networked information resources when traveling outside of their home nation. We will see international resource sharing consortia, and also see institutions in one nation licensing access to resources in other nations.

It should be noted that virtually any strong access management system that incorporates general purpose cryptographic services will be illegal for export since all strong cryptographic implementations for general encryption/decryption are export controlled in the United States under current laws governing trafficking in arms. Note however that it may be possible for members of a user community traveling abroad to export cryptographic software for temporary personal use under some specific limitations; depending on where they are traveling it may or may not be legal for them to use it under the laws of the country they are in at the time. Matters are more complex than they may seem, however, because US export control laws are mostly concerned with cryptography that can support encryption (for confidentiality or concealment); export licensing of systems specifically for authentication or digital signatures which do not serve dual use as encryption systems has been much less of a problem. Consideration of the legality of developing, importing, exporting, and operating of access management systems outside the US needs to be analysed on a country-by-country basis; laws vary considerably.

3.3 Granularity and Extensibility

There is a need for fine-grained access control where institutions want to limit resource access to only individuals registered for a specific class; this arises in electronic reserves and distance education contexts, especially when a class may be offered to students at multiple institutions. Other variations are also possible: limiting access to law students, to faculty, to graduate students and faculty in physics. This sort of fine-grained access management is likely to be very complex, since there will be great variation from institution to institution in how groups of users are identified, named and specified. There is also some overlap between fine-grained authentication and demographic information that may be needed to generate management information (discussed below).

Granularity of access has been one of the most controversial issues in the discussions of the first draft of this paper and related issues. Without arguing against the need for fine-grained access control for some applications, I will summarize a few observations:

- At present, most access to network information resources is *not* controlled on a fine-grained basis. There is a very real danger that by accommodating all of the needs for fine-grained access management into the basic access management mechanisms we will produce a system that is too complex and costly to see wide-spread implementation anytime soon.
- The information needed to support fine-grained access management probably needs to be kept within institutions for privacy reasons, and should be treated as attributes to an identity rather than expressed as additional identities (in other words, one should record that a user with a given identity happens to be enrolled as a member of course X, rather than issuing the user an identity as member-21-of-course-X). This also has

implications for the locus of authorization decisions for fine-grained access management.

- In many – but certainly not all – cases, the resources (such as electronic course reserves) that are subject to fine-grained access management will be within an institution, or within one of the institutions in a consortium of institutions that are collaborating closely through shared courses or similar projects. The case where an external commercial networked resource will be access controlled to members of a small group like a class will be rare.

- In some cases, the presence of fine-grained access management mechanisms may encourage irrational license economics. For example: suppose there is an electronic journal that prices based on the number of people that have access, rather than on the number of people that actually use it. This would encourage an institution to define a fine-grained group of authorized users to this journal in order to save money. Such an arrangement is complex and sets up barriers to access for the rest of the university community. It would probably make more sense to initially price access for the entire university community based on the approximate number of people who will actually use the journal, and then if it turns out a few more people are using it than were originally expected, negotiate a slightly higher fee at license renewal rather than defining a special access group. Revenues to the publisher will be roughly the same in either case, but additional use would be encouraged rather than discouraged. Note that of course this reasoning doesn't apply in cases where there is wide demand for a resource, and the licensing institution is making a policy decision to deliberately and systematically limit access to the resource to a specific closed user community; but this is, reviewers believed, the exception rather than the common case.

3.4 Cross-Protocol Flexibility

Some approaches work for a wide range of applications protocols that might be used for accessing information. Others are designed to work only with specific protocols, or would require the development of special software extensions or modifications in order to support a full range of protocols. For our purposes, HTTP-based web access is the critical application protocol; we will also consider Telnet terminal emulation and the Z39.50 information retrieval protocol, although these are far less critical. The main locus of concern here is the user's desktop machine, which normally uses HTTP or Telnet to connect to machines that are part of the system of networked information resources; Z39.50 is seldom used at the desktop today and finds its main application in linking major networked information resources together.

Reviews of the earlier draft of the paper felt that the X Window protocol was not an issue, as this was primarily a local access application. The ability to sign electronic mail messages is certainly an issue for email-enabled networked information applications, though probably not a major one. Secure email *access* – authenticated SMTP, POP, or IMAP, for example – are viewed as primarily issues within an institution rather than cross-organizational questions; while it is certainly useful to have an authentication infrastructure which will support these applications, as well as local administrative applications, this is again not central to the cross-organizational problem. Directory access protocols such as LDAP are also potentially serious issues.

CORBA and DCOM are potential questions, though it is not clear to what extent these will be used from desktop machines in the future. There are also a set of issues involving authentication in conjunction with JAVA applets and systems like Authenticode or PICS which are not well understood at this point. Many of the authentication and authorization problems in this area deal with a user's machine making decisions about what applets it is willing to accept and to execute, and what authorizations it is willing to assign them; these are similar to questions about document authenticity and integrity and are out of scope for this paper. The other set of problems center around an applet making decisions about a *user's* rights; while technology and standards in this area are still in flux, most of the current approaches seem to assume some kind of certificate infrastructure. This is an area where more work is clearly needed.

3.5 Privacy Considerations

The application scenarios here involve access to information resources. In many cases libraries will pay for these licenses to electronic resources as a replacement for physically acquiring information in paper form.

The licensee institution, in the print world, has a set of internal policies about record-keeping and use reporting (both who used it and how often it was used); generally these are very restrictive and stress user privacy. The institution then has a separate set of policies (which may in fact never have been explicitly codified) about sharing this usage information with the content supplier: in general this policy has been very simple – the supplier got no information about usage other than that which the institution chose to make public for other reasons.

In the electronic environment, the situation changes. Because information is often accessed at the publisher site, the publisher may know a great deal about who is accessing what material and how often. Aggregators and service bureaus may also complicate both the collection and flow of information. To some extent the collection, use, retention, and even potential resale of this information can be covered by license contract; and should be. Institutions will have to develop realistic policies about privacy of readers in the networked information environment which are acceptable to their user communities and well understood by readers. However, some authentication and access management approaches offer licensee institutions much greater flexibility than others to limit the amount of information that can technically be collected by the resource operator. In general, it is desirable that the amount of privacy at risk which needs to be controlled by contractual provision be minimized.

Clearly, one strategy for ensuring user privacy is to ensure that users remain anonymous in their use of information resources. We can distinguish several common situations:

- Repeat users cannot be identified; each session is completely anonymous. We will call this anonymous access.
- Repeat users can be identified, but the identity of a user cannot be determined. The resource operator knows only that some specific individual is accessing the resource repeatedly, not who that individual is. The user may be identified by some arbitrary identifier, such as USER123. We will call this pseudononymous access.
- Demographic characteristics of users can be determined, but not actual identities. We will call this pseudonymous access with demographic identification.
- Actual identities can be associated with sessions. We will call this identified access. It may be supplemented with demographics; just because the resource operator knows who someone is does not mean that they automatically know the user's demographic characteristics as well as his or her name.

Note that many users choose to identify themselves in order to obtain added value services, such as electronic mail notification of changes to a resource, or to preserve context from one session to the next, or to maintain a user profile at a resource. It's important to distinguish voluntary user self-identification from automatic identification that is generated as a byproduct of an authentication and access management system. It is also worth considering, at least briefly, how an institution might provide services for its community that permits community members to enjoy these added value services without identifying themselves to resource operators, and whether it's worth going to the trouble to make this possible.

Understanding the coupling between pseudononymous or identified access as provided by an access management system and the desire to implement such capabilities as part of an information access system is a crucial issue. A given information resource may rely on an authentication and access management system to provide identified or pseudononymous access automatically, or it may offer some weak or strong higher level functions (using a user ID/password or cookie scheme, for example) that give the already authenticated and authorized user the option of identifying him or her self (literally or pseudononymously) in order to obtain personalized services from the information resource. In the latter case, assuming that it's a real choice and the level of service offered to the anonymous user is meaningful, this isn't an authentication and access management system issue at all: it's a choice that users of the information resource are free to make on an individual basis.

Privacy is not a purely political or moral issue. To the extent that researchers are pursuing patents, developing grant applications in a competitive environment, or seeking precedence for discoveries, confidential access to information resources is a critical issue with potentially significant economic consequences. Many higher education institutions are bound by laws about privacy of student records; some public libraries may face legislative constraints on patron privacy; and medical institutions (including university hospitals) may have to consider issues involving privacy of medical records. And, of course, beyond the United States – for example in Europe – the overall legal framework grants stronger privacy rights for all citizens.

Finally, in discussing privacy, we should recognize the overall need for a secure environment; this goes beyond authentication and access management. If user interactions with networked information resources are conducted in the clear, they are subject to eavesdropping by other machines on a local area network near the user (for example, by sniffer-based attacks within the campus network) or by attackers anywhere along the network path to the resource. Very few information resources today support searching and information retrieval (as opposed to ordering) via encrypted

SSL-secured HTTP. If privacy is to be honored in the licensing of networked information resources, then contractual arrangements, resource sharing designs, and procurements must recognize the importance of providing such support.

In some situations privacy and confidentiality issues go beyond access management and session encryption. Some users may be concerned that even knowledge that they are using a resource (not necessarily what they are doing with it) becomes known through traffic analysis. Link level encryption helps with this to an extent, but is not widely deployed and is unlikely to be widely deployed anytime soon. Very large scale aggregating proxies and experimental systems such as Crowds, which build on work done with anonymizing emailer systems such as Mixmaster also help to address these needs. Robust protection against traffic analysis in the public internet requires very large overheads. We will not consider this problem further here, other than to observe that credential-based approaches seem likely to be most flexible in these environments, and that if they are used it will be necessary to consider traffic analysis vulnerabilities created by the credentials verification process as well as the submission process. Similarly, there are situations where some users are unwilling to permit a resource operator to know what sort of information they are searching for (even beyond contractual restrictions on the collection and use of this information); in these cases it may be necessary for such users to locally replicate an entire resource or large subsets of it.

3.6 Accountability

In negotiating a license agreement, all parties recognize that the resource being licensed is of value and that the rights of the licenser must be respected. Typically, a licensee institution will agree to educate members of the user community about the license terms and restrictions relevant to the information resource in question, and to work with the resource operator to identify, investigate and put a stop to improper use of the resource. Thus, both the resource operator and the licensee institution share a common interest in having some individual user accountability as part of an authentication and access management system, so that if inappropriate use is detected (for example, if a single user seems to be accessing the resource thousands of times a day from computers on three continents) the organizations know where to begin investigating.

Of course, there's a tension between accountability and privacy; to the extent that privacy is achieved through anonymity, there is no accountability. Note that this balance may be managed by compartmentalizing information, for example: if a specific user is identified to the resource operator simply as USER2345, and the licensee institution knows who USER2345 actually is (but the resource operator does not) then the resource operator could call for an investigation of what USER2345 is doing, and the licensee institution might then follow its own due process in that investigation, which might result in internal disciplinary action but might never result in revealing the individual's actual identity to the resource operator. In a real sense, the obligation of the members of the user community are to the licensee institution, and the licensee institution in turn has obligations to the resource operator to ensure that members of its user community behave responsibly; it is not at all clear that it's appropriate for the resource operator to be dealing with individual members of the user community directly.

Accountability will also have some interactions with institutional policies about inappropriate use of network resources, particularly to the extent that interaction with these resources may go beyond simply retrieving information to participation in interactive communications. For example, policies that typically govern the use of electronic mail may come into play. But even if resources are used purely for information retrieval purposes some accountability (coupled with management data) may be desired in support of policies prohibiting use of university resources for personal commercial gain, for example; a useful analogy may be drawn to practices and policies in areas such as telephone logs.

3.7 Ability to Collect Management Data

The licensing institution has a legitimate need to gather management data in order to guide future decisions; if it is spending a great deal of money to license access to a resource, or to participate in a consortium resource sharing arrangement it is only reasonable that it will want to know how much various resources are being used and what sectors of the user community is making use of them. For public institutions, in particular, collection of management data is an essential part of institutional accountability, and some collection of management data may even be considered part of public records responsibilities for these institutions.

There are many reasons to collect management data besides guiding licensing or resource sharing decisions. These include the allocation of costs within a licensing organization or even the development of enhanced services such as collaborative filtering systems.

It's useful to define some terms. Management data can be faceted in two ways. The first is by user: this might include faceting by source IP address, by identity (name), or by user attributes that figure into a contractually based authorization decision (i.e. a resource is limited to faculty and graduate students; this user had the faculty attribute), or by demographic information that the licensee institution knows and wants to correlate with usage patterns (i.e. this is a first year graduate student in civil engineering, or even, in theory though likely not in practice, this is a male student). The second way to facet management data is by the objects being accessed or the services being used: which pages of which articles are being read, which one of several different databases on a server is being searched, how often searching is by author rather than by date, etc.

Collecting highly aggregated data is not particularly problematic; there's no way to prevent the resource operator from having aggregated data (although its use can obviously be managed by contract). The only question is whether the licensee institution can collect its own aggregate data or whether it must take it as a return feed from the resource operator; in the latter case, there are a whole series of scaling issues related to standards, since it will be a significant burden for the licensee institution to receive use statistics feeds from potentially hundreds of resource operators in different formats, reflecting different conceptual models about what is being counted, and with different delivery schedules.

The larger problems arise when one wants demographically faceted use data, or even individual use data. In the case of demographically faceted data, either the licensee institution must use the authentication and access management system to pass demographic faceting to the resource operator so that it can become part of the usage data that the resource operator returns, or the licensee institution must be able to capture its own demographically faceted use data. Privacy considerations begin to emerge when demographic data must be passed to the resource operator.

In the case of individual use data the problems become even more sensitive. Clearly, if users are individually tracked by the resource operator (whether or not their identities are known – i.e. whether they are pseudononymous or identified) then the resource operator can collect individual level data and return it to the licensee institution. The resource operator may even get supplemental demographic data about the individuals from the licensee organization. There are also a series of institutional policy problems having to do with individual level data at the licensee institution: who can see this data – for example, can a faculty member look at the statistics for his or her students' use of specific information resources? Under what procedures are usage records subject to audit to detect misuse? Again, we need to consider when these issues should be defined by policy and trust in implementation of policy as opposed to being managed by technical means.

While many scenarios are possible, I suspect that the most common practical situations today will be these:

- usage is tracked on an aggregated basis either by the institution or the resource operator; I suspect tracking by the resource operator will be more common since the resource operator will be able to count events that are more meaningful in measuring resource utilization (for example, by journal rather than just page accesses).
- usage is tracked on an individual (pseudononymous or identified) basis by the resource operator, who then passes use logs back to the institution, which processes them to factor in demographic data and obtain a demographically faceted usage report.
- institution and resource operator agree on some very simple demographic faceting and demographic data is passed to the resource operator by the access management system; these demographics are then factored into the usage reports developed by the resource operator.

Management data is a major problem in the current access framework. Part of the problem is the conflict between privacy and a desire for demographic or individual data. Most of this is going to have to be sorted out at the institutional policy level, and may involve making sacrifices in order to ensure privacy. Some institutions may be legally limited in their ability to collect certain management data. It would be very useful to have some real-world examples of how this trade-off has been settled.

A very insightful comment was made at the meeting to review the first draft of this paper. From the perspective of the licensing institution, particularly when facing difficult collection and resource allocation decisions, the observation was 'there's never enough management information – this issue here is to define what you absolutely have to have, not would you would ideally like'.

4.0 Approaches to Access Management

Having summarized the many and sometimes conflicting requirements that an access management system must address, we now consider a number of actual schemes currently in use or under consideration and analyse how well they meet these requirements.

It's important to recognize that in solving real-world problems more than one approach may be relevant at a single institution; one might use one scheme for one class of users and a different scheme for another class. For example, an institution might choose to manage access for kiosks and public workstations by IP source address, and to use a credential scheme for other users. Indeed, virtually all of the major institutional systems that are currently being deployed combine multiple approaches. Also, note that approaches can be cascaded in a hierarchy; for example, a resource might be set up to first check whether a user could be validated by an IP source filtering approach but if the IP source address isn't valid for access, the resource might then apply a credential-based access management test.

At the most general level, there are three approaches – proxies, IP source filtering, and credential-based access management.

Basically, with IP filtering, the licensee institution guarantees to the resource operator that all traffic coming from a given set of IP addresses (perhaps all IP addresses on one or more networks) represent legitimate traffic on behalf of the licensee institution's user community. The resource operator then simply checks the source IP address of each incoming request.

In the case of a proxy, the licensee institution has deployed some sort of local authentication system, and users employ specific proxy machines to send traffic to the resource and receive responses back from that resource; the local authentication system (which is invisible to the resource operator, except that the resource operator knows that it is in place in order to guarantee that traffic coming from the proxy machines is legitimate) is used to control who can have access to the proxy machine. As a business matter, the resource operator may want to know something about how the local authentication system works in order to have confidence in the proxy, but this does not enter into the actual authentication which is performed operationally by the resource operator. The resource operator will most commonly identify the proxy machines by their IP addresses (or some variation such as reverse DNS lookup), and for this reason from the resource operator's point of view proxies are often just considered to be a special case of IP source address filtering – a resource operator who is set up to do IP source address filtering can accommodate a licensing institution employing proxies with essentially no additional work. However, proxies can actually be identified using either IP addresses or any credential-based cross-organizational authentication scheme (such as certificates). Because of this, and also because many of the policy and technical issues surrounding proxies at a higher level are quite distinct from those involved in IP source address filtering, we will treat proxies as a separate approach.

The third approach is credential-based. Here the user presents some form of credential – a user ID and password, or a cryptographic certificate, for example – to the resource operator as evidence that he or she is a legitimate member of the user community. The resource operator then validates this credential with some trusted institutional server (or third party server operating under contract to the institution) before deciding whether to allow access. Note that there needs to be advance agreement (most likely as part of the license contract or resource sharing agreement) as to how the mutually trusted institutional servers or third parties (such as certificate authorities) are identified and authenticated themselves.

For completeness, it is worth noting that there is one other possibility: the resource operator assigns credentials to individual members of the licensee community (perhaps in co-operation with the licensee institution). This is what was done historically when small numbers of users needed access to a few specialized information resources. The trouble is that it does not scale manageably to large numbers of users or large numbers of resources, and particularly not to both. While it's reasonable for an institution to distribute one set of credentials to each member of its user community (for example, in conjunction with an internal authentication system) it's not reasonable to distribute hundreds of different credentials for different resources to each user, or to expect the users to manage them or to keep straight which credentials are for use with which resource. Thus, we will not consider this model further, other than to recognize that it may have its place for specialized resources that serve only a handful of users.

4.1 IP Source Address Filtering

Currently, IP source address filtering is the major mechanism used to implement authentication and access management for cross-institutional resource access. The way this works is that the licensee institution provides the resource operator with a list of IP addresses that are authorized access; this can include some wildcarding to permit entire subnets or networks to have access, and also occasionally incorporates exclusion lists (all hosts on a given net or subnet EXCEPT for the following specific hosts). There is general agreement that it is unsatisfactory for a number of reasons, and it is instructive to evaluate it against our seven functional requirements both to see where it works and where it actually falls short.

Feasibility and Deployment: This is relatively easy to deploy and manage from the perspective of both the institution and the resource operator. No special software is needed at the user side, and at the resource operator side the support is not difficult. There is some maintenance involved in keeping the tables at the resource providers up to date, but this is not unmanageable. It is necessary for the licensee institution to perform some analysis on access and use policies for the machines within the institution to make sure that machines that aren't access-limited to the institutional community are excluded where necessary, and to educate members of the community that giving outsiders an account on a machine also gives them access to institutional resources that they may not be entitled to; there are some real dangers of access control breaches by the creation of proxies either through ignorance of the implications or deliberately.

The major problem, from a feasibility point of view, is that many legitimate users are not coming through the institutional network at all times; they may want access through commercial ISPs, at their workplaces outside of the institution, or from home. Some other solution is needed to handle these users.

One should not underestimate the management complexities of IP source address-based access management, particularly from the point of view of a resource operator. Configuration changes are frequent, and configurations for a large licensee institution can be quite complex. Also, the move from the older class-based network addresses owned by institutions to classless IP network addressing with the address space managed by the ISP has introduced new problems; not only must the licensee institution get the network masks right, but there's no easy way for the resource operator to independently verify this (for example, that an institution's network is a /18 rather than a /19).

Authentication Strength: Source IP filtering is actually relatively strong. While it's not difficult to introduce packets to the network with spoofed source addresses unless appropriate packet filters are in place (and this has become a major problem in the context of network denial of service attacks), getting responses back to a spoofed network address is much harder, and basically involves hijacking entire network addresses within the routing infrastructure. This is relatively unlikely; it's a sophisticated and complex attack, and is very likely to be noticed quickly. Resolving the threat of IP spoofing needs to be addressed at the network routing infrastructure level, and considerable work is going on in this area (packet filters and authenticated BGP peering, for example).

A specific machine with an excluded source IP address that sits on a generally authorized network can circumvent that restriction more easily, if the machine isn't under institutional administration (for example, its owner can just give it a new IP address on the same network).

Source IP filtering isn't subject to systemic compromise, and doesn't come with export control restrictions.

Granularity and Extensibility: To the extent that membership in specific groups can be linked unambiguously to specific network addresses (for example, in an office, a dorm room, or a computer lab) fine-grained access is feasible. Such direct linkage is often not the case, however; students in a class may share use of a computer lab, or need to use public workstations in a library.

Cross-Protocol Flexibility: Since all protocols of interest run on top of IP, source IP address-based access control is quite universal.

Privacy Considerations: To the extent that source IP addresses can be linked to individuals (for example, personal workstations in offices) there are some privacy issues. And certainly source IP addresses are correlated to demographics, if the resource provider is willing to invest in understanding the campus network architecture. Access in a source IP filtering authentication environment is probably somewhere between anonymous and pseudononymous, with some ability to move from pseudononymous to identified access in individual cases if the resource provider is willing to go to the trouble to do so (this is the case of personal workstations used primarily by a single individual).

Accountability: There is limited accountability – at the level of machines rather than people – which mirrors the privacy situation. One has relatively good accountability for individually owned personal workstations and relatively poor accountability for everything else; for a large, shared machine one gets accountability to the machine level, and then has to work with the administrator of that machine to identify a specific user or users. If dynamic IP address idress assignment is used (as is often the case for laptops in public areas, for example), then accountability is particularly weak.

Management Data: An institution can collect some usage data at a highly aggregated level that is not well correlated to application-level constructs through a border router, or get aggregated usage data from the resource operator. Demographic data can be obtained to the extent there is correlation between IP address blocks and demographics (for example, there might be a campus subnet for a medical school); this demographic data will be sketchy and imperfect at best, and some differentiations (such as students as opposed to faculty) will be very hard to extract. Individual level usage data will be possible only in the case where there are personal workstations, and all work by an individual is done on that workstation.

Summary: IP source address-based access management tracks the activities of machines rather than people. To the extent that there's a very close correlation between the two, it works reasonably well. Unfortunately, the correlation has never been that good and many trends (such as the move from institutional modem banks to purchase of commercial dial up access to the internet) continue to weaken this correlation. IP source address access management may work particularly well for fixed-location, institutionally managed public terminals, such as public workstations in libraries or computer labs.

There are several additional issues and variations on source IP filtering which deserve some additional comment.

Many organizations are moving to dynamic assignment of IP addresses, either for limited situations such as laptops that may be docked in classrooms, computer labs, or public areas such as library reading rooms, or in some cases, campus wide in order to simplify address management. This dynamic assignment weakens accountability, strengthens privacy, and complicates the collection of meaningful management data. However, since dynamic IP addresses are assigned within an organizational network number, use of dynamic IP addresses does not invalidate the use of IP source address-based access management.

To mitigate the problems with access via dial-up ISP connections, a few universities have negotiated special arrangements with specific ISPs so that members of their community are assigned addresses on a specific (private) net or subnet when connecting via the ISP (since the ISP does authentication on the users as part of the establishment of the dial-up connection, this is feasible if the ISP can maintain this information as part of its user attribute database). While this makes it possible to extend IP source authentication to dial-up users obtaining service through the ISP, it should be clear that this approach will not scale reasonably to offer users a wide range of choice in the ISP marketplace (including wireless and cable TV-based ISPs); it is most practical in situations with large educational institutions who have the marketplace power to negotiate such arrangements and where members of the institution's user community are willing to select from at most a small number of competing ISPs.

Approaches using IP tunneling and/or Mobile IP type support can be used to mitigate some of the limitations of traditional source IP-based access management schemes, though they may have considerable performance and complexity drawbacks. The next revision of the paper will include a discussion of these approaches.

Some organizations have used reverse Domain Name System (DNS) look-ups on source IP addresses and then checked the DNS name in order to perform access management. This changes matters very little except that it means that access management must also rely on the security of the DNS system itself (which can be a problem; secure DNS is not yet deployed widely) and requires that all hosts have DNS names tabled, which is often not the case. This approach also does not work well with DHCP (dynamic assignment of IP addresses) which is often used to support laptop machines.

4.2 Proxies

In some sense, proxy-based approaches simply shift the problem, since an institution will still have to deploy an internal authentication and access management system in order to control use of the proxy servers. However, it may be easier to implement an internal system than to implement a system that must be used by a wide range of resource providers; proxies modularize and compartmentalize the authentication problem.

Let us assume for the time being that an institution has implemented a viable internal authentication system and analyse various proxy schemes under that assumption. Our comments, then, will only cover the proxy scheme itself, not the institutional authentication system necessary to support the proxy.

We need to distinguish between two different kinds of services that are sometimes referred to as proxies. The first, which we will call mechanical proxies, are services which make use of facilities designed directly into implementations of protocols such as HTTP. To use a web proxy server, one configures a browser to pass all HTTP requests not directly to the destination host, but instead to a proxy server, which intercepts these requests and when necessary retransmits them to the true destination host. In this case, the operation of the proxy should be invisible to the end user.

The second type of proxy is what we will call an application-level proxy (historically, these have often been called 'protocol translation systems' or 'gateways'). An application level proxy functionally forwards requests where appropriate, but does not rely on protocol mechanisms. An example might be a Telnet proxy, where in order to reach an access-controlled Telnet-based resource, one telnets to an institutional system; this might engage the user in an authentication and authorization dialog, and then manage a Telnet session to the remote resource, with some editing. In the web environment, a service such as the anonymizer (www.anonymizer.com) is a good example; here, one accesses the web page of the service and provides the URL of the remote resource one really wishes to access. The anonymizer service not only forwards requests on, but also dynamically re-writes each page coming back from the remote resource prior to presenting it to the end user, for example, replacing each URL in the retrieved page with a URL that accesses the anonymizer with a parameter of the actual remote page that is being requested. As the environment becomes more sophisticated, applications proxies become increasingly problematic: for example, an applications-level proxy generally will not handle pages that contain Java applets properly.

Feasibility and Deployment: This is not entirely straightforward. Proxies introduce a considerable amount of overhead, and the institution will need to invest in the installation and operation of proxy servers. Some overhead may be mitigated by having the proxy server perform caching operations as well as access management, although this introduces a range of other responsibilities and problems. Also, proxy servers become mission critical systems; they need to be available and reliable, and to be sized so that they do not represent a performance bottleneck.

Proxies – and in particular application level proxies – have scaling problems not only in terms of computational resources to support a large user community, but also in terms of configuration management and support as the number of resources available to the user community multiply. Each resource needs to be configured, and as resources change, configuration changes will be needed in the proxy.

In the case of mechanical proxies, user browsers have to be properly configured to make use of the proxy rather than communicating directly with resources on the network. This will be a particular problem when pre-configured browsers are supplied by sources other than the licensee institution; for example, cable TV-based internet service providers like @home make extensive use of proxies and caching within their own networks, and supply browsers that are configured to use the ISP's network.

In the case of applications level proxies, users will have to be taught to go through the application in order to reach remote information resources.

Integrating a local authentication system with a commercial (usually mechanical) proxy server may be non-trivial. Programming for an application level proxy can become quite complex. One useful distinction is the locus and complexity of decision making that the proxy must perform. At the simplest level, a proxy can just screen all potential users without regard to the resource that they want to access; essentially there's a single authorization to use the proxy, and through it all of the resources that it permits access to. At a more complex level, the proxy might consider both the user and the resource in order to make an authorization decision; at the most complex level, it may track in detail the user's interaction with various resources and make very specialized decisions about what requests it will and will not pass through to the resources.

Telnet application proxies are tricky to build (consider problems like the handling of break signals as they are propagated across the proxy), and as far as I know, standard commercial software to support construction of such proxies doesn't exist. For Z39.50 applications, it's certainly possible to construct custom proxies, although I am not aware of general purpose software to do this. The proxy strategy is a very general one architecturally.

From the point of view of the resource operator, proxies are easy to work with; they usually just look like a particularly simple form of IP source address authentication. However, they may raise some user support problems; if an institutionally provided proxy is out of service or overloaded, the resource operator can expect complaints about bad service for reasons that are outside of its control.

Authentication strength: obviously, this depends on the local authentication system. There is the danger of systemic compromise if the proxy server is successfully attacked (that is, the local authentication built into the proxy server is broken) or the proxy is misconfigured. A breach of the local authentication system is likely to be a very high visibility event which will receive rapid response from the licensing institution; a breach of the proxy may be more insidious and more difficult to detect. The communication between the proxy server and the resource can be very strongly secured and authenticated using certificates and session level encryption.

Granularity and extensibility: in theory, anything is possible if enough work is done on the proxy server. For fine-grained access control, however, it's necessary for the proxy to consider who is trying to access what, rather than just having the proxy server authenticate members of the user community prior to any use of the proxy. It's not clear how hospitable commercial proxy software is to this kind of application, or how complex the institution-specific programming will have to be; the more complex it gets, the more likely there are going to be security vulnerabilities.

Cross-Protocol Flexibility: Because the authentication mechanism used between proxy and user and between proxy and resource need not be the same, there's a particularly high level of cross-protocol flexibility. In the worst case, the proxy can use a very general authentication approach like source IP filtering to support protocols between the proxy and the resource, and can use specialized methods (even embedded within application proxy code) to authenticate users to the proxy server.

Privacy: proxies can provide real anonymity of use if they are set up properly; the resource operator need not even get a source IP address for the end user. On the other hand, they provide a choke point for potential systematic institutional monitoring of what the user community is doing, which may be some cause for concern.

Accountability: in general, proxies provide poor accountability, since they offer anonymous access. At best, some level of accountability can be provided by correlating local logs at the proxy (which is tied into the local authentication system) and monitoring at the resource. In theory it would be possible for the proxy to pass some pseudonym or identity to the resource, but it's not clear how this would be accomplished in a standard and interoperable fashion.

Management data: just as a proxy is a choke point for monitoring, it is also a choke point for collecting management data, including demographically faceted data or individual data since it authenticates users and then sees all of their requests to resources. Of course, correlating this to applications-level events and terminology is hard. It is not clear how a proxy could pass demographic data along with requests to a resource to permit faceted statistics collection at the resource side.

Summary: it's hard to fully evaluate the proxy approach for two reasons. To some extent it just moves the authentication problem because it presupposes the existence of an institutional authentication system, and the problems of deploying such a system really need to be considered. Second because a proxy – particularly an applications level proxy – is a point at which custom programming can be inserted almost anything is possible, at least in theory, but it's hard to evaluate the implementation and maintenance cost of such a system, and the extent to which it demands custom interfaces to the resources themselves, as opposed to using completely standard interfaces.

4.3 Credential-based Approaches

In a credential-based approach, the user interacts directly with resources on the net rather than working through an institutionally provided proxy intermediary. The key problems here are:

- What are the credentials that the user presents to the resource?
- how are these credentials presented securely?
- how are the credentials validated with the issuing institution?

For a credential-based approach to scale, all of these activities need to take place in a standardized fashion. The most commonly discussed credentials are X.509 certificates, which are attractive because browsers and servers already have some support for them (designed to enable electronic commerce) and because other software components needed for an X.509 public key infrastructure are already becoming available on the marketplace. However, many other forms of credentials are possible, including user IDs and passwords, one time passwords, and the like. Indeed, it's useful to differentiate between application-level credentials – where the collection of the credential and its validation is packaged into the application itself, such as obtaining and checking a user ID and password – and credentials which are built into protocol mechanisms, such as the use of certificates with HTTP and SSL. The protocol-based mechanisms are more general and often require less work to implement on the part of the resource operator, but are less familiar to end users, calling for a larger investment in infrastructure and user education.

Credentials can be confusing to analyse because they can potentially carry both authentication and attribute information together, or they can be used purely (or almost purely) for authentication.

We will analyse two credential-based approaches: a user ID/password scheme at the application level, and a certificate-based approach.

4.3.1 Password-based Credentials

Assume that institutions simply maintained databases of (pseudonymous or identified) user IDs and passwords. Note carefully that the idea here is that a member of the institutional user community has a single user ID and password for access to all licensed resources, and not a separate user ID and password for *each* licensed resource.

Using SSL-encrypted forms (which eliminates the problems of transmitting passwords in the clear), it would be fairly easily for a resource to ask for this user ID and password securely; one could then have a special purpose protocol so that a resource could securely check whether the user ID and password were valid by querying an institutional user ID/password database server. Note that SSL can set up an encrypted connection with a server certificate but no client-side certificate.

The special purpose user ID/password checking protocol doesn't exist today, but is not hard to design or implement, and since it only needs to be implemented by the resource operator and by an institutional server or two at each licensee institution, it might be much less problematic than making all licensee community users go through the complications of obtaining and installing certificates on their machines. Further, similar protocols for user ID/password checking are already in use for validating users to terminal servers (i.e. TACACS, RADIUS); these might be used, or at least adapted.

Users are already familiar with user IDs and passwords, including the need to keep passwords secure, to change them, and to pick them well (or at least they are more familiar with these issues than, for example, certificate use). User IDs and passwords can be carried in the minds of people rather than being installed on specific machines the way that certificates are; this helps with kiosks, computer labs, libraries and other shared machine settings – assuming that one can teach the user to log off when he or she is finished, rather than just leaving the machine signed on. Probably the biggest problem with this approach – which is not shared with certificates – is that the resource operator obtains a set of globally valid credentials for the user, and has to be trusted to keep them secure. There are also some secondary problems – Trojan horse resources that capture user IDs and passwords under false pretenses, for example, are a much more serious threat than they are in a certificate exchange environment.

Let's consider passwords and user IDs carried over SSL encryption from the perspective of our requirements definition. It's clear that they are feasible and deployable. Assuming that a protocol for verifying user IDs and passwords with an institutional server is standardized and deployed, the amount of work faced either by a licensee institution or a resource operator is quite manageable. Special desktop software is not required for web access; for other protocols, such as Telnet, an SSL-capable Telnet is needed (my understanding is that some of these are under development). Z39.50 credentials are a particular problem because no Z39.50 interface to a service like SSL is currently defined. User IDs and passwords are clearly linked to people rather than network addresses of machines. One problem with user IDs and passwords is that they don't encourage seamless navigation among resources; each resource is going to explicitly annoy the user by asking for his or her user ID and password on each visit.

While passwords represent relatively weak security, a system can be put in place to require them to be difficult to guess (by forcing the use of pass phrases rather than passwords, or avoiding use of words in a dictionary), and also insisting that they be changed frequently. The use of an SSL-based transport removes the security problems of transmitting them in the clear. The protection provided by SSL will depend on whether US-only (long key) or international (short key) versions of SSL are supported by the user's browser. User IDs and passwords are subject to systemic compromise from two perspectives; if the institutional password verification server is compromised, new passwords would have to be issued to all members of the user community. Also, each resource operator now shares in the responsibility for keeping user IDs and passwords secure; if any resource operator's site is retaining user IDs and passwords, and is compromised, this will compromise all other resource operators as well as the home institution (if the institution is using the same user ID and password for internal and external authentication and authorization purposes).

Granularity and extensibility. An institutional password server will just verify that a particular user ID/password combination is valid (it would also know what resource operator was asking). In situations where an access management decision needs to be made that goes beyond validity of the user ID/password pair, the key question is the locus of that decision. The resource operator will either have to maintain a list of valid IDs (identities) or the password server will have to keep information about what resources a user ID has access to. Or the institution would have to offer resource operators access to a user attribute database keyed on user ID.

Cross-protocol flexibility: because passwords operate at a higher level of abstraction than protocols they are general. Telnet and Z39.50 support should be straightforward, assuming that there is encryption on the link over which the passwords are transmitted, as discussed above.

Privacy and accountability. The use of user IDs and passwords transfers personal information directly to the resource operator. This information may be pseudononymous or identified; it will not be anonymous. To this extent, it undermines privacy but offers accountability. Management data faceted by demographic categories will be available from the resource operator only to the extent that the licensee institution provides demographic data as a byproduct of user ID/password validation. There is no opportunity for the licensee institution to collect statistical information directly, other than a count of how often user ID/password pairs are validated by the various resource operators.

Summary: to the extent that an institutional password verification server controls the export of individual and demographic information, passwords could work surprisingly well in an SSL-protected context. A primary benefit is that users are familiar with the model. There are important missing pieces here, particularly the protocol to permit resource operators to verify user ID/password pairs with institutions that issued them. Probably the greatest weakness of this approach is the dependency on each resource operator to protect user ID/password pairs, and the danger of systemic compromise due to a security failure on the part of a single resource operator.

Further comments: clearly, by issuing different passwords and user IDs for different resources, it is possible to reduce the interdependence among resource operators and the dependence on each resource operator in maintaining security. However, large numbers of passwords and user IDs are extremely unfriendly and confusing for users, and probably impractical. For users who only use a single machine (or who are willing to store a cookie file in a network file system), and for resources that don't require high security, it's certainly possible to store user IDs and passwords as cookies on the user's machine (though many users have become 'cookie-phobic' due to the overly dire publicity surrounding cookies); once stored, the user doesn't have to enter them at all, improving seamless cross-resource navigation. This is the approach that is taken by many low-security commercial services in the consumer marketplace today.

4.3.2 Certificate-based Credentials

X.509 certificate-based credentials are substantially more complex than passwords, but offer a number of advantages. In essence, an X.509 certificate (plus the private key that goes with the certificate) gives a machine credentials that support its right to make use of a name, and allows this assertion to be verified by checking with a certificate authority (which might be operated by the licensee institution, or operated by a third party under contract to the licensee institution). X.509 certificates include expiration dates, and certificate authorities can also provide revocation lists to invalidate certificates prior to their expiration date (though checking such lists can involve substantial overhead, and not all systems supporting certificates currently check revocation lists.)

Rather than making a complete analysis of certificate-based credentials, we will simply highlight how they differ from the password-based credential approach already discussed.

X.509 certificates and corresponding private keys are messy to distribute (much more so than, for example, a starter single use password for a local authentication system), and complicated for users to install, particularly in cases where the certificate needs to be installed in multiple machines owned by a single user. Backup and recovery needs to be considered carefully lest a user loses his or her certificates permanently as a result. They are highly intractable in cases where users share machines, such as public workstations. X.509 certificates can contain demographic data (though there are standardization problems here about how to encode them in the certificate payload) which could be used for resource operator-based statistics gathering or fine-grained authorization decisions.

In contrast to passwords, there is already a well defined protocol/process which can be used to validate an X.509 certificate-based credential that has been presented to a resource operator.

Note that an X.509 certificate-based credential does not consist of simply the certificate itself, but rather a complex object that includes the certificate and is signed with the (secret) private key corresponding to the certificate; since this is computed anew each time a credential is needed, X.509-based certificates do not share the password-approach problem that security depends on each resource operator carefully protecting the user's credentials.

User IDs and passwords are application level constructs; they can be designed into an application using any protocol, assuming only that the connection can be encrypted. The exchange of X.509 certificates is a lower level, protocol-integrated operation and does not rely on encryption. Thus, there is work involved in extending the use of X.509 certificates to work with protocols other than HTTP, such as Telnet (Z39.50 already contains facilities for certificate exchange). There is also still a need for an SSL-type service to encrypt the connection where confidentiality is desired; SSL can also handle many aspects of certificate exchange without the need for upper level protocol engineering, if it is available (though the application – if not the applications-level protocol – still needs to know something about certificates). One advantage of certificates is that they are more flexible than most other mechanisms; they can be used for signing electronic mail messages, for example (though generally a separate key is used for signing). And much of the current work on new protocols and services – for example in the Java environment – seems to be based on certificate models.

The issues involving privacy, accountability and management data change little from the password scenario already discussed. One point worth noting is that if the user has several certificates – for example, an identified one for use with an internal institutional authentication and authorization system and a pseudononymous one for use with external services – he or she must select the correct certificate for presentation in order to maintain privacy.

4.4 Proxy/Credential Hybrid Schemes

There are several interesting and confusing schemes that after much discussion the initial reviews of the paper recognized are really hybrids of the proxy and credential approaches. In these schemes, the user contacts an applications proxy in order to gain access to the resource. The proxy authenticates the user, checks his or her authorization, and then prepares and submits a set of credentials to the resource. After the user's connection to the resource is established through these credentials, the proxy steps out of the way (via an HTTP redirect) and the user interacts directly with the resource. This has several useful results. It greatly reduces the overhead generated by use of a proxy, and minimizes the resource requirements for the proxy machines. It reduces some of the privacy concerns related to the proxy. And it means that short-lived rather than long-lived credentials (something perhaps more akin to a Kerberos ticket, philosophically, though it may be embodied in a certificate-based credential) can be sent to the resource operator; further, it may avoid the need to store these short-term credentials locally on the end user's machine.

5.0 Conclusions

Both proxies and credential-based authentication schemes seem to be viable approaches. Proxies have the advantage of compartmentalizing and modularizing authentication issues within an institution. But they also place heavy responsibilities upon the licensee institution to operate proxy servers professionally and responsibly. Proxy servers will become a focal point for policy debates about privacy, accountability and the collection of management information; successful operation of a proxy server implies that the user community is prepared to trust the licensee institution to behave responsibly and to respect privacy. Similarly, resource operators have to trust the licensee institution to competently implement and operate a local authentication system; anomaly monitoring of aggregated traffic from a proxy server by a resource operator is very difficult, and the resource operator will have to largely rely on the institution to carry out a program of anomalous access monitoring.

A cross-organizational authentication system based on a credential approach has the advantage of greater transparency. Resource operators can have a higher level of confidence in the access management mechanisms, and a much greater ability to monitor anomalous access patterns. The downside is much greater complexity; issues of privacy, accountability and the collection of management statistics become a matter for discussion among a larger group of parties. Further, it seems that a credential system means that there has to be cross-organizational interdependency in order to avoid systemic compromise of the authentication system, as opposed to a simple relationship of trust – recognized in a contract – for the proxy approach.

One point that seems clear is that an institutional public key infrastructure may not extend directly to a cross-institutional one; it may be desirable to issue community members a set of pseudononymous certificates for presentation outside the institution as well as individually identified ones that are used within the institution in order to provide a privacy firewall while still maintaining some level of accountability.

IP source filtering does not seem to be a viable general solution, although it may be very useful for some niche applications, such as supporting public workstations or kiosks. It can be used more widely – indeed today it usually is the basic access management tool – but it definitely cannot support remote users flexibly in its basic form. Most real-world access management systems are going to have to employ multiple approaches, and IP source address filtering is likely to be one of them.

Reviewers of the first draft of the paper were very concerned with the costs of deploying access management systems and the supporting authentication infrastructure. There is relatively little good data on this, though some early adopter institutions are seeing rather high costs, particularly for public key (certificate) based approaches. There is an urgent need to develop a better basis for estimating the initial deployment and operating costs of the various approaches, and this need should be addressed in any follow-on work to the white paper.

A final issue: this white paper has focused on interinstitutional issues in authentication and access management. It should be clear that the role of the licensee institution as a mediator adds some very significant value for the members of the user community. There are many users of networked information resources who do not have a natural affiliation with a licensee organization, and who thus do not have a way to obtain these benefits. We can expect these users to seek affiliations – such as that of alumni – which allow them to obtain these benefits. The idea of being able to have a single ID that allows access to a vast array of networked information resources is a very powerful one, and it is one that today is available only in an institutional context.

Appendix: Notes on the State of the Art in Available Software

This appendix provides a snapshot of the currently available state of the art for key software components in terms of their support for authentication, authorization and access management. One of the key issues that the white paper has identified is the need for off the shelf software to provide the needed facilities, particularly at the user's desktop.

Web Browsers

Two web browsers – Netscape Navigator and Microsoft's Internet Explorer – currently dominate the browser marketplace. Both support a wide range of platforms, including Microsoft windows, the Mac OS, and various varieties of UNIX.

Both browsers support SSL for encrypting forms that include passwords. It is worth noting that while both browsers support 128-bit encryption in their US-only products, users must take special action to obtain these versions and the vast majority of users probably are still running the much less secure 40-bit export qualified versions that are available as the default distributions. Both browsers support proxy servers as a configuration option. Both browsers support the incorporation of X.509 certificates. The browsers do not yet support certificate revocation lists (verify this).

There are many problems with certificates. They are not simple for the average user to import. Certificate backup and recovery (for example, in the case of a disk crash) is a problem. Certificates may not be moved smoothly as part of an upgrade; they definitely won't move if a user switches between Netscape and Internet Explorer (Netscape will import IE certificates via explicit action, but neither browser will simply make use of certificates installed in its competitor).

Both browsers include a built-in Telnet. This Telnet does not support SSL for protecting the transmission of user IDs and passwords. Both browsers can be configured to use independent Telnet helper applications rather than the build it Telnet. I am aware of work going on in the Mac world to provide a stand-along Telnet application which incorporates SSL encryption. Reconfiguration of any browser to substitute an external Telnet is non-trivial for the average user.

One issue that was identified during early reviews of this paper was the Lynx character-based web browser. Lynx is important for two reasons: because there is still a large installed base of trailing-edge character-based terminal technology, and, perhaps more compellingly, because Lynx, in conjunction with other specialized assistive software, is a key part of many institutional strategies for meeting the needs of disabled users and the requirements of the Americans with Disabilities (ADA) law. Lynx capabilities remain to be researched.

Web Servers

Commercial web servers from Netscape and Microsoft support SSL, as does Stronghold (commercial Apache); Apache proper supports SSL only on a limited basis with the addition of the shareware SSLeay module.

Need to review X.509 support, including what Certificate Authorities are supported/will issue, support of Certificate Revocation Lists, etc.

Index